COMPULSORY
FIGURES

COMPULSORY FIGURES

Essays on Recent American Poets

HENRY TAYLOR

LOUISIANA STATE UNIVERSITY PRESS
Baton Rouge and London

Designer: *Glynnis Phoebe*
Typeface: *Goudy Old Style*
Typesetter: *G & S Typesetters, Inc.*
Printer and binder: *Thomson-Shore, Inc.*

Library of Congress Cataloging-in-Publication Data

Taylor, Henry, 1942–
    Compulsory figures : essays on recent American poets / Henry
Taylor.
        p.   cm.
    Includes bibliographical references and indexes.
    ISBN 0-8071-1755-2 (cloth : permanent paper)
    1. American poetry—20th century—History and criticism.
I. Title.
PS325.T36   1992
811'.5409—dc20   92-5464
                                                          CIP

To the memory of DAYTON KOHLER

CONTENTS

PREFACE

Like William Jay Smith's "Mr. Smith," I cut a poor figure on skates, but years ago I spent many hours in a secluded meadow, riding horses until the circles I was asking for were as round, or the halts as square, as they were going to get. Toward the end of my serious riding days, I enjoyed practice of "compulsory figures" at least as much as I enjoyed competition; that was about the time that I discovered writing, as opposed to the vague wish to be a writer. Process, and the discovery of something previously unknown, may sometimes lead to finished products, but those diminish in importance, receding before the onset of another bout with process.

It is a commonplace that writers do not usually read in quite the same way that we would like to be read; we are said to keep a sharp eye peeled for what we can learn for use in our own work. That way of reading, and a number of kind invitations and extensions of hospitality from various editors, have resulted in these essays, about poetry to which I have felt compelled to return countless times over the past twenty-five years or more (Richard Dillard gave me my copy of *Traveling Through the Dark* on my twenty-first birthday).

There are other poets to whom I return as often as I return to these; for several reasons, they are not treated here. There are some about whose work I have become accustomed to saying no more than "voilà"; some are already so thoroughly scrutinized that my discoveries or opinions about them strike me as redundant; some, however often I reread them, have attracted me in ways I cannot yet explain. I have regretfully omitted an essay on Richard Wilbur, because his publisher and I could not agree on an appropriate fee for permission to quote from his work. An earlier version of that essay appears in Wendy Salinger's collection, *Richard Wilbur's Creation* (Ann Arbor, 1983). Finally, I have not written extensively about poets who are my age or younger, or about poets to whose work I return reluctantly.

I have given no thought to selecting, from among those poets who have done their best work since 1945, the seventeen poets most worthy of discussion. Nevertheless, I have enjoyed reflecting that a few of the poets treated here are rarely considered by such critics and anthologists as seem to know which poets deserve notice. I have enjoyed some transient enthusiasms from time to time, and may even occasionally have predicted that this or that poet would be read a couple of centuries hence. But such a question interests me far less than the qualities that draw me repeatedly back to a particular poet over several years.

The order in which the essays appear is guided more by intuition than by considerations such as the chronological order of their composition or of the poets' dates of birth. A recurring theme in the essays is the relationship between technique and the poet's developing notions of what poems should try to be and do. Rather than provide an implicit history of the changes in my preoccupations with such questions, I hope the arrangement of these essays might reflect my present conviction that it does not greatly matter whether a poet works in open or closed forms, or whether a poet's career is clearly divisible into formalist and free-verse eras, or whether a poet is, by some reckoning or other, distinctly loyal to older traditions or notably interested in exploring frontier territory. It matters a great deal more that the poet know how the grip closes around the selected implement. The poets discussed here have taken their lives in their hands.

Living writers continue to work after one has written about them. I have added to a few of these essays since they first appeared in periodicals, but I am grateful that most of these poets continue to outdate my remarks.

ACKNOWLEDGMENTS

In writing these essays, I have received generous assistance of various kinds, sometimes from the subjects themselves, always from the editors for whom they were first written, and occasionally from friends, students, and colleagues who have helped me unravel a puzzle, unearth a fact, or find a suitable phrase. I thank especially Patrick Bizzaro, Staige Blackford, Preston Browning, Kevin Cantwell, Jim Clark, Vince Clemente, R. H. W. Dillard, Troy Elliot, Stuart Friebert, Laurence Goldstein, Marilyn Hacker, Michael Haggerty, Richard Harteis, Judson Jerome, Jon Maney, Richard McCann, Mary Jay Michel, John Rees Moore, Dave Smith, Jack Wright, Stuart Wright, and David Young. I am also grateful to Julie Schorfheide, Louisiana State University Press's production editor, and to Jane Taylor, whose copy editing was a model of alertness, diligence, and sensitivity.

Grateful acknowledgment is made to the editors and publishers who granted permission to reprint the following selections, which first appeared in their publications:

"Enter the Dark House: The Poetry of William Jay Smith," *Michigan Quarterly Review* (Fall, 1991); "The Fun of the End of the World: David R. Slavitt's Poems," *The Virginia Quarterly Review*, LXVI (Spring, 1990); "Letting the Darkness In: The Poetic Achievement of John Hall Wheelock," *The Hollins Critic*, VII (December, 1970); "Home to a Place Beyond Exile: The Collected Poems of May Sarton," *The Hollins Critic*, XI (June, 1974); "In Charge of Morale in a Morbid Time: The Poetry of William Meredith," *The Hollins Critic*, XVI (February, 1979); "The Example of J. V. Cunningham," *The Hollins Critic*, XX (October, 1983); "In the Grip of Days: The Poetry of John Woods," *The Hollins Critic*, XXIII (October, 1986); "Great Experiments: The Poetry of Louis Simpson," *The Hollins Critic*, XXVII (June, 1990); "John Hall Wheelock's Last Poems," in *Paumanok Rising: An Anthol-*

ogy of *Eastern Long Island Aesthetics*, ed. Vince Clemente, Graham Everett, et al. (Port Jefferson, N.Y., 1981); "Millions of Intricate Moves," *Field*, No. 41 (Fall, 1989); "In the Mode of Robinson and Frost: James Wright's Early Poetry," in *The Pure Clear Word: Essays on the Poetry of James Wright*, ed. Dave Smith (University of Illinois Press, 1982); "The Brutal Rush of Grace: George Garrett's Poetry," in *To Come Up Grinning: A Tribute to George Garrett*, ed. Paul Ruffin and Stuart Wright (Huntsville, Tex., 1989); "Forms of Conviction," *The Southern Review*, n.s., XXVII (Winter, 1991); "The Gift of the Waters: The Poetry of Brewster Ghiselin," *Quarterly West*, No. 25 (Spring, 1987); "Everything We Cannot See Is Here: The Poetry of Robert Watson," *The Greensboro Review*, XLVI (Summer, 1989).

Grateful acknowledgment is also made to the poets whose work has been reprinted here and to the following publishers for permission to reprint excerpts from various collections:

Dragon Gate, Inc., for excerpts from John Woods, *The Valley of the Minor Animals* (1982) and *The Salt Stone* (1985); Louisiana State University Press, for excerpts from *The World Between the Eyes: Poems by Fred Chappell*, copyright © 1963, 1964, 1966, 1969, 1970, 1971 by Fred Chappell, for excerpts from *Midquest: A Poem by Fred Chappell*, copyright © 1981 by Fred Chappell, for excerpts from *Castle Tzingal: A Poem by Fred Chappell*, copyright © 1984 by Fred Chappell, for excerpts from *Source: Poems by Fred Chappell*, copyright © 1985 by Fred Chappell, and for excerpts from *First and Last Words: Poems by Fred Chappell*, copyright © 1989 by Fred Chappell; St. Martin's Press, Inc., New York, N.Y., for excerpts from *Brighten the Corner Where You Are*, by Fred Chappell, copyright 1989 by Fred Chappell, and for excerpts from *The Fred Chappell Reader*, by Fred Chappell, copyright 1987 by Fred Chappell; Duke University Press, for excerpts from Fred Chappell, "Familiar Poem," in *Under Twenty-five: Duke Narrative and Verse, 1945–1962*, ed. William Blackburn. Copyright 1963 by Duke University Press, Durham, N.C. Reprinted by permission. Excerpts from Gwendolyn Brooks, *Blacks* (The David Company, Chicago, and Third World Press), copyright © 1987, 1989, 1991 by Gwendolyn Brooks; University of Utah Press, for excerpts from the work of Brewster Ghiselin; University of Michigan Press, for excerpts from William Stafford, *Writing the Australian Crawl* (University of Michigan Press, 1978), copyright © 1978 by the University of Michigan, and for excerpts from William Stafford, *You Must Revise Your Life* (University of Michigan Press, 1986), copyright © 1986 by the University of Michigan; HarperCollins Publishers for excerpts from "Brother" and "Some Notes on Writing," from *An Oregon Message* by William Stafford. (These excerpts appear in the essay that begins on p. 139.) Copyright © 1987 by William Stafford. Reprinted by permission of HarperCollins Publishers, Inc. University of South Carolina Press, for excerpts from R. H. W. Dillard, *Understanding George Garrett* (Columbia, S.C., 1988); Wesleyan University Press by permission of University Press of New England, for excerpts from James Wright, *Above the River*, copyright 1990 by Anne Wright; Alfred A. Knopf, Inc., for excerpts from *Partial Accounts: New and Selected Poems*, by William Meredith, and from *Earth Walk: New and Selected Poems*, by William Meredith. Reprinted by permission of Alfred A. Knopf, Inc.; Alfred A. Knopf, Inc., for excerpts from *The Transparent Man*, by Anthony Hecht, and from *The Collected Poems*, by Anthony Hecht. Both works copyrighted © 1990 by Anthony Hecht. Reprinted by permission of Alfred A. Knopf, Inc. Excerpts from *Collected Poems (1930–1973)* by May Sarton are reprinted by permission of the author and W. W. Norton & Company, Inc. Copyright © 1974 by May Sarton. Reprinted by permission of A M Heath & Company, Limited, Authors' Agents. Wesleyan University Press by permission of University Press of New England, for excerpts from "The Runner" and "To the Western World," from Louis Simpson, *A Dream of Governors*, copyright 1959 by Louis Simpson, and "Lines Written Near San Francisco" and "In the Suburbs," from Louis Simpson, *At the End of the Open Road*, copyright 1963; Houghton Mifflin Company, for excerpts from *The Best Hour of the Night* by Louis Simpson. Copyright © 1983 by Louis Simpson. Reprinted by permission of Ticknor & Fields, a Houghton Mifflin Company imprint. All rights reserved. Franklin Watts, Inc., for excerpts from "Caviare at the Funeral," "Working Late," and "A Bower of Roses," from *Caviare at the Funeral*, copyright © 1980 by Louis Simpson. Used with permission of the publisher, Franklin Watts, Inc., New York. Paragon House, for excerpts from "Carentan O Carentan," "Lazarus Convalescent," "Periodontics," "Sacred Object," and the Preface from Louis Simpson, *Collected Poems* (New York, 1988), and for excerpts from "Trouble," from Louis Simpson, *Selected Prose* (New York, 1989). Excerpts from "Lancelot to Guinevere," "Silence," "Mr. X (_____ State Mental Hospital)," "In the Dark City," and "The Part Called Age," reprinted with permission of Charles Scribner's Sons, an imprint of Macmillan Publishing Company, from *By Daylight and in Dream: New and Collected Poems, 1904–1970*, by John Hall Wheelock. Copyright © 1970 by John Hall

COMPULSORY
FIGURES

J. V. CUNNINGHAM   The Last Variation Is Regularity

I

I will establish at the outset that I am indebted beyond measure to the work and advice of J. V. Cunningham; I trust that his example will have enough force to keep me from unsupported panegyric.

In October of 1962, Fred Bornhauser, one of my teachers at the University of Virginia, took me to a few sessions of the National Poetry Festival at the Library of Congress. That spectacle included some thirty brief readings by actual humans who seemed to have stepped from the pages of my textbooks—even Oscar Williams was there—and several panel discussions: the role of the poetry journal, the poet and the public, and the problem of form. This latter session was moderated by John Crowe Ransom, and the three speakers were Léonie Adams, Allen Tate, and J. V. Cunningham, of whose name and work I had up to then been ignorant. His remarks on that occasion were brief, learned, and, on me anyway, profoundly effective. I had not previously heard a formal discussion of poetic theory that demonstrated an extensive factual knowledge of poetry, put to uses other than graduate orals or trivia games. A year and a half later Cunningham came to Charlottesville and delivered on successive evenings a lecture—subsequently published as "The Styles and Procedures of Wallace Stevens"—and a reading of his poems. I knew immediately, and with emotional force, that he spoke to my condition, but I did not foresee how heavily, over the succeeding decades,

I would depend on him not only as a source of classroom example and anecdote—it is useful to tell students that he once said of one of my poems, "It
has a dry, muted, uncertain music, that ultimately is forgettable"—but as a
touchstone, a kind of conscience. On those occasions when I write un-
metrically, it is thanks largely to Cunningham that I have considered my
decision to do so—and, for that matter, that I have had the choice, instead
of being forced to free verse by the ignorance of metrics that many young
poets have considered sufficient equipment.

II

"The Problem of Form" appears in Cunningham's *Collected Essays*. It is of
course based on the literary practice of the Modernist era, but its concluding
paragraphs still raise interesting questions about the poetry of the past twenty
years:

> Indeed, it is the inherent coincidence of forms in poetry, in metrical writ-
> ing, that gives it its place and its power—a claim for poetry perhaps more
> accurate and certainly more modest than is customary. For this is the poet's
> Poetics: prose is written in sentences; poetry in sentences and lines. It is
> encoded not only in grammar, but also simultaneously in meter, for meter
> is the principle or set of principles, whatever they may be, that determines
> the line. And as we perceive of each sentence that it is grammatical or not,
> so the repetitive perception that this line is metrical or that it is not, that
> it exemplifies the rules or that it does not, is the metrical experience. It is
> the ground bass of all poetry.
>
> And here in naked reduction is the problem of form in the poetry of
> our day. It is before all a problem of meter. We have lost the repetitive
> harmony of the old tradition, and we have not established a new. We have
> written to vary or violate the old line, for regularity we feel is meaningless
> and irregularity meaningful. But a generation of poets, acting on the prin-
> ciples and practice of significant variation, have at last nothing to vary
> from. The last variation is regularity.[1]

"Naked reduction" is sometimes misleading, for elsewhere in his critical
writings Cunningham takes note of those larger claims for poetry that have

1. J. V. Cunningham, *Collected Essays* (Chicago, 1976), 250. Hereafter cited in the text
as *CE*, followed by a page number.

characterized poetic discussion at least since the Romantics; though he had some things in common with his former teacher and colleague, Yvor Winters, he did not, as Winters did, succumb to the belief that what he was right about made everything else wrong. At first glance, the passage above might seem to be the sort of thing around which self-consciously old-fashioned poetasters might rally; but most of them are not among that ever-dwindling "we" who might "perceive of each sentence that it is grammatical or not."

Furthermore, in recent years the discussion of meter among poets has resulted not only in ill-informed analogies—Pope is to the Newtonian world-view what Olson is to the Einsteinian—but also in remarkably competent metrical writing by several poets now barely into their thirties. The debate goes on, and even seems to produce the most interesting results when it has been conducted between the two impulses as they declare themselves in the mind of a single poet.

But it is not merely the metrical decision that set Cunningham's poetry apart from much of the rest of the poetry of our time. For example, in *Poet's Choice*, Paul Engle and Joseph Langland assembled poems chosen by their authors, along with the poets' explanations of their choices. Cunningham chose his "Epitaph":

> When I shall be without regret
> And shall mortality forget,
> When I shall die who lived for this,
> I shall not miss the things I miss.
> And you who notice where I lie
> Ask not my name. It is not I.

His explanation: "I like the poem because it is all denotation and no connotation; because it has only one level of meaning; because it is not ironic, paradoxical, complex, or subtle; and because the meter is monotonously regular."[2] In the March, 1983, *Critical Inquiry*, Alan Shapiro writes that Cunningham "is in an important sense a poet of denials," and a few pages later he cites this poem as an example. Certainly his description is apt; he demonstrates the ways in which the poem withholds what we customarily

2. Paul Engle and Joseph Langland, *Poet's Choice* (1962; rpr. New York, 1966), 105. The poem appears also in Cunningham's *Collected Poems and Epigrams* (Chicago, 1971), 112. Hereafter cited in the text as *CP*, followed by a page number.

expect from epitaphs in order to say that "death is the total obliteration of personality."[3] And Cunningham's sentence about the poem is characteristically brief, thorough, and acerbic in its denial of customary expectations; poets do not usually talk this way about their own work.

But an expressed preference for regularly metrical statement did not keep Cunningham from letting metrical patterns perform subtle modulations of his statements. Here is Epigram 28:

> Dark thoughts are my companions. I have wined
> With lewdness and with crudeness, and I find
> Love is my enemy, dispassionate hate
> Is my redemption though it come too late,
> Though I come to it with a broken head
> In the cat-house of the dishevelled dead.
> (CP, 114)

It is not the additional twelve syllables alone that make this poem seem more complicated than "Epitaph." The former poem contains no images, no run-on lines, and only one significant caesura, and that exactly in the middle of the last line. By contrast, this poem seems fraught with imagery; the first three lines are run on; and the distribution of pauses and stresses is noticeably at variance with the iambic norm, though in no pattern that could not be illustrated by examples from the sixteenth century. Toward the end of this poem, line-ends coincide more neatly with phases of the statement. At its most assured, then, this voice says that the redemption of dispassionate hate comes only with death. Love, be it enemy or not, and passionate hate, are inescapable in life. The metrical tentativeness of the first three and a half lines foreshadows the conclusion.

It has often been noticed, by both admirers and detractors, that Cunningham's is chiefly a poetry of statement, rather than of image and suggestion. In an essay called "Several Kinds of Short Poem," Cunningham describes his own concerns in ways that enlarge on his pronouncements in "The Problem of Form:"

> I do not, for example, ordinarily think of poetry as vision, although I know
> it sometimes is, and so I have no vision. I have no intuition into the heart

---

3. Alan Shapiro, "'Far Lamps at Night': The Poetry of J. V. Cunningham," *Critical Inquiry*, IX (March, 1983), 612, 615.

of things; I have no special way of seeing. I think of poetry as a way of speaking, a special way of speaking. As a poet I speak in meter, and sometimes in rhyme; I speak in lines. It follows naturally that I am a formalist and that anything that can be said in metrical lines is subject for poetry, even vision, and that anything worth saying should sometime be said. This last adds a principle of value, the principle of what is worth saying as distinguished from what is not. And to this, formalism adds another principle of value, for the aim of the formal is the definitive. A poem, then, on this view is metrical speech, and a good poem is the definitive statement in meter of something worth saying. (CE, 431)

And it follows from this, he goes on to say, that the poet who thinks of poetry in this way is likely to become an epigrammatist. Cunningham's prose style is so lean and precise that it has the sound of fact when what it expresses is opinion; it is worth remembering the first-person pronouns and the phrase "on this view," lest the tone of the passage persuade us that Cunningham had no room in his sensibility for poetry much different from what he describes. One might even profitably belabor the obvious point that "what is worth saying" is often made to seem so by the way in which it is said.

The fact remains that Cunningham's style changed little, and came to him, or he to it, early in his career; his first published poem (February, 1932), now called "In Innocence," is in many ways scarcely distinguishable from his more recent work:

In innocence I said
'Affection is secure.
It is not forced or led.'
No longer sure

Of the least certainty
I have erased the mind,
As mendicants who see
Mimic the blind.
(CP, 23)

This is the version of the poem that appears in *Collected Poems and Epigrams;* earlier, under the title "Retreating Friendship," the first line had read "When I was young I said," and the fourth word of the sixth line was "my" instead of "the."[4] These revisions are of course considerable—just over 11 percent, by syllable count—and the changes may be said to reflect Cunningham's mature style, as they eliminate two first-person pronouns and add one abstraction. But the structure of the thought is only slightly complicated by the introduction of "innocence"; the paradoxical effect of the last two lines has not been altered. The poem says that the mind has been erased only to the extent that the speaker's loss of certainty, and his will, can bring about this defense against disillusionment.

In *Forms of Discovery*, Yvor Winters, despite a tendency to veer off unpredictably into somewhat paranoiac digressions, makes several penetrating observations concerning the force of emotion in Cunningham's poetry. Having noticed that several of Cunningham's poems "define truths which cannot be avoided," and offer only the solace of clear understanding, he continues, "There is another kind of matter, not wholly unrelated to this last, which may give the reader trouble unless he can consider it dispassionately. This is the matter related to the doctrine of hatred or anger. The doctrine, briefly, and as nearly as I can understand it, is that hatred is the only cleansing emotion and the most moral of emotions. Baldly put, the doctrine is not beguiling and may even seem shocking, but it is not without a justification in experience."[5]

The word *doctrine* is too heavily loaded to describe accurately the ambiguous place of hatred in Cunningham's poetry; as we have seen, dispassionate hate redeems, but comes too late. If hatred is a cleansing emotion, it may also be adulterated, as in Epigram 55:

> I had gone broke, and got set to come back,
> And lost, on a hot day and a fast track,
> On a long shot at long odds, a black mare
> By Hatred out of Envy by Despair.
> (*CP*, 119)

Handicappers learn by bitter experience that previous performance, the class of the competition, and so on, need as much attention as pedigree.

4. J. V. Cunningham, "Retreating Friendship," *Commonweal*, XV (February 10, 1932), 408.

5. Yvor Winters, *Forms of Discovery: Critical & Historical Essays on the Forms of the Short Poem in English* (Denver, 1967), 305.

In a few poems scattered throughout his career, Cunningham mingled statement of abstraction with various forms of fiction, or possibly autobiography. He himself described "The Phoenix" as one of these, and "An Interview with Doctor Drink" makes another interesting example:

> I have a fifth of therapy
> In the house, and transference there.
> Doctor, there's not much wrong with me,
> Only a sick rattlesnake somewhere
>
> In the house, if it be there at all,
> But the lithe mouth is coiled. The shapes
> Of door and window move. I call.
> What is it that pulls down the drapes,
>
> Dishevelled and exposed? Your rye
> Twists in my throat: intimacy
> Is like hard liquor. Who but I
> Coil there and squat, and pay your fee?
> (CP, 78)

The violent compression of a phrase like "the lithe mouth is coiled" is unusual in Cunningham's work; yet this nearly surrealistic image is worked out by the end of the poem in a manner that seems almost formally logical: "Your rye / Twists in my throat." The startling proposition that "intimacy / Is like hard liquor" is hard to understand to the extent of paraphrase, but it is, in the context of this poem, momentarily believable. The speaker of this poem may have a few understandably fuzzy thoughts, but the intelligence behind the poem has not succumbed to easy temptations.

III

Cunningham's impatience with easy ways of doing things finds memorable expression throughout his critical writings. The preface to *Tradition and Poetic Structure* (1960) begins, "I have attempted in this book to be brief, clear, and cold-blooded, to make a number of positive contributions to the field of literary scholarship, and to present a consistent and no doubt unpoetical attitude toward poetry. I should, perhaps, have practiced more the higher and easier art of literary criticism."[6]

A few years earlier, in "Plots and Errors: *Hamlet* and *King Lear*," he writes: "And the difference in aesthetic effect between two plays with approximately the same quantity of plot but with greater and less digression and episode will be, as Coleridge noted of *Hamlet* and *Macbeth*: 'the one proceeds with the utmost slowness, the other with a crowded and breathless rapidity.' Or, to put it less perceptively: the one in a school text I have at hand runs to fifty pages, the other to thirty" (CE, 215).

These remarks are clearly calculated to be provoking, but they make a point about literary study that is exemplified in virtually all of Cunningham's prose. The point is that it is relatively easy to have an emotional response to a text, and to contrive ways of discussing the response; it is more difficult to establish reliable texts and to discover what their authors meant by them. This is not to say that emotional responses are irrelevant, but only that one must be alert to the response the text engenders, and to the response conditioned by the reader's experience.

As an example of these two ways of responding, Cunningham discusses the phrase "Ripeness is all" (*Lear*, 5.2.11) at the beginning of his monograph called *Woe or Wonder: The Emotional Effect of Shakespearean Tragedy*. He cites several modern reactions to the phrase, and then carefully establishes that Shakespeare meant "that the fruit will fall in its time, and men die when God is ready."[7]

What are we to do, then, with the modern reading of the phrase, in which it seems so profoundly expressive of "an inner and emotional completion in life that is attainable and that will resolve our tragedies"? Cunningham concedes that many of us cherish some such reading of the phrase, and that we may continue to do so, if we do not also insist on believing that Shakespeare intended us to. "If we are secure in our own feelings we will accept our own meanings as ours, and if we have any respect for the great we will penetrate and embrace Shakespeare's meaning as his" (CE, 7).

In describing Cunningham's scholarship as an act of generosity and love, Alan Shapiro justly quotes the sentences that follow those above.[8] They are

6. J. V. Cunningham, *Tradition and Poetic Structure* (Denver, 1960), 5.

7. J. V. Cunningham, *Woe or Wonder; The Emotional Effect of Shakespearean Tragedy* (Denver, 1951), reprinted in CE, 1–129.

8. Shapiro, " 'Far Lamps,' " 624n20.

as succinct and clear a statement of the value of literary study as I have seen; if Cunningham is often acerbic or sarcastic, he is often eloquent as well: "For our purpose in the study of literature, and particularly in the historical interpretation of texts, is not in the ordinary sense to further the understanding of ourselves. It is rather to enable us to see how we could think and feel otherwise than as we do. It is to erect a larger context of experience within which we may define and understand our own by attending to the disparity between it and the experience of others" (CE, 7).

This passage comes early in the monograph, which is a brilliantly sensitive and careful exploration of the meaning, in Shakespeare's era, of words like "tragedy," "wonder," and "woe." Cunningham recapitulates the content and the pervasiveness of the definition of tragedy given by Donatus in his commentary on Terence, and searches the plays for pertinent definitions and descriptions. The final chapter, "Reason Panders Will," establishes the Renaissance conception of man's ability to determine his fate, and contrasts this view with more modern ones, which are informed by theories of evolution and psychology. Modern readers, for example, whose expectations may be conditioned as well by the pace of fiction, find improbabilities in Othello where the Renaissance audience may not have found them. "Such critics make the optimistic assumption that men are not likely to go wrong unless there is sufficient cause. But this is modern, and not too well founded in fact. The general assumption of the Renaissance was that men were not likely to go right unless there was a supernatural cause" (CE, 111).

The careful historical scholarship in this study may have aroused some unfavorable New Critical reactions; in any case, the monograph in its present state is followed by two appendixes, "The Ancient Quarrel Between History and Poetry" and "Tragedy as Essence." In both, Cunningham deals with his having chosen to determine, if possible, the intentions of the author of a literary work. The New Critics knew this approach to be fallacious; Cunningham is persuasive to the contrary, and seems to foreshadow some of the complaints of recent writers like Gerald Graff when he attacks that brand of criticism that is concerned with "timeless" responses to a work of literature: "So the multiplicity of wild and inconsistent interpretations of Macbeth . . . testify to the virility of the Macbeth-stimulus, and not at all to the stupidity, confusion, and selfishness of the interpreters" (CE, 123).

In arguing that historical and aesthetic interpretation must of necessity be the same thing, since every statement is made with an intention discoverable from the statement itself and from the circumstances in which it was made, Cunningham offers a principle of morality: "For the understanding of an author in the scholarly sense involves the exercise under defined conditions of the two fundamental principles of morality in the Western tradition: 1) the principle of dignity, or of responsibility to the external fact, in the special form of respect for another person as revealed in his works; and 2) the principle of love, the exercise of sympathetic insight, or of imaginative transformation" (CE, 126).

The kind of imaginative transformation Cunningham is talking about is the central theme of one of his early poems, "Lector Aere Perennior." It is necessary to recall that a doctrine of the transmigration of souls has been attributed to Pythagoras:

> Poets survive in fame.
> But how can substance trade
> The body for a name
> Wherewith no soul's arrayed?
>
> No form inspires the clay
> Now breathless of what was
> Save the imputed sway
> Of some Pythagoras,
>
> Some man so deftly mad
> His metamorphosed shade,
> Leaving the flesh it had,
> Breathes on the words they made.
> (CP, 16)

Cunningham paraphrases this poem in "The Quest of the Opal," a third-person exposition of the background and meaning of some of his early poems. He is clear enough on the poem's central statement that a writer survives not by the reputation of his name, but by the labor of that reader who can see what he meant, who has "the irrational trick of assuming the spirit of the author" (CE, 409). This phrase is less powerful than the nearly oxymoronic "deftly mad," but both remind us that if logic and rational attention are essential to literary interpretation, they may not be sufficient in themselves. I hesitate to ascribe even deft madness to Cunningham's own exemplary acts as a reader, but if it describes the thoroughness and sympathetic insight of his criticism, perhaps it applies.

Once in a while, however, Cunningham's logical mind and singleness of purpose lead him to conclusions that surprise even the reader who is convinced, as I am, that he is usually right. In an essay called "How Shall the Poem Be Written?" he takes up at some length what he calls the "dangerous fiction" of the metrical norm. Rejecting the theory that one may perceive and respond to tensions between the abstract metrical pattern and the actual stress-contour of a line, he says, "Meter is perceived in the actual stress-contour, or the line is perceived as unmetrical, or the perceiver doesn't perceive meter at all" (CE, 262). He then quotes a singularly un-iambic ten-syllable line from Donne to demonstrate how it feels to perceive an unmetrical line.

A few pages later, after a virtuoso display of bits of casual conversation that fall into standard iambic pentameters and tetrameters, he repeats his assertion from "The Problem of Form" that the metrical experience is the perception that a line is metrical or not, and adds: "It follows that metrical analysis is irrelevant to poetry; metrical perception is of the essence. . . . It follows, also, that the notion of norm and variation is not relevant to traditional meter. There are alternative patterns, each of which satisfies the metrical requirements, some more common, some less. You may begin 'To be or not' or 'Whether 'tis nobler'; the choice is metrically indifferent" (CE, 268).

In this essay, Cunningham is concerned to discredit what he calls "parasitic meter," the method championed by Eliot of establishing a norm, departing from it by as much as six or seven syllables, and returning to it from time to time. So he has a point of view. He may also have been made impatient by those excessively ingenious metrical analyses that seem to suggest that sound alone, in the absence of denotation, can convey meaning. "Desperate staccato trochees," "portentous spondees," and the like, arouse skepticism toward analyses mentioning them; most of us have learned that the metrical pattern of the limerick suggests humor only to those who recognize it.

But in short poems in which metrical variations are few, there may be effects different from those produced by acceptable alternative patterns in narrative or dramatic verse. It is possible to produce metrical variations that operate significantly on the words in which they occur. In the twelfth poem of a sequence which I will shortly discuss in more detail, Cunningham's speaker returns to New England from a sojourn in the West, where he had become involved in a love affair:

Absence, my angel, presence at my side,
I know you as an article of faith
By desert, prairie, and this stonewalled road—
As much my own as is the thought of death.
(CP, 103)

The third line gets the traveller across the continent, from the vastness of desert and prairie to the more enclosing landscape of New England, where straying from the road will bring him up against stone walls. It is emotionally right that the final three syllables of this line receive more stress than the three preceding them. Admittedly, this rightness has to do with the meaning of the words; in a line describing someone's vocal affectations, a similar metrical pattern will be of little interest: "my secretary in his phone-call mode."

Significant metrical variations are rarer than many metrical analysts like to believe, but they are not nonexistent; and when brief poems like the one above, or like "Dark thoughts are my companions," display metrical movements that parallel or even amplify their statements, it is a pleasure to take notice of them.

IV

In the late 1950s and the early 1960s, Cunningham conducted a couple of experiments that resulted in his most impressive poetic work up to that time. One of these seems relatively simple: he composed a few poems in syllabic meters. Yvor Winters chides him for this in *Forms of Discovery*, hazarding a guess that Cunningham may have been "converted" to syllabics during a visiting semester at Santa Barbara, where the confirmed syllabicist Alan Stephens was working; but he adds that one of Cunningham's syllabic poems is "the best poem so far in an unfortunate mode."[9]

9. Winters, *Forms of Discovery*, 351. In a letter dated December 8, 1983, Cunningham offered me the following clarification: "[O]n syllabics and Al Stephens: an early poem in syllabics was for years on Winters' brief list of my best poems (and he himself wrote & published syllabics). Several of the syllabics in *To What* were written, and published, before I went to Santa Barbara in the winter of 1963. And the one he praises (#15 in the sequence) is in fact unrhymed octosyllables."

The poem thus characterized is the last in a sequence of fifteen entitled *To What Strangers, What Welcome.* It constitutes the second experiment, which was to try to compensate for his poems' usual brevity by arranging some of them within a narrative structure that might allow some enlargement of scope.

As first published in its entirety,[10] the sequence carried an epigraph from E. A. Robinson's *Merlin,* in which Merlin recalls the Lady Vivian after he has returned to Camelot; he asserts that she will remember him, and say:

"I knew him when his heart was young,
Though I have lost him now. Time called him home,
And that was as it was; for much is lost
Between Broceliande and Camelot."

It is a moving passage; unfortunately, it was dropped from the sequence as it appears in *Collected Poems and Epigrams* because, as Cunningham explained in a letter in September of 1972, it was too expensive to acquire reprint permission. An epigraph, of course, is rarely integral to the work it precedes; it acts only as a signpost of some sort. But in this case, the choice was apt and effective.

The story line of the sequence is predictable and potentially trite: a man goes west, has a few brief adventures in places like Las Vegas, achieves the Coast and falls in love, and then returns home, as Merlin had. So the story itself is primarily a framework in which the poems may have their resonance.

But considerable narrative skill has gone into the composition of several of these poems. The first is formally like most of Cunningham's four-line epigrams, but though it closes formally, it launches us toward the essential narrative question about what may happen next:

I drive Westward. Tumble and loco weed
Persist. And in the vacancies of need,
The leisure of desire, whirlwinds a face
As luminous as love, lost as this place.
(CP, 91)

10. J. V. Cunningham, *To What Strangers, What Welcome* (Denver, 1964), reprinted in CP, 91–106.

Next, a poem whose management of sensory detail recalls that in "Interview with Doctor Drink":

> On either side of the white line
> The emblems of a life appear
> In turn: purpose like lodgepole pine
> Competitive and thin, and fear
>
> Agile as aspen in a storm.
> And then the twilit harboring
> In a small park. The room is warm.
> And by the ache of travelling
>
> Removed from all immediacy,
> From all time, I as time grows late
> Sense in disordered fantasy
> The sound and smell of love and hate.
> (CP, 92)

The speaker is ready for something to occupy some emptiness, to fill some need. After two poems exploring in an abstract tone the forces that drive people together or apart, there is a brief epigram describing a pickup in a bar, and then the startling "It was in Vegas":

> It was in Vegas. Celibate and able
> I left the silver dollars on the table
> And tried the show. The black-out, baggy pants,
> Of course, and then this answer to romance:
> Her ass twitching as if it had the fits,
> Her gold crotch grinding, her athletic tits,
> One clock, the other counter clockwise twirling.
> It was enough to stop a man from girling.
> (CP, 97)

There is nothing like this elsewhere in the sequence; the violent satirical tone suits Las Vegas, but we must push on to discover what will come to a character who talks this way, if only for a moment. What comes to him is a

love affair, movingly portrayed in the ninth poem, where a perennial difficulty is memorably posed and resolved:

> Innocent to innocent,
> One asked, What is perfect love?
> Not knowing it is not love,
> Which is imperfect—some kind
> Of love or other, some kind
> Of interchange with wanting,
> There when all else is wanting,
> Something by which we make do.
>
> So, impaired, uninnocent,
> If I love you—as I do—
> To the very perfection
> Of perfect imperfection,
> It's that I care more for you
> Than for my feeling for you.
> (CP, 100)

In the next poem he asks whether this encounter must be sin, and says
it is something

> That happens because it must happen.
> We live in the given. Consequence,
> And lack of consequence, both fail us.
> Good is what we can do with evil.
> (CP, 101)

The statements that conclude these two poems have seemed to me, since
I first heard them in 1964, among the most convincing utterances ever to
have arisen from such circumstances. But their value as insight arises from
their more specific context; the speaker may find himself in a difficult situation, but he has retained the ability to think about it, and about the feelings
it arouses.

The eleventh poem of the sequence turns the speaker homeward, in a
haunting union of sound, image, and statement:

> I drive Eastward. The ethics of return,
> Like the night sound of coyotes on a hill
> Heard in eroded canyons of concern,
> Disposes what has happened, and what will.
> (CP, 102)

The poem ends, as Cunningham said in a commencement address in 1978, "with the acceptance of the rejection of the valued experience."[11] The speaker addresses himself:

> I sit in the last warmth
> Of a New England fall, and I?
> A premise of identity
> Where the lost hurries to be lost,
> Both in its own best interests
> And in the interests of life.
> (CP, 106)

Aside from its meeting Cunningham's own standards, by containing many definitive, metrical, worthwhile statements, this sequence quite firmly settles the question whether a poet who tries to think thoroughly, factually, and abstractly about poetry may write poems of emotional power as well as intellectual clarity. In fact, it is the steady intellectual attention given to the experience that gives the experience its value. To What Strangers, What Welcome is a rare achievement, a fusion of the human and the durable.

Cunningham's later epigrams tended away from learned restraint toward more immediate and bawdy humor; but in certain longer poems, and in a few translations from Latin, he was at his best. In the 1970s he completed his last extended critical work, having expanded two lectures given at UCLA in 1973 into Emily Dickinson: Lyric and Legend. In this brief and extraordinarily beautiful example of book production, Cunningham again combines deep sympathy with the object of his attention, and scrupulous care in establishing, from contemporaneous texts, letters, and so on, some of the usages in Dickinson that we might misconstrue if we read them by contemporary lights.[12]

---

11. J. V. Cunningham, "Commencement Address, Lawrence University, June 11, 1978," Folio, XVII (Spring, 1980), 18.

12. J. V. Cunningham, Emily Dickinson: Lyric and Legend (Los Angeles, 1980).

Great care, great patience, and steadfast attention to the craft and tradition of poetry are unusual qualities in any era; it is superfluous, if tempting, to hold Cunningham up as an example to our age only. If his work is not as widely known as some of us think it should be, his uniqueness surely does not reside in that fact. Fashion is whimsical, and it is sometimes self-destructive to try to flow with it; it is healthier to work from a fact Cunningham mentions in his introduction to *The Collected Essays:* "If my poems are not of their time, they are nevertheless part of the evidence for what the times are" (*CE,* ix). The evidence is greatly enriched by his having stated, with astonishing precision, his opinions of what poetry is, and by his having written some two hundred poems that fulfill his exacting definitions.

ANTHONY HECHT   Forms of Conviction

I

In the *Times Literary Supplement* of May 6, 1988, Edwin Morgan wrote, "It is one of the oddities of English usage that a longer poem is shorter than a long poem, in the same way as a younger poet is older than a young poet."[1] Similarly, few of the poems in Anthony Hecht's *Collected Earlier Poems* (1990) can be called *early*. This collection reprints *The Hard Hours* (1968; Pulitzer Prize, 1969), *Millions of Strange Shadows* (1977), and *The Venetian Vespers* (1979); *The Hard Hours* contains fifteen poems carried forward from Hecht's first book, *A Summoning of Stones* (1954). These, the only early poems in this collection, display the symmetry and brilliance for which they are widely known, even to their detractors. We are to notice that the first poem in *The Hard Hours*, "A Hill," though somewhat elevated in tone and rhythm, is unmetrical, as if to let us know right away that Hecht had taken a fresh direction. Nevertheless, as his range has deepened, the contrast between his early poems and later work has come, paradoxically, to seem less startling than it did.

Hecht has from the beginning written at an extremely high level of what is now, alas, called cultural literacy; his early poems are often elaborate

1. David R. Slavitt brought this to my attention; it is the epigraph to his *Eight Longer Poems* (Baton Rouge, 1990).

in their formality, carrying tradition to such extremes as a "Double Sonnet"—two rhymes in a sixteen-line "octave," three in the twelve-line "sestet," each stanza a single sentence. They easily accommodate a range of diction that some would find burdensome, in syntactical sinuosities learned, in all likelihood, not only from Milton, but also from those to whom Milton bent in his apprenticeship. They move securely among art treasures, classical myths, neoclassical literature, history, and, somewhat surprisingly, colloquialism and slang.

"The Gardens of the Villa D'Este" is a strong representative of the early poems, not only because of its superb finish, but because it explicitly rejects the cut-glass stasis that has sometimes been said to characterize *A Summoning of Stones*. A description and meditation set in the gardens of the dukes of Ferrara, it establishes the difference between these and the clockwork rigidity of French gardens; this is not an attempt to vanquish nature:

> Actually, it is real
>   The way the world is real: the horse
>   Must turn against the wind, and the deer feed
> Against the wind, and finally the garden must allow
> For the recalcitrant; a style can teach us how
>   To know the world in little where the weed
>   Has license, where by dint of force
>   D'Estes have set their seal.
>
> . . . .
>
>
>   For thus it was designed:
>   Controlled disorder at the heart
>   Of everything, the paradox, the old
> Oxymoronic itch to set the formal strictures
> Within a natural context, where the tension lectures
>   Us on our mortal state, and by controlled
>   Disorder, labors to keep art
>   From being too refined. [2]

These are the only stanzas containing repetitions as substantial as those of "against the wind" and "controlled disorder"; emphasis falls on the struggle

---

2. Anthony Hecht, *Collected Earlier Poems* (New York, 1990), 94, 95. Hereafter cited in the text as *CEP*, followed by a page number.

to maintain tension and on the difference between "formal strictures" and strangleholds.

The Henry Ford philosophy of poetry (*History is bunk; any color as long as it's blank*) has kept some readers from valuing the liveliness in Hecht's use of metrical patterns; one of the more memorable attacks on it appears in Kenneth Koch's exciting and hilarious jeremiad, "Fresh Air" (1955):

> Where are young poets in America, they are trembling in
>   publishing houses and universities. . . .
> Sometimes they brave a subject like the Villa D'Este or a
>   lighthouse in Rhode Island,
> Oh what worms they are! they wish to perfect their form.[3]

Dualistic views of American poetry have seemed increasingly oversimplified since the 1950s, when *raw* and *cooked* or *academic* and *non-academic* were terms that could pretend to some inclusiveness; but in those days such views were widely held, and intelligence and talent could be found on both sides. Even in such a climate, Hecht's sophistication was unusual; *A Summoning of Stones* may be the only American book of poems that twice employs the peruke as a symbol of artifice and restraint. Rooted confidently in the past, the poems sometimes seem removed from the present tense in which most of them are written. Though much that is described was made a long time ago, the poems only rarely dwell on any personal preoccupation with time's passing, or with mortality. They continue to exist in a timeless state, somewhat remote but durably elegant.

Though *The Hard Hours* opens with an unmetrical poem concerning a couple of personal recollections, most of the poems are cast in formal stanzas. Yet they have other qualities that led admirers, at the time, to make reckless statements of the sort that greeted James Wright's *The Branch Will Not Break*. Among the laudatory paragraphs reproduced on the jacket of *Collected Earlier Poems* is Ted Hughes's reaction to *The Hard Hours*, which reads, in part, "this most fastidious and elegant of poets shed every artifice and began to write with absolute raw simplicity and directness." Fortunately for Hecht and his readers, this is inaccurate; "absolute raw directness" is incompatible with metrical composition—if not with language itself.

3. Donald M. Allen, *The New American Poetry* (New York, 1960), 231.

It is true, however, that the diction of *The Hard Hours* is more often conversational than that of the early poems, and that many of the poems present speakers, or a speaker, aware of his helplessness in the face of forces beyond his control. "Adam," the poem which contains the book's title phrase, provides an example of some of these tendencies, and further demonstrates what can be achieved, not by shedding artifice, but by keeping it in its place. In it, a father addresses an absent son; they are separated for an unspecified reason. The following lines are in the middle of the poem:

> Where you are men speak
> A different mother tongue.
> Will you forget our games,
> Our hide-and-seek and song?
> Child, it will be long
> Before I see you again.
>
> Adam, there will be
> Many hard hours,
> As an old poem says,
> Hours of loneliness.
> I cannot ease them for you;
> They are our common lot.
> During them, like as not,
> You will dream of me.
> (CEP, 31)

In form, the first five of the poem's six stanzas resemble the one immediately above: eight lines, the first and eighth rhyming, and the sixth and seventh. Other rhymes and slant rhymes appear less predictably from stanza to stanza. The final stanza, however, is a small miracle of unobtrusive craft; the absence of rhyme within the stanza is all but unnoticeable. This is partly because four of the end-words more or less distinctly echo end-words located earlier in the poem, but chiefly because these lines convey flawlessly the speaker's wish for connection:

> Think of the summer rain
> Or seedpearls of the mist;
> Seeing the beaded leaf,

> Try to remember me.
> From far away
> I send my blessing out
> To circle the great globe.
> It shall reach you yet.
> (*CEP*, 32)

This poem and "The Vow" (in which the speaker makes promises to the spirit of a miscarried child) treat personal griefs with a directness that Hecht had previously avoided, but they do not depend, as confessional poems do, on the shock value inherent in certainty that they are autobiographical. "The Vow" begins starkly enough: "In the third month, a sudden flow of blood." But from there, the poem moves with control and assurance through echoes from the Bible, and from Sophocles ("For truly it is best of all the fates / Not to be born"), to the moving conclusion. Grief, dignity, and affirmation are so thoroughly married to art in this poem that a reader who pities the speaker, let alone the poet, misses the point entirely.

Sophocles turns up twice more in *The Hard Hours*—once in "The Dover Bitch," the wonderful nymph's reply through her spokesman in which the silent listener in Arnold's poem is at last portrayed, and again in "Three Prompters from the Wings," an extraordinary recasting of the Oedipus story, in which each of the three Fates discourses on aspects of it, and expresses resignation that she will be blamed for the events she has been at pains to explain in other ways. It has lately been unfashionable so to incur indebtedness to ancient authors, partly because many poets do it clumsily, making offhand references that cannot sustain the weight put on them. But Hecht has clearly absorbed that tradition as deeply as one can in our time; when he invokes it, he nearly always does so both with immediacy and with awareness of its cultural and temporal distance from us. The Fates speak in three-stress lines, their voices shifting rapidly between the formal and the colloquial; here Clotho, representing the present, speaks:

> Some sentimental fool
> Invented the Tragic Muse.
> She doesn't exist at all.
> For human life is composed
> In reasonably equal parts
> Of triumph and chagrin,

And the parts are so hotly fused
As to seem a single thing.
This is true as well
Of wisdom and ignorance
And of happiness and pain:
Nothing is purely itself
But is linked with its antidote
In cold self-mockery—
A fact with which only those
Born with a Comic sense
Can learn to content themselves.
(CEP, 25–26)

This idea informs the most powerful poems in *The Hard Hours*, some of which deal with subjects so nearly unbearable that they caused sensitive readers momentarily to forget how well made they are. "Behold the Lilies of the Field," "Rites and Ceremonies," "'More Light! More Light!'," and "'It Out-Herods Herod. Pray You, Avoid It.'" are various in formal treatment, but they all take time to look hard at examples of the hideous things humans can do to one another. That the voice remains steady and controlled through descriptions of men dying at the stake, or at the hands of SS officers, is among Hecht's unique accomplishments. No other recent poet has been able to meditate on such atrocities without posturing. Hecht's strength resides largely in his poetic resources, of course, but also in his detachment. As it is written in "Rites and Ceremonies," "The contemplation of horror is not edifying, / Neither does it strengthen the soul" (CEP, 43). And at the end of "Clair de Lune," "The heart turns to a stone, but it endures" (CEP, 21).

The heart's endurance is as mysterious as outrageous wickedness. But Hecht writes as convincingly of momentary or illusory pleasures as he does of mortality and torture. His third book, *Millions of Strange Shadows*, is framed at beginning and end by poems that capture moments of concentrated grace. "The Cost" contrasts the perilous grace of an Italian couple circling Trajan's column on a Vespa and the futility of the emperor's military exploits, especially the Dacian Wars. "The Lull" dwells on the moment when a sunlit July morning is transformed by an approaching storm:

            the air
Came to a sudden hush, and everywhere

> Things harden to an etched
> And iron immobility, as day
> Fades from a scurry of color to crosshatched,
> Sullen industrial tones of snapshot gray.
> (CEP, 178)

In the midst of such description, it is almost a lesson in poetry writing to come upon the statement that "the trustful eye" is "content to notice merely what is there." I think of Richard Wilbur's "Grace," in which Nijinsky explains his apparent ability to hang in mid-air: "I merely leap and pause."[4]

The detachment with which Hecht confronts evil, and his deepening interest in rendering a particular moment as clearly and fully as possible, have resulted in several poems of more than usual length. In recent years, these have chiefly been blank-verse monologues or narratives. *Millions of Strange Shadows* contains two superb and very different examples, though neither is as concerned with the invention of fictional characters as are the later long poems. "Apprehensions" recalls episodes in the speaker's boyhood, when he was young enough to be protected from understanding his family's fear and unhappiness, but old enough to know that they were there. He recalls his "Teutonic governess," a reader of sensationalist newspapers:

> My primary education was composed
> Of daily lessons in placating her
> With acts of shameless, mute docility.
> (CEP, 155)

He took refuge in the Book of Knowledge, and then in something else—a vision, or a keen awareness of what was truly there one afternoon, when an approaching thunderstorm altered the light on the street and made everything "distinct and legible"; a taxicab, in particular, took on "the absolute, parental yellow." This moment of clarity and stillness, broken by the storm itself, has stayed with him, like other moments Hecht has recalled in such poems as "The Lull," "A Hill," and the later "Auspices," and gathered significance in the faint light of subsequent realizations, which

> seemed to prove, in a world where proof
> Was often stinting, and the clues ominous,

4. Richard Wilbur, *New and Collected Poems* (New York, 1988), 384.

That the *Journal-American* after all was right:
That sex was somehow wedded to disaster,
Pleasure and pain were necessary twins,
And that the Book of Knowledge and my vision
(Or whatever it was) were to be put away
With childish things, as, in the end, the world
As well as holy text insist upon.
(CEP, 159)

The shadowy nature of the things that matter to the household—a brother's illness, the vagaries of Wall Street, the father's attempt at suicide, the peculiar cruelty of the governess, and her departure—are rendered in this poem with an amazing blend of precision and dreamlike vagueness, as if one were to apprehend a painting by looking at details from it. The gradual accretion of connections builds toward the conclusion, in which the speaker's dreams of encountering "Fräulein" combine with the actual nightmare of the *Reich*.

Vision and metaphor are also the means by which "Green: An Epistle" transcends mere self-excoriation. It begins with apparent directness:

I write at last of the one forbidden topic
We, by a truce, have never touched upon:
Resentment, malice, hatred so inwrought
With moral inhibitions, so at odds with
The home-movie of yourself as patience, kindness. . . .
(CEP, 117)

Only in the poem's last line does it become clear that the speaker of this meditation addresses himself, though there are a couple of earlier hints. The gradual burgeoning of hatred and malice is presented as the evolutionary development of plants; for some fifty lines, the fortunes and struggles of single cells, small plants and grasses, and at last trees, are described almost as they might be in one of Loren Eiseley's essays; this green prospect masks what it contains. The following passage, at the beginning of the penultimate verse paragraph, draws the metaphor more explicitly (and makes mordant allusion to what motivates some kinds of horticulture):

Consider, as one must, what was to come.
Great towering conifers, deciduous,

Rib-vaulted elms, the banyan, oak, and palm,
Sequoia forests of vindictiveness
That also would go down on the death list
And, buried deep within alluvial shifts,
Would slowly darken into lakes of coal
And then under exquisite pressure turn
Into the tiny diamonds of pure hate.
The delicate fingers of the clematis
Feeling their way along a face of shale
With all the ingenuity of spite.
The indigestible thistle of revenge.
And your most late accomplishment, the rose.
(CEP, 120)

The end of this poem, with its admission that the speaker confronts himself, opens into a spirit of reconciliation and peace, in which "the long ache / Of motives twisted out of recognition" (CEP, 121) can be recalled with some detachment and relief, though there is still a gap between the two selves; the addressed "you" sometimes contemplates the image "of some-one, a stranger, quite unknown / . . . Writing this very poem—about me" (CEP, 121).

In The Venetian Vespers, Hecht takes a new direction, though it partakes of some of his earliest excellences. "The Short End" and "The Venetian Vespers" are long narratives—or longer narratives, at least—running to about 385 lines and 850 lines, respectively, and they somewhat resemble the explorations of "Green: An Epistle" and "Apprehensions." But in these more recent poems, the speakers are clearly fictional characters, and the poems are more leisurely, though economical, in presenting elements of plot and character.

"The Short End" opens with a twenty-two-line sentence describing a large and astonishingly vulgar collection of souvenir pillows. We are far from the Villa D'Este. The first of the poem's five sections continues to set the scene: in late middle age, Shirley Carson is a drunk, and her husband, Nor-man, is the disillusioned owner and operator of an automobile body shop. He has long since given up on Shirley's drinking; he comes home, empties ash-trays and thinks about staleness, and goes to bed long before Shirley does:

She would sit up till late, smoking and drinking,
Afloat upon a wild surfeit of colors,

The midway braveries, harlequin streamers,
Or skewbald, carney liveries of the macaw,
Through which, from time to time, memories arose.
(CEP, 193)

"Of these," the second section begins, "two were persistent." Sections II and III detail the first, a wretched compound of nostalgia and humiliation, from the early days of the marriage; at a convention in Atlantic City, they are inveigled into a party by three other couples, who, when they discover that the Carsons are newlyweds, engage in a devastating round of bawdy toasts, songs, and suggestions. It is on this evening that Norman gains his lifelong nickname, Kit. Finally, when Kit and Shirley are released, it is made clear that they are the only married couple present, and that they have a lot to learn about conventions. The accuracy and dark humor of Hecht's narrative are scarifying:

The merriment was acid and complex.
Felix it was who kept proposing toasts
To "good ol' Shirl an' Kit," names which he slurred
Both in pronunciation and disparagement
With an expansive, wanton drunkenness
That in its license seemed soberly planned
To increase by graduated steps until
Without seeming aware of what he was doing
He'd raise a toast to "good ol' Curl an' Shit."
They managed to get away before that happened,
Though Shirley knew in her bones it was intended,
Had seen it coming from a mile away.
(CEP, 196–97)

With the opening of section IV, the second persistent memory is introduced; it is a bizarre item, like something out of Flannery O'Connor. This time, Shirley and Kit are somewhere south of Wheeling,

driving through a late day in November
Toward some goal obscure as the very weather,
Defunctive, moist, overcast, requiescent.
(CEP, 197)

Around a curve, they discover a long line of parked cars and a billboard announcing a live entombment. A smaller poster proves more expository, if not quite explanatory; in a coffin rigged with a viewing glass and a tube through which words and food may pass, one George Rose lies in apparent boredom, having "forsworn the vanities of this world." The promotion is being managed by John Wesley Rose, George's brother; contributions are requested. While Kit prepares to ask a few questions of John Wesley, Shirley wanders off to the edge of a ragged field and gradually comes to something like a hallucination; the voice of her old Latin teacher, long since dead, instructs her to stand right there forever:

> "Consider deeply why as the first example
> Of the first conjugation—which is not
> As conjugal as some suppose—one learns
> The model verb forms of 'to love,' *amare,*
> Which also happens to be the word for 'bitter.'[5]
> Both love and Latin are more difficult
> Than is usually imagined or admitted.
> This is your final exam; this is your classroom."
> (*CEP*, 200)

The final section of "The Short End" returns to the present, finding Shirley drunk among her pillows at three o'clock in the morning, looking at a Drambuie ad in *The New Yorker.* She lingers over the formally clad couple descending from a hansom cab, but what most holds her attention is the lantern on the cab; in its flame she sees "the figure *redivivus* of George Rose." This dissolves to a flood of red, and she dies.

Most poetry is ill served by plot summary, and "The Short End" is not much of an exception. But plot and characterization, rare in recent poetry, are among this poem's prime ingredients. Its scope and sympathy are remarkable by any standard; in our time they are virtually unique.

The nine poems that round out the first section of this book are short poems and translations of brilliant polish; they are overshadowed, perhaps, by "The Short End" and "The Venetian Vespers," but two or three of them stand out sharply, even so. "Still Life" is a perfect evocation of a predawn landscape heavy with fog and dew; the intentness with which it is described

---

5. Hecht's note on this line (*CEP*, 271): "Strictly speaking it is the adverbial 'bitterly,' but this lapse is to be explained by the imperfect memory of a former student in an hour of stress."

and the feeling of anticipation that it generates are explained in the final
lines, when it becomes clear that this scene has aspects of the *déjà vu*:

I stand beneath a pine-tree in the cold,
Just before dawn, somewhere in Germany,
A cold, wet, Garand rifle in my hands.
(CEP, 211)

Two witty "versions" of poems by Horace deftly combine freedom and
fidelity; "Application for a Grant" (*CEP*, 208) alters the letter, but perhaps
not the spirit, of the first of the Odes, in which Horace presents in sequence
a few of mankind's better-known aspirations, saving his own—perfection
of his art—for last. Hecht emphasizes the patron-seeking side of this poem
and brings it up-to-date, addressing it to the "Noble executors of the munifi-
cent testament / Of the late John Simon Guggenheim," and listing among
human aspirations occupying the White House and being known by the
headwaiter at the Tour d'Argent. The poem is funny enough before the original is consulted, but the wit of the substitutions is delectable when it is
discovered.

The same is true of "An Old Malediction" (*CEP*, 217), a somewhat
slighter poem subtitled "freely from Horace." Taking off from the short
Ode V, addressed to a coquette, Hecht plays with a few details, as when
Horace asks, literally, "For whom do you tie back your blonde hair / in simple
elegance?" Hecht renders this "Dazzled though he be, poor dope, by the
golden looks / Your locks fetched up out of a bottle of *Clairol.* . . ."

It is possible that the extended narrative range of this book has been
nurtured by Hecht's experience as a translator of Greek tragedy. With Helen
Bacon, he has produced a magnificent version of Aeschylus' *Seven Against
Thebes*, and his translation of Sophocles' *Oedipus at Colonus* can safely be
called "long-awaited." The Greek Tragedies in New Translations series established by the late William Arrowsmith and published by Oxford University
Press, of which they are a part, has so far proven an uneven enterprise, but
Hecht's contribution has about it as much permanence as translation is likely
to have.

Though the short poems and translations in this book are clearly equal
to Hecht's deservedly high reputation, it is the stunning title poem for which
the collection is to be cherished. "The Venetian Vespers" is a monologue,
less spectacular in episode than "The Short End," but more thorough in its
concentration on the tension between a life's momentary consolations and
its hopelessness. The speaker is an expatriate from Lawrence, Massachusetts,

of immigrant stock. When he was a child, his father went west to seek a better life for his family and was not heard from again; it was many years before anyone but an uncle knew that he had spent the rest of his life in a hospital after an accident, with no proof of his identity. This uncle's success in business was largely due to his secret refusal to acknowledge his brother; the speaker now lives on an annuity inherited from his uncle, thus sharing in the fruits of a peculiar crime. At extravagant and absorbing leisure, he muses upon Venice, his orphaned childhood and vaguely troubled youth, his non-combatant service during World War II, his frail health and approaching death:

> I wander these by-paths and little squares,
> A singular Tyrannosauros Rex,
> Sauntering towards extinction, an obsolete
> Left-over from a weak *ancien régime*
> About to be edged out by upstart germs.
> I shall pay out the forfeit with my life
> In my own lingering way. Just as my uncle,
> Who, my blood tells me on my nightly rounds,
> May perhaps be "a little more than kin,"
> Has paid the price for his unlawful grief
> And bloodless butchery by creating me
> His guilty legatee, the beneficiary
> Of his money and his crimes.
> (*CEP*, 246)

Despite the grim pessimism and shame with which the speaker regards himself, he rejoices in the sound of language, coating pain with artifice, and thereby draws attention to the fleeting pleasures that make his life—or the thought of it, at least—bearable. This magnificent poem braids strands that weave through much of Hecht's other work; some of them he had not taken up since A *Summoning of Stones*.

II

The Transparent Man (1990) continues this tendency to move simultaneously toward and away from preoccupations of Hecht's early poems. "Terms" is cast in the most tightly repetitive form Hecht has ever employed. From among the several manifestations of the canzone, he has chosen the most challenging: five twelve-line stanzas and a five-line envoy, employing only five end-words or their homophonic substitutes; in each stanza one appears six times, two twice, and two once, all according to a rigid pattern; of course each appears once in the envoy. It makes a double sonnet look like a pleasant before-breakfast exercise. Sestinas, in which adjacent repetition of end-words occurs only across stanza breaks, may almost conceal their patterns. "Terms," by contrast, makes graceful peace with a rising tide of teleutonic audibility, as end-words close with increasing tightness around a vision of the world grown old and ill.

There is also a sestina here. "The Book of Yolek" recounts a five-year-old boy's walk to the death camps in 1942. In its quiet conviction that the memory of Yolek will endure, the poem is somewhat less shocking than some of Hecht's earlier poems on the Holocaust, but there is elemental force in its relative simplicity. The same may be said for another treatment of a familiar point of departure, a translation of a choral ode from *Oedipus at Colonus,* in which the line quoted in "The Vow" is cut down to "Not to be born is, past all yearning, best."[6]

Still, seekers after elaborate and allusive play will be delighted with "A Love for Four Voices," in which the couples from *A Midsummer Night's Dream* are set down in a masque that takes its structure from a Haydn quartet. The form is merely analogous, of course, since words do not blend simultaneously as well as musical notes do; but the wordplay, sexual and otherwise, carries the poem handsomely over several pages. Hecht has always had a place in his work for humor, ranging from serious satire to pure fun; "The Dover Bitch" is now a minor classic, and a few double-dactyls are still lurking about, ready to call Hecht father at some inopportune moment. But the somber and the light-hearted are more deeply blended in *The Transparent Man* than in Hecht's earlier books.

Among the light-hearted poems is a wonderful sonnet, "Naming the Animals"; the octave recalls the legend of Adam as First Poet, and the sestet presents him as a real beginner:

Before an addled mind and puddled brow,
The feathered nation and the finny prey

6. Anthony Hecht, *The Transparent Man* (New York, 1990), 5. Hereafter cited in the text as *TM*, followed by a page number.

Passed by; there went biped and quadruped.
Adam looked forth with bottomless dismay
Into the tragic eyes of his first cow,
And shyly ventured, "Thou shalt be called 'Fred.'"
(*TM*, 58)

But here as in *The Venetian Vespers*, Hecht is at his best in two extended monologues, the title poem and "See Naples and Die." The speaker of the latter recalls, years after the fact, how his marriage began to dissolve during a vacation in Naples. Unwittingly, he reveals enough about himself to convince the reader that he will never understand the depth of the difference between himself and his wife; he is troubled by her emotional reactions to things, and she arouses in him some guilt concerning his relative lack of feeling. He refers several times to the necessity "To form for ourselves a carapace of sorts, / A self-preservative petrific toughness" (*TM*, 29). He echoes the speaker of "The Venetian Vespers," who says, "The mind / Can scarcely cope with the world's sufferings, / Must blinker itself to much or else go mad" (*CEP*, 233). But this former husband sometimes reveals that he has been all too successful in this conscious and nearly willed fall from innocence:

We were both
Decent and well-intentioned, capable
Of love and devotion and all the rest of it.
(*TM*, 33)

It is only at the end of the poem, when he arrives at a private vision of what hell is, that he rises to a fusion of language and belief that transcends his pettiness. That he does so convincingly is one of the strongest moments in this book. Recalling a visit to a place called the Elysian Fields, which turned out to be little more than an ugly thicket dotted with bare headstones, he says,

What sticks in the mind, what I cannot escape,
Is the setting in which we found ourselves that day
I first began to see us as outcast:
The ugliness of the landscape, the conviction
That no painter would think it worth a glance.
There are both places and periods in life

That are tolerable only as transitions;
Hell might consist in staying there forever,
Immobile, never able to depart.
(*TM*, 34)

Here is someone so imprisoned by his views that he can think of places and periods in life that are not transitional. There is one, of course; our knowledge of it is limited, considering its population, but this poem ends with a vision of it that both derives and sets itself apart from Milton. Almost incredibly, the speaker's recollection of the Elysian Fields is deepened by his having read a passage in the Younger Pliny concerning the Elder Pliny, who calmly walked about, protected for a time by a pillow on his head, studying the eruption of Vesuvius that destroyed Pompeii. The concluding lines of the poem report what he saw before he himself was destroyed; the last two words make an excruciating oxymoron:

Of all those strange sights the most ominous
Was perhaps the sudden vision of the sea
Sucked out and drained away by the earthquake
That was part of the eruption, leaving a sea-bed
Of naked horrors lighted now and then
By jets of fire and sheet-lightning flares,
Only to be folded back into the dark.
One could make out in such brief intervals
An endless beach littered with squirming fish,
With kelp and timbers strewn on muddy flats,
Giant sea-worms bright with a glittering slime,
Crabs limping in their rheumatoid pavane.
(*TM*, 34)

"The Transparent Man" teeters on the brink of sentimentality, but stays this side of it. Its speaker is a woman just thirty, lying in a hospital and awaiting death from leukemia. The diction ranges convincingly between chattiness and majesty, as she reveals the language that can come to one who has elected to dwell at length upon small things—among which, finally, she can place her own impending death. Her companions are the trees outside her window, in whose branches she has seen the circulatory system of the brain, recalled from a plastic model she played with as a child.

The vaguely tangled branches of the trees, though they are less threatening in this poem, echo the several instances in Hecht's work of fallow, ragged winter landscapes, in which weeds persist despite the weather. The field where Shirley Carson hears her old Latin teacher, the hellish Elysian Fields of "See Naples and Die," and the childhood recollection in "A Hill" are images of chaos only temporarily held in abeyance by the season. In "Auspices," Hecht says of them, "These are the wilds / Of loneliness, huge, vacant, sour and plain" (*CEP*, 207). The speaker of "The Transparent Man" finds a consoling way of looking at them; elsewhere, Hecht's descriptions of them recall the "controlled disorder" of the D'Este gardens, as the formal voice and structure of the poems hold the vision at bay.

Beyond the trees in the foreground, she can see a wood, but cannot distinguish individuals; she knows that winter and snow might make that seem easier:

> Of course I know
> That within a month the sleeving snows will come
> With cold, selective emphases, with massings
> And arbitrary contrasts, rendering things
> Deceptively simple, thickening the twigs
> To frosty veins, bestowing epaulets
> And decorations on every birch and aspen.
> And the eye, self-satisfied, will be misled,
> Thinking the puzzle solved, supposing at last
> It can look forth and comprehend the world.
> That's when you have to really watch yourself.
> (*TM*, 71–72)

It is Hecht's singular achievement that he can contemplate the human tendency to confuse the important and the trivial, without Swiftian outrage at foolishness and delusion. I suppose that a poet of such profound refinement must have found some realm of our experience that he considers unspeakable, but I do not know what it could be. No other poet of our time has been able to find such beautiful language for our peculiar joys and horrors.

LOUIS SIMPSON Great Experiments

In 1988, Louis Simpson published his *Collected Poems*. At the head of the table of contents, he says, "These are not all my poems—they are the poems I would like to be remembered by."[1] Fortunately, however, Simpson has been more generous here in selecting from his early work than he was in his previous retrospective collections, *Selected Poems* (1965) and *People Live Here: Selected Poems 1949–1983* (1983). There are no new poems, since a new collection, *In the Room We Share*, followed this one in 1990. But these 179 poems not only provide ample evidence of the poet's changing concerns and ways of doing things; they also give more pleasure, poem by poem, than do most lifetime collections. *Collected Poems* is the record of a triumphant progress.

In addition to the two selected volumes, Simpson has published nine books of poems up to now. According to certain milestones of a poetic career, they fall into two groups. In 1969, Richard Howard noted that the story of a career might be deduced, "perhaps unfairly," from the titles of the first four collections: *The Arrivistes* (1949), *Good News of Death* (1955), *A Dream of*

1. Louis Simpson, *Collected Poems* (New York, 1988), vii. Hereafter cited in the text as CP, followed by a page number.

Governors (1959), and *At the End of the Open Road* (1963; Pulitzer Prize, 1964). "It is," Howard wrote, "a sad, successful story."[2] After twenty-seven years, and the addition of five more "lines" to this cryptic "narrative," the success is untarnished, but the sadness, if it was ever evident, is harder to discern: *Adventures of the Letter I* (1971), *Searching for the Ox* (1976), *Caviare at the Funeral* (1980), *The Best Hour of the Night* (1983), and *In the Room We Share* (1990) make a series that might be battered into suggesting some movement toward closure, but not without good humor.

Simpson was born in Jamaica, in the British West Indies, and came to this country when he was seventeen. He did not become an American citizen until he had been through several major engagements as an American soldier during World War II. The discovery of America, then, is a theme that recurs frequently in Simpson's poetry; the treatments of that theme become increasingly complex and rewarding as the poet himself becomes more thoroughly American.

Simpson's first book, *The Arrivistes*, was published in Paris at his own expense. It contains poems arising from the landscape of Jamaica, from the oddity and emptiness that can characterize life in New York, and from episodes recalled from the war. "Carentan O Carentan" is a bitter recollection of the young soldier's introduction to battle; the ballad form, with its slightly antique diction, lends a haunting wistfulness to the gruesome narrative details:

> There is a whistling in the leaves
> And it is not the wind,
> The twigs are falling from the knives
> That cut men to the ground.
> (CP, 24)

Most of the subjects of these poems are matters that have often engaged the poet since; even some relatively minor images have a noticeable persistence in his work. In *The Arrivistes*, for example, there is this stanza, from "Lazarus Convalescent":

2. Richard Howard, *Alone with America* (New York, 1969), 452–53.

The water laps, the seagulls plunge and squawk
And lovers lock in wind that makes him shiver.
"I'll have to learn to use a knife and fork
Again. Look there above us!
Spry's for Baking . . . starry spectacle.
For Frying. More, a miracle."
(*CP*, 10)

In *The Best Hour of the Night* (1983), the blinking advertisement for Spry turns up again, in "Periodontics." In this four-page poem the speaker's thoughts make apparently casual leaps of association; the poet has linked them with consummate subtlety. Trying to ignore the pain of having his teeth cleaned, the speaker studies the initials on the dental unit; they are also those of Paula Chapman, a high school sweetheart who lived across the street from the Spry sign. A recollection of their humiliating night at the prom ends with the speaker "drinking quantities / of pink lemonade out of paper cups" (*CP*, 353). On the next page, back in the present and the dentist's chair, he accepts from the hygienist "the paper cup / with the liquid that's bright red / and bitter."

The poem ends with an account of a brief and unsatisfactory reunion between Paula and the speaker; after twenty years,

The magic, as they say, was gone,
like a song that used to be on the hit parade.

But there is always a new song,
and some things never change.
Not long ago, visiting a friend
who lives on Riverside Drive
I saw that the sign for Spry
is still there, shining away.

"Spry for Baking." It blinks off
and on again . . . "For Frying."
Then the lights run around in a circle.
(*CP*, 355)

While Simpson's prosody has changed dramatically, traces of an earlier manner continue to appear, along with the occasionally recurring images. In

the third and fourth lines above, there is an echo of such ballad rhythms as
Simpson mastered early.

Along with a variety of excellent short lyrics, Simpson has experimented
from the beginning with ways of expanding a single poetic work. The title
poems of his first two books are effective pseudodramas that take witty advantage of the literary self-consciousness their conventions inspire. *A Dream of
Governors* contains "The Runner," a narrative of just over 700 lines of flexible blank verse, set in Holland and France in the fall of 1944. Dodd, the
protagonist, is a soldier with the 101st Airborne; he is called "the runner"
because his primary responsibility is to carry messages. He has a wish to be
brave, then an hour or so of bravery, followed a few weeks later by a moment
of destructive panic, after which he endures some weeks of humiliation; finally he is given a second chance. Much of the plot and detail are reworked
around a character named Bell in Simpson's novel, *Riverside Drive* (1962).

The poem opens with a half-page note declaring the poem to be fiction
based on historical events, which are briefly recounted. The first few lines of
the poem itself are repetitious and harshly suggestive of military routine:

> "And the condemned man ate a hearty meal,"
> The runner said. He took his mess kit over
> To the garbage can. He scraped his mess kit out,
> Then dipped it in the can of soapy water,
> And swished it in the can of clean, hot water,
> And came back to his place.
> (CP, 100)

With the exception of a few passages, the style of the whole poem is very
much like this, if less dependent on verbal repetition. The sentences are
short; in none of the poem's twelve sections does the ratio of lines to sentences rise much beyond one and one-half to one; in the final section, there
are more sentences than lines. The welter of authentic detail carries the
narrative, along with the interaction among Dodd and a handful of secondary
characters, some of them not visualized; they are little more than bits of
dialogue.

Dodd is set apart from most of his compatriots. He is better educated
than most of the men with whom he speaks, and some of his conversational
gambits, such as the first line, arouse their irritation. His being a runner,

furthermore, sometimes puts him in a curious limbo where he is regarded as somehow not fully a combat soldier. On a messenger's errand one night, he ponders his status:

> A man could be a runner all his life
> And never be shot at. That's what they thought.
> But how about the shelling? He'd been shelled
> As much as anyone. And back in France,
> At Carentan, he had been shot at—plenty!
> It wasn't his fault he never had a chance
> To fire back. Now, right here on this road,
> He might be killed by accident. But still,
> That wouldn't be the same as being brave.
> He had no chance to be thought so, no part
> In the society of riflemen.
> So, as he went, he reasoned with himself.
> (CP, 109–10)

This passage, like many another in this understated poem, captures with touching precision the young soldier's vacillation between childishness and maturity. The following day, Dodd's company comes under fire:

> He felt a sting between his shoulder blades.
> I'm wounded! he thought, with a rush of joy.
> (CP, 110)

He then delivers boxes of ammunition to a mortar crew, at considerable danger to himself, and lies down that evening without a care, having done "all that could be expected" (CP, 111).

Some weeks later, however, he returns to camp by a way he does not know, wanting to avoid a field full of corpses. He gets lost, is challenged in German, and panics, running across the battlefield yelling the company's password. He falls into a hole, and is discovered by men from his company. There follows a period of humiliation, while the division is camped at Rheims during a lull; this section, IX, is curiously visionary. Dodd falls asleep in his tent, listening to men outside at drill, making fun of him; he dreams odd snatches from literature and French history, which distance and dream render inaccurate and meaningless. When he wakes he goes out for a walk and finds a trench, apparently dug during World War I, and comes to feel the presence of the men who fought there. Like the actual men, the shadows fade; the same moment, described in *Riverside Drive*, concludes with a brief meditation in the spirit of much of Simpson's later poetry. Portions of the novel are reprinted in Simpson's *Selected Prose*:

> The greater part of life has not been expressed. The simple and illiterate, those who sustain the labor and pain of existence, those who carry out the orders, are never themselves heard. History neglects to mention them; most art admits little of their existence. Yet on the hill near Rheims, and at other times in my life, I have seen for a moment into the depth of this life, and it has given me an instinctive distrust of expressed ideas. If most of man's life has passed into silence, is not truth itself silent?[3]

Something like this is behind "The Runner," with its insistence on the daily boredom, grubbiness, and gradual distortion of emotion that character-ize much of life for the infantryman. When the 101st moves in around Bas-togne, Dodd finds himself in the trenches again, firing his rifle at an oncom-ing tank, which is finally disabled by some stiffer firepower. The poem ends with Dodd once more a trusted messenger, the moment of panic forgiven; but as he sets off on another errand, the inconclusiveness of the situation is emphasized:

> Dodd waved his hand, although it was too dark
> For the other to see him. And set off
> In what seemed to be the right direction.
> (CP, 123)

"The Runner" is a compelling narrative on its own terms; furthermore, it reveals Simpson's deepening interest in concealing artifice. It was written before Simpson stopped writing in traditional meters, but in its insistence on the importance of apparently trivial detail, and of external routine as a

---

3. Louis Simpson, *Selected Prose* (New York, 1989), 132. Hereafter cited in the text as *SP*, followed by a page number.

dehumanizing force, it points energetically in a direction Simpson would soon take.

The war, the poetry of young love, and the mastery of strict form run like a current from *The Arrivistes* through *Good News of Death* and *A Dream of Governors*. In his third book, Simpson handles these with an authority that seems to lift the best of his poems out of time, as in "To the Western World," a poem of fifteen lines that recapitulates the discovery of America by European explorers and, later, by immigrants. The third stanza memorably characterizes an age and a way of life:

> The treasures of Cathay were never found.
> In this America, this wilderness
> Where the axe echoes with a lonely sound,
> The generations labor to possess
> And grave by grave we civilize the ground.
> (CP, 90)

There are few examples of this mode in *At the End of the Open Road;* Simpson's shift to free verse was swift and dramatic, and such poems in quatrains as "My Father in the Night Commanding No" and "The Riders Held Back" seem at first out of place in the collection. But they are fine poems, and they offer a kind of ballast for the bold voyage into a more deeply confronted America. If the meters of "To the Western World" are generally absent, its themes are present.

Five of the poems Simpson has collected from *At the End of the Open Road* refer to Walt Whitman, or address him directly. Whitman's assertions—about poetry, people, and America—are tested in poems that acknowledge their indebtedness to him without sounding like him. In "Lines Written Near San Francisco," Simpson presents a landscape that seems to have skipped some of the history behind other civilizations. This country seems to have gone from the promise of wilderness directly into late decline:

> While we were waiting for the land
> They'd finished it—with gas drums
> On the hilltops, cheap housing in the valleys
>
> Where lives are mean and wretched.
> . . . .

Whitman was wrong about the People,
But right about himself. The land is within.
At the end of the open road we come to ourselves.
(CP, 166–67)

On the other hand, Whitman reminded his readers that writing poetry
was not always a matter of excising the extraneous; he demonstrated, and
preached, that poems could be inclusive in difficult, ill-mannered ways. From
this notion Simpson fashioned a six-line poem that has perhaps been more
often quoted than any other poem in *At the End of the Open Road.* "American
Poetry" must be able to digest all kinds of things, and "It must swim for miles
through the desert / Uttering cries that are almost human" (CP, 154).

For Simpson, the suburbs seemed at that time a useful analogy to the
desert. "In the Suburbs," another well-known six-line poem, seems hopeless
enough:

There's no way out.
You were born to waste your life.
You were born to this middleclass life

As others before you
Were born to walk in procession
To the temple, singing.
(CP, 136)

This small poem is brilliantly balanced between the idea of the first line, and
the ideas of nobility conveyed by the two ways of life; the inescapable condition of the singers is not emphasized.

The Preface to *Collected Poems* ends with a few words about making
poems in an unpoetic age:

In recent years I have written about occurrences, sometimes very ordinary
ones, in which there is a meaning hidden beneath the surface. Bringing out
such meanings, it seems to me, is a road poetry can take in a world that, as
it grows more industrial, seems less beautiful in the old sense. The more
banal and "anti-poetic" the material, the more there is for the poet to do.
For this work a sense of humor is as necessary as an awareness of the drama,
the terror and beauty of life. (CP, xiv)

Simpson has always made occasional use of an odd, sometimes surrealistic humor; it is not absent from *At the End of the Open Road*, the most baleful of his collections (I think immediately of the hilariously threatening atmosphere of "On the Lawn at the Villa"), but he is right to note its increasing usefulness in the four books that followed his prizewinner.

Two of the themes that most often recur in Simpson's later work are the mystery of a lost, imagined past, and the triviality and despair of much suburban life. The poems that invent the past are partly based on family history. Simpson's mother, he explains in the preface, was born in Russia, and told him stories. These Simpson has remembered and used to shape an imaginary Russia, populated with people who were his relatives, and by people who were created by such writers as Tolstoy and Chekhov. Most of the poems about Russia appear in *Adventures of the Letter I*, though there are a few in both *Searching for the Ox* and *Caviare at the Funeral*. In these, anecdote and character, the need for a story, are central—so much so, in fact, that the "actual" and "fictional" characters are equally alive, just as Huckleberry Finn and Abraham Lincoln are equally "real" in most American imaginations.

The title poem of *Caviare at the Funeral*, for example, expands imaginatively on an epigraph from Chekhov's "In the Ravine": "This was the village where the deacon ate all the caviare at the funeral." The deacon's bold commitment to what began as carelessness is funny and touching, though its results are disastrous:

Next morning he was seen at the station
buying a ticket for Kurovskoye,
a village much like ours, only smaller.
(CP, 298)

Chekhov himself becomes a character in "Chocolates," which immediately follows "Caviare at the Funeral." According to Simpson, "The poem is based on an actual incident" (SP, 348). During a visit from some admirers, Chekhov briefly endures talk about himself and his work, and then shifts the conversation to chocolates—a topic on which everyone has strong opinions. The visitors are suddenly at ease. The poem is not without humor, but its more serious point—that people are happier discussing what they can than what they think they ought to—is of a piece with Simpson's own love of particulars, and his suspicion of "expressed ideas."

At the End of the Open Road attracted attention partly because of Simpson's relatively sudden shift to poems in more relaxed and open forms. For various reasons, most of them private, a number of other poets of roughly the same generation—James Wright, W. S. Merwin, Galway Kinnell, and Adrienne Rich, for example—were making similar shifts at about the same time. Various cultural forces contributed to this phenomenon, but the work of each of these poets provides, in itself, specific reasons for that poet's having sought a new way of working. Simpson addresses his dissatisfaction with meter and rhyme in a brief essay about the composition of "Walt Whitman at Bear Mountain," which "marked a turning point in [his] work." Simpson says that in *A Dream of Governors* he had contended successfullly with certain difficulties of writing in form, and continues:

> But now I felt that my skill was a straitjacket. . . . It was time, I felt, to write a new kind of poem. I wanted to write a poem that would be less "willed." I would let images speak for themselves. The poem would be a statement, of course—there really is no such thing as a poem of pure metaphor or image—but I wanted the statement to be determined by the poem itself, to let my original feeling develop, without confining it in any strict fashion. . . .
>
> My groping toward a poetry of significant images and spoken lines enabled me to say certain things that I had not been able to say before. ["Walt Whitman at Bear Mountain"] was followed by others in which I was able to deal with material that interested me—poems about history, my own personal life, America. (*SP*, 337)

This commentary is immediately followed in *Selected Prose* by a short piece written much later. "The terms of Life Itself: Writing 'Quiet Desperation,'" first published in 1985, reveals that Simpson has continued to ponder the uses of various prosodies: "The stresses within the lines are so variable that I would not call them feet. I do observe, however, a preponderance of lines with three or four stresses. The lines vary in length, and I pause at the end of a line or run on as I would if I were speaking. This kind of verse isn't entirely free and it isn't written in meter. The term I think best describes it is 'free form'" (*SP*, 346).

It is hard, even in our time, to imagine how verse might be "entirely free"; Simpson is obviously correct in saying that his is not. "Free form," however, is a term that applies less effectively to verse than it does to palette-shaped coffee tables and theftproof motel ashtrays. Simpson is writing free verse, but it is firmly controlled, and the preponderance of three- and four-stress lines creates important reverberations.

The absence of regular rhyme and meter in Simpson's later work is certainly noticeable, but it is not total. Throughout the poems collected from Simpson's four later books, there are brief passages in which something like common measure, or like an anonymous ballad, makes a fleeting but effective appearance. In Simpson's early work, the ballad stanza is often an occasion for "ballad language," a slightly archaic and literary diction, such as characterizes "Carentan O Carentan"; that kind of language appears in the later poems very rarely, and then only to satiric or ironic effect.

In free verse composed largely of three- and four-stress lines, there will of course be brief passages of iambic tetrameter and iambic trimeter. Such passages can appear where they will be noticed, and where they will not. They can in rare cases be reinforced by rhyme. But if they appear too often, they create an uncomfortable tension, a feeling that less rhythmical passages are less "finished."

A few examples, taken out of context, faintly suggest the effectiveness with which they appear:

And the light that used to shine
at night in my father's study
now shines as late in mine.
("Working Late," CP, 265)

He supposed this was what life taught you,
that words you thought were a joke,
and applied to someone else,
were real, and applied to you.
("A Bower of Roses," CP, 276)

He cannot bear the sun
going over and going down . . .
the trees and houses vanishing
in quiet every day.
("Quiet Desperation," CP, 335)

Though I have prayed with Eliot,
"Teach us to sit still,"

> this could be laziness,
> and life could be very dull.
> ("The Champion Single Sculls," CP, 364)

> And there were streets and ruins
> in the weedy ooze below . . .
> the pirate town that vanished
> in an earthquake long ago.
> ("A Fine Day for Straw Hats," CP, 365)

Passages like these, along with numerous shorter and less obvious rhythmical echoes of old ballads, have beautiful and somewhat mysterious effects. In Simpson's poems, they make nearly subliminal connections between his narratives and older ones, and they create a rewarding tension between themselves and the less traditionally rhythmical passages. The marvel is that Simpson can do this with such delicacy as to keep the less metrical passages from seeming too flat. His control of tone is complete; the nonmetrical passages have no less "finish" than the metrical ones. It has been suggested that free verse is inferior to metrical verse because it provides nothing against which to make variations. Simpson's ear is so good that some of his poems suggest an opposite possibility, quite at odds with certain rules of the workshop thumb: that free verse can be rewardingly varied by the occasional use of meter.

Simpson allows himself a certain self-consciousness in the poems about suburbia, which range from the despairing, through the wickedly satirical, to the hopeful. He includes himself, or a character who must be seen as standing in for him, in many of these poems, and directly treats some of the problems of being a poet in such a context. "Sacred Objects," from *Adventures of the Letter I*, begins with a mildly zany self-deprecation:

> I am taking part in a great experiment—
> whether writers can live peacefully in the suburbs
> and not be bored to death.

> As Whitman said, an American muse
> installed amid the kitchen ware.
> (CP, 218)

This passage makes it hard to take seriously the notion of the "great experiment," but in fact a large number of Simpson's recent poems display its amazingly successful results. Putting out the garbage, paying bills, riding the commuter train, stripping paint from woodwork, and so on, would seem to put a poet in danger of stultifying repetitiveness, but the equipment that Simpson has been selecting and honing for more than forty years continues to stand him in good stead. These poems are astonishing not only for the frequently daring banality of their surfaces, but even more so for the range of their tones and the depth of their emotional resonances.

On the one hand, there is sharp satire, as in "The Unwritten Poem," which characterizes "a life beginning with 'Hi!' and ending with 'So long!'" On the other, there is the extraordinary complexity of "The Previous Tenant," a fourteen-page poem containing more people and events than are contained in many novels. It winds confidently among various attitudes—regret, affection, contempt—toward an array of suburban characters. The narrator might at first be thought to stand for the author, but his various ineptitudes increasingly interfere with this reading.

The poem is in ten sections of varying lengths; the style is flat, even by Simpson's standards. The tone is constantly in danger of seeming inappropriate; most of the time, the narrator is like a low-key, monotonic comedian. In the opening section, he establishes himself in a cottage still somewhat encumbered by things the previous tenant has left behind. On a visit, the landlord begins to talk about that person, a doctor named Hugh McNeil. As background is supplied, there is a subtle blurring of point of view, so that the attitudes of neighbors, co-workers, wives, and so on, appear to come through clearly. McNeil was liked and admired; once, at a village meeting, he failed to persuade his neighbors to retain a Latin teacher. He accepts this defeat with grace, and earns more of his neighbors' respect and affection:

> The residents of Point Mercy
> are proud of their village
> with its beautiful homes and gardens
> and wild life sanctuary.
> Contrary to what people say
> about the suburbs, they appreciate culture.
> Hugh McNeil was an example . . .
> doing the shopping, going to the club,
> a man in no way different from themselves,

husband and family man
and good neighbor, who nevertheless spoke Latin.
(CP, 338)

It is nearly possible to take this at face value, but even intensive study of Latin rarely results in the ability to speak it. This is but one of many satiric exposures of the narrowness, anti-Semitism, and complacent ignorance of most of the upper-class suburbanites who populate the poem.

McNeil's life becomes complicated by his affair with one Irene Davis. There is damaging gossip; he is assaulted by Irene's brothers, who appear to be gangsters; finally, his wife sues for divorce, and he moves into the cottage now being occupied by the narrator. In the sixth section, the narrator's knowledge of the place, and of his own habits, inform his imaginings of McNeil's life there; the two of them almost blend into one character—lonely, expert with frozen food, deeply knowledgeable of late-night television.

Writing, and the reactions of one's neighbors to one's being a writer, come in for a fair drubbing in this and a few other poems, though the effect is rarely to suggest that the writer should do anything but what he does. In "The Previous Tenant," however, the writer takes on some of the stereotypical habits and attitudes of bad writers. He goes through a batch of letters he has turned up, and learns more about the affair between McNeil and Irene; his pronouncements on some of the details reveal a pedestrian imagination:

I copied some of the passages.
They might come in useful. There was an idea for a novel
I'd had for years: A Bovary of the Sierras . . .
The Bovary of Evanston . . . The Bovary of Green Harbor.
(CP, 343)

By the end of the poem, the writer-narrator has edged back a little nearer our respect, so we can look from both sides at the ending, in which one of the suburban wives is quoted, self-righteously dismissing the narrator's novel and insisting on the sufficiency of the New Yorker, Time, and the Book of the Month. As our belief in the narrator's writing talent wanes and waxes, along with the confidence with which we can equate the narrator and the author, Simpson's lines about the "great experiment" might remind us that the pressures of suburban mentality could make even a poet like Simpson think, now and then, of writing a Bovary of Green Harbor.

Simpson regularly insists that the poet writes from where he is, and makes what can be made from there. "At the end of the open road we come to ourselves": depending on the poetry one writes, this statement could be either hopeful or despairing. Simpson has clearly not found himself in a cul-de-sac whose confines threaten to silence him, or to turn him inward on his own self, to the exclusion of others, though he writes, in both prose and verse, of some difficulties attendant on writing poetry in our time.

He is not always solemn about this. *Selected Prose* concludes with a poem, "Trouble," as an afterword; in it, the poet worries for a while about his happiness, and its tendency to keep him from writing. The poem concludes with the poet looking out a window, imagining what the "powers that be" have decided about him:

> "no more poetry for this fellow,
> just life, since he likes it so much.
> .   .   .   .
>
> What we like is a burnt offering . . .
> not just cooked, scorched black,
> a heart turning on a spit
> over the fires of greed
> and lust and self-loathing.
>
> But a white birch by a door,
> sunlight breaking from a cloud,
> yellow and purple tips
> pushing up from the ground,
> and the woman he's so fond of . . .
>
> if that's all he wants, let him have it,
> there's nothing we can do for him."
> (*SP*, 516)

The speaker may seem to wonder how he can go on, but the absurdly melodramatic images of sacrifice, and Simpson's continuing work itself, provide all the necessary answers to that question.

JOHN WOODS In the Grip of Days

Several fine poets, including David Wagoner and James Wright, have remarked over the years that the poetry of John Woods has not received the critical attention it deserves. Less responsible commentators have overstated the case for his work, doubtless with the honorable intent of helping to rectify the situation; for some time, it was possible to find on the jackets of his books a kind of label—"America's best poet"—which had been offered in something called *New American and Canadian Poetry.* This is not the place to make a detailed argument against the possibility of identifying America's best poet; it is enough to say that the diversity and range of contemporary poetry in this country are so great that consensus about the best is increasingly hard to reach, and that to pretend otherwise, for the sake of championing a particular poet, is likely to arouse more derision than assent.

There remains the question of Woods's reputation; he has published eight books and a few chapbooks, and most of these have received praise from people who know what they are talking about; a reading of all his books of poems leads me to the conclusion that his art has developed along lines that can only be followed by paying vigilant attention to the most difficult choices a poet faces—when to keep going in a vein one seems to have mastered, when to attempt poems in an unfamiliar manner, when to decide that a poem, however obscure, has reached its optimum clarity, which poems to keep and which to abandon when making a selection from earlier work. No poet has made unarguably right decisions about these matters at all times; certainly Woods has written his share of poems I would prefer not to have seen, or has tried too many times to work in ways that seem to me inimical to his deepest tendencies; but those of his poems to which I regularly return are always as good as I expect them to be, and retain the capacity to surprise even on repeated readings.

The characteristic voice of John Woods's poetry is steady and honest. In a career spanning more than thirty years, it has deepened, and sometimes veered off momentarily in flashes of exuberance, parody, or failed experiment; but it has remained unusually free of posturing, or the phony "development" inspired by fashion.

Like most good poets, of course, Woods has a voice that adapts to the poem at hand; but there are moments, some of them in poems that he has chosen not to keep in print, which embody many of his excellences in a short space. Here, for example, is a passage from "The Unemployed Blacksmith," a poem about his grandfather from *The Cutting Edge* (1966):

> When I went to the army,
> he kissed my face. He died
> when I was studying the machinegun.
> Mail Pouch signs flake from the barns,
> in a world of show horses,
> horseshoe-playing firemen,
> and grandchildren, standing far back
> from the great, twitching flanks
> of Percherons.[1]

And here is "In South Chicago," from *Keeping Out of Trouble* (1968):

> At night, the freight cars stack
> in the great yards of South Chicago.
> They carry fading names

1. John Woods, *The Cutting Edge* (Bloomington, 1966), 25.

of Santa Fe, Chesapeake and Ohio, Wabash,
dim and wistful in the tart fogs
of Rinso and Bethlehem.
Certain old men with faces
knotted as the history of unionism
bang at the wheels,
pull the smell of oil into the yard office
to the young college men.
Later, they stretch their blue selves
into the red caboose
where they shuffle pinochle,
eat dry sandwiches
made in unknown meat from Kroger's.[2]

The first impression is of a flat but economical factuality, a directness in
the use of declarative sentences. The brand names evoke a lost era, but something more complicated than nostalgia is at work here. The speaker of the
first passage certainly sees the present of "show horses" as somehow inferior
to the world in which the grandfather put shoes on workhorses, and it is easy
to imagine barns sinking a little closer to the ground as the signs flake away
from their sides. In the second poem, the dim wistfulness of the railroad
names is partly caused by the effluents from factories; the criticism here is
again of the present, characterized by young college men and Kroger's, in
which the old men try to persist in their old ways.

But it is Woods's unobtrusive yet absolute mastery of sound joined with
evocative images that makes these passages haunting. In the first passage, the
primary effect is achieved through progressions like *army, barns, horses, fire-
men, grandchildren, Percherons,* and through close sequences of stressed monosyllables—"Mail Pouch signs flake from the barns." The second passage,
being a whole poem rather than an excerpt, is more complicated, but the
internal rhyme between *freight cars* and *great yards* is noteworthy, as are the
assonance of *tart fogs* and *yard office,* the progression through all five vowel
sounds, and, in the second half of the poem, the several *l* sounds that lend a
mitigating euphony to the sternness of the description.

Woods's first book, *The Deaths at Paragon, Indiana,* appeared in 1955 from
Indiana University Press, which later published four more collections of new

2. John Woods, *Turning to Look Back: Poems, 1955–1970* (Bloomington, 1972), 106.

poems, and one book of selected poems, *Turning to Look Back* (1972), which scatters nineteen new poems among those selected from the earlier books. His most recent books have been published by Dragon Gate, one of several small presses in the Pacific Northwest that produce beautiful books; the first of these was *The Valley of Minor Animals* (1982); the second was *The Salt Stone: Selected Poems* (1985), a purely retrospective selection from the six books published by Indiana University Press.

Neither *Turning to Look Back* nor *The Salt Stone* provides any indication of which individual collections contained which poems; nor are all the new poems in *Turning to Look Back* identified as such. Investigation reveals that chronology is less important than theme in determining the arrangement of poems in these two volumes. Though the 121 poems in *The Salt Stone* may be said to tilt generally in the direction of chronological order—more early poems toward the beginning, more late poems toward the end—there are many instances of poems placed well out of chronological order, for the sake of thematic coherence. Furthermore, Woods has been unusually evenhanded in making his selections; he has included roughly half of each earlier collection (the heaviest proportional representation being 19 of the 32 poems from *The Deaths at Paragon, Indiana*). The thematic arrangement has one distinct advantage over the historical: Woods has been able to work toward perfecting a single collection, and has found fresh juxtapositions of poem to poem that enable his older work to stand free of whatever notions the reader might have concerning the way people wrote poems in the mid-1950s. Less charitably, one might remark that the thematic arrangement also conceals the relative strengths of individual collections; Woods may not care to demonstrate that his first book is considerably better than his second, though he has made formidable advances since.

The Deaths at Paragon, Indiana introduces a poet of unusual accomplishment; many of the tones, forms, and themes that Woods explored more deeply later are first sounded in this collection. Like a few other first books by relatively young men, it contains a remarkable number of poems touching on human mortality and earthly change; it is a topic that makes the young man gloomy most of the time. Over the years, Woods has softened in his attitude toward some of these changes, but he has rarely spoken of them more memorably.

The book opens with one of Woods's strongest poems, "The Visits of My Aunt," held together with just enough narrative to support the superb description:

> The visits of my aunt in Martinsville
> were invasions. I see the webby arbor
> and the tottered shed full of kindling
> and games, the willow lacing the pause
> of afternoon, and townsmen rocking
> under wasp shells and locust husks.
> Then my aunt's car would startle dogs
> to ragged challenges as she blew her horn
> down Grant Street.[3]

The speaker puts himself in the present tense, thus earning the sophistication of "the willow lacing the pause/of afternoon," the one image here that goes beyond literal description, and that most strongly hints at the poem's urge to interrupt the progress of time; the poem is like a series of treasured snapshots, whose backgrounds contain objects Woods has continued to find evocative of the midwest in the 1930s—deteriorating buildings, various empty shells, the parts of old machines:

> That rusting crankcase filled with rain,
> half-hidden in the weeds, held no
> more rainbow than she stroked from air.
> (SS, 34)

The stillness of those summer days first explodes into action under the influence of this aunt, and then, paradoxically, she imposes her own kind of stillness:

> While she spoke
> clouds held their rain, and August
> lay like lambs beneath her spell.
> (SS, 34)

The poem ends with a balancing act between two propositions that have recurred regularly in Woods's poetry; there is a touch of self-consciousness here in the use of the first person, the explicit pointing to high-sounding

---

3. John Woods, *The Salt Stone* (Seattle, 1985), 34. Hereafter cited in the text as SS, followed by a page number.

conclusions; but the pressure of statement is slight compared to the weight of the images:

> When she died
> under the glass tent, I grew into an answer:
> life, as well as death, can last forever.
> There is a heaven of things: car doors,
> uncles, the ashtray from the Exposition.
> But as she withered in the tilted bed,
> I came with first frost to another meaning:
> something of brown leaves, withered grapes,
> the ganged birds exploding from the oak;
> that someday the easy wind would knot,
> and I'd be helpless in the grip of days.
> (SS, 34–35)

There is a paradox between life's lasting forever, and one's being caught in the grip of days; Woods extends that throughout the passage, with the contrast between "heaven" and "things," and the two kinds of autumnal imagery, one conventional ("brown leaves") and one startling ("the ganged birds exploding from the oak"). It seems to me that Woods's "heaven of things" is here on earth; certainly his love for tangible objects pervades his poems; he writes like someone who knows the feel of a well-made axe handle or the steering wheel of a tractor. Even time's ravages can be lovingly evoked; the last four lines are phrased with a wistfulness beyond rage or helplessness.

The "easy wind" here brings to mind the several poems in which Woods recalls a youthful fascination with kites. Sometimes, in *The Deaths at Paragon, Indiana,* the kite suggests a boy's relatively carefree afternoon on a hill; but there are later poems in which the kite gives rise to threatening description, as in "Turning to Look Back," first collected in *Keeping Out of Trouble* (1968). This is a wonderful poem in several parts, spoken by versions of people from the poet's past—a grandfather, a father, a brother who died in infancy, a series of women. The grandfather has the opening and closing sections, and seems to want to explain how he foresaw the poet in the child. At the end of his first monologue, he recalls the boy flying a kite over the town, and the views of the town it might have had are given with the same touch of nostalgia that rises from the simple illustrations in classic children's books:

Here, on this hill, I see you
letting out the kite like a far eye
over the scatter of smokehouses,
at the field's edge where the town
thins out into corncribs and fishing shacks,
old Fords driving a wood saw,
out past the cannery whistle.
(SS, 18)

But the creation of characters seems to be a tough business: the section concludes with the reeling-in of the kite, and a last line of unexpected violence:

Then, hand over hand, pulling it close,
struggling with the wind in it,
hugging it like the frail ribcage of a young girl;
and on this morning you made us all,
holding it to your face until the trees
stood up red through the tearing tissue.
(SS, 18)

Here, as in "In Touch with Wind," "Saying the Wind," "Flying Kites in
March," and "Looking Both Ways Before Crossing," the obvious symbol-
ism—the string between the earthbound and the sky—is complicated by
intimations of the creative process. From the imagined view the kite has of
the village, to the act of looking through the tissue to a world tinged by its
color and fragmented by the tissue's tearing, there is a deeply suggestive and
complex portrayal of the poet caught between two worlds and trying to make
the best of the tensions between them, as in the final stanza of "In Touch
with Wind":

Only Grandma knew, with her cakes and dimes,
that I would pause under gliding leaves,
seized from within by halving time
that, for all my anger, takes and twins:
this for heart and this for mind.
The heart grows up, and can no longer touch.
(SS, 10)

The heart's urge to touch, to recover something from the past for use in the present, is a constantly recurring theme in Woods's best poetry. The first poem in *The Cutting Edge*, for example, is called "Three Mornings in September"; its three sections are titled "1936," "1946," and "1956," and each begins with the same line: "I wake in my father's house."

The use of the present tense in each of the three sections gives each recollection an immediacy amounting almost to urgency; in the first section the blend of the peaceful and the threatening is almost subliminal, until the explicit first reference to war:

> My dog lifts his ears at a neighborly bark,
> scrabbles off through the arbor.
> . . . .
>
> Now the sun strikes through the window,
> the blind cracked like a blueprint,
> through the web-woven barn window
> to the searing edge of the scythe.
> . . . .
>
> My father tries to cough up the war
> in the shallow trench of his sleep.
> (SS, 143)

The next decade, of course, takes us through World War II; the speaker, having served, is home again, gradually letting the military life lift from his body:

> Uniforms die in the closets,
> with shoulder patches, stripes and ribbons
> already turning to Greek.
> A far sun lifts from my tan,
> old commands ease from my muscles.
> The earth aches for the harvest
> in the first full year of peace.
> (SS, 144)

By 1956, the speaker is thirty, and has a wife and children; his sense of life's cycles has deepened, and he lies beside his wife, offering a prayer:

We are between wars again.
Snow sends its first, white scouts
into the dreaming valley.
I send this prayer out into the light.
May children wake, in ten years' time,
on the full brink of harvest,
safe in their father's house.
(SS, 144)

With extraordinary subtlety, Woods uses verbal repetition in this poem
to reinforce the vision of life as a series of progressions and repetitions;
though the first line of each section, and the slightly altered version of it
which concludes the poem, are quite obvious, the use of smaller phrases and
of single words in repetitive patterns connects the three sections. Dogs bark-
ing, suntans, uniforms, and the idea of harvest, all recur unobtrusively, until
the poem begins to resemble more highly formal repetitive constructs like the
villanelle or the sestina (Woods has published two sestinas); the unity of the
three recollections as one vision is rendered strongly and memorably, in language that never strays from the conversational.

Woods's recollections of past scenes are not always so solemn, nor are
they always presented realistically; he uses both humor and the surrealism of
dreams to enrich what might otherwise become a series of sepia postcards.
"Days," for example, opens with a description of his grandmother lighting a
stove by a method that federal guardians of our safety would doubtless not
approve:

Pouring coal oil on the stubborn mass
she'd throw a match and jump back. Whoomph.
Each morning would begin dangerously.
(SS, 14)

And "The Sleepwalker" contains a stanza whose rapid description, suggestive of time-delay photography, presents the view that all things yearn to
go back to what they were:

On a curled country road
where the field shakes loose,
where the shack wood spirals from paint,

a billboard peels its decades;
each bright, accessible image
flowers, sickens and falls
back through the wars, the depressions,
until the screen stutters black.
Then, in the boards, the whorls
contract, drawing the wood back
into boles, into trees, into seeds.
(SS, 126–27)

The image of one thing peeling from another, or fading away to reveal what lies under it, shows up frequently in Woods's poems of recollection; like the Mail Pouch signs on the sides of barns, the crusts of maturity fall away as the memory works its way more deeply into the past. Many of Woods's poems detail the slow decline of human beings and the things they make. Not surprisingly, perhaps, there are more such poems in Woods's earlier work than there have been recently; *The Deaths at Paragon, Indiana* contains several of the best of these, though *The Cutting Edge* also explores this theme in several ways.

However, a poem that Woods published in the Autumn, 1986, issue of *Poetry Northwest* extends the sequence of September mornings; "The Fourth Morning in September" is dated 1986, and begins, "Time is a bomb. The old barns of the county / lean on whatever can take it." In a controlled inclusiveness of tones, the poem is an elegy for

the cows, for Spot
(the dog's dog), for the hired hands,
trucked over from Morgantown,
glaring into the haying sun.
They all stood there
on the last Sunday of a world,
shadows burning into stone.[4]

The presence of these poems concerned with mutability seems at first to be balanced by the presence, from the earliest work to the most recent, of a

4. John Woods, "The Fourth Morning in September," *Poetry Northwest*, XXVII (Autumn, 1986), 3–4.

great variety of poems about love. There are a few fairly straightforward love
lyrics whose directness and simplicity of design rule out any considerations
beyond the two lovers they celebrate; in a few others, like "How So Lovely
Walks the Wind" or this passage from "Every Barley Tongue Is Loose," there
is a declaration that love survives the decline of the year:

> Our summer love was touch and go.
> But when the sky goes blind with snow,
>   within our hearts we'll tend a storm.
> Between our hands we'll keep love warm.
> (SS, 76)

In many other love poems, however, Woods confronts the tension between "the full time / that seemed the death of time" ("In the Full of Love,"
SS, 74) and the surer knowledge that change and decline are inevitable.
Even this can be celebrated, as in "Happily because April"; the present tense
of the first main clause is important:

> Happily because April wore
> your flashing pelt, I sing
> this praise of everything:
> water, sycamore,
> the breathing of the wine
> across your lips to mine.
> (SS, 73)

Though the third and final stanza details the descent that comes with
time, the poet still sings his praise:

> But yellow takes the oak.
> And autumn takes the heart.
> Love and counterpart
> fall away in smoke.
> I celebrate the stone,
> the limits of the bone.
> (SS, 73)

"The limits of the bone" can be thought of as one guide to the earthly
processes in which all humans are caught, or in which they willingly partici-

pate; how one sees it is a matter of temperament. Woods celebrates love and sexuality as a part of what Richard Wilbur, in "Running," calls "that great going"; for Woods, the simultaneity of the beautiful and the dreadful is, finally, beautiful, though it is only in death that humans approach a state of permanence.

"Lie Closed, My Lately Loved" directly treats the unity of human sexuality with other natural processes; indirectly, by means of the almost funereal phrasing of the opening few lines, even the knowledge that life ends in death is handled tenderly:

> Lie closed, my lately loved, in the far bed
> at the foot of the moon, barred by sash and shade.
> Now your eyes are shells adrift in shadow.
> (SS, 78)

The wakeful lover admires the sleeping body on the bed, and then reflects on what has passed between them, even referring to the lovers of an hour ago as "themselves" rather than as "ourselves"; the end of the poem brings much of the world into the picture:

> One hour away from sweating animals,
> afraid to wake the children or themselves,
> we're locked apart, though something of your shape
> still molds my hand. I breathe you still.
>
> A heavy stallion rumbles in the straw,
> stud for all the trembling mares.
> Around his yellow mouth hang crumbs of flowers.
> (SS, 78)

The concluding stanza presents the tension between the stallion's animal force and his delicacy, and makes clearer the speaker's complicated reaction to the quiet body and the recollection of its having recently been one of two "sweating animals."

The unity of life and the forces of evolution are perhaps most economically taken up in "The Woman Who Is One Woman"; it begins with a direct statement that we must accept or reject:

> The woman who is one woman
> remembers the egg time, the time
> of the blind fish.
>   She remembers
> herself as one, long body
> rising from the beginning.
> (SS, 99)

If we accept this for the purposes of continuing to read, we are of course no different from most readers of recent poetry; but we will have to pause over the comma in the second sentence, and consider the import of this usage. Is it a redundant comma, as in "long, red hair," or is it meant to suggest that the woman remembers herself as a blind fish? The poem is unchanged from its appearance in *Striking the Earth,* so a misprint is unlikely; furthermore, Woods occasionally truncates parallel clauses. The line is an interruption of the poem's calm assurance, but it takes us beyond the literal to the idea that the long trail of evolutionary progress can be thought of as a single body.

The poem continues to characterize someone more usual, and ends in spooky prophecy:

> But the woman who is two women
> will keep pressed flowers,
> fossil cake, a motel key.
> The neuter angel, glorying at the womb
> of Eden, will press a gold ring
> on her hand. One will stay
> in the dying forest, and one
> will set forth, and they
> shall be apart forever.
> (SS, 99)

It is the human tendency to separate ourselves from the rest of the natural world; Woods opens *The Salt Stone* with "Coming to the Salt Lick," a brief poem first published in *Keeping Out of Trouble.* The poem begins by emphasizing this separateness through description of a herd of cows; the details are precise, yet suggestive of a remoteness from our lives. The ending, however, makes the connection at the same time that it reminds us of the schism men have made between themselves and animals:

They will have it.
But not in the fodder
blowing ropily green
from their yellow mouths.

Now they are coming down from the pasture,
the swinging bell, the milky blaze,
heavy, imprecise, to the acrid stone.

Why do they want it?
Why do we need it?

It is our blood, remembering its own taste,
and when we took different paths
in the forest.
(SS, xi; page unnumbered)

The emergence from the forest has not, in Woods's view, been always toward enlightenment. "Lying Down with Men and Women" begins with a frighteningly brief history of that journey:

When we came up from water, our eyes
drew to the front of our heads,
and we had faces. When we came up
on our knuckles, we held fruit to our mouths,
and wanted to know the chemistry
of sweetness.
        Then as we walked down
the earth's curve, trees and hills
got in our way, so we moved them
for roads and newsprint and wreckage.
(SS, 190)

The rest of the poem constructs a myth to explain parts of our behavior; we lie down a little every day, Woods says, because we must "honor our lost / tails and gills" (SS, 190). But lying alone, on our backs or on our faces, forces us to confront terrifying distances or nearnesses.

            And so
we lie down with men and women

because we are terrified, and sometimes,
for that reason, we stand up and kill.
(SS, 190)

The proposition that love and violence are frequent companions also
appears in poems that begin, not as love poems, but as poems explicitly about
war and other violent manifestations of human nature. The most complex of
these recall World War II; former soldiers, whatever they have come to think
of war, are often fond of recalling episodes of their own military lives. Woods
deals with this tendency in "The Closing of the Victory Bar and Grill," a
poem that moves rapidly, yet without loss of control, among surprisingly disparate tones. The poem begins with a series of "outrages and illusions" that
pass through the memories of a veteran as he sits in a bar; then the reader,
or perhaps the dedicatee, Richard Hugo, is addressed directly by the poet:

You are thinking this is a long poem.
It was a long war,
and the Victory Bar and Grill
is here to testify that a drinking veteran
dreams a long gullet. He listens close,
hearing what's coming and going,
explosions behind his eyes,
the whip of blood.
If you sing through this gullet,
it takes a while
to come out fabulous.
(SS, 136–37)

This brusquely conversational tone is modified a couple of stanzas later,
when the speaker becomes more deeply satirical; veterans of that war feel
diminished in many ways:

We were lost in that war
and live on the other side of life
with the others that blew up,
where the joyless are gently restrained,
no causes to die for,
where the powerless grow steadily beautiful,

where we tell poems
about the underside of grass.
(SS, 137)

"Ode to the Smith and Wesson Revolver" confronts more directly the
notion that "we stand up and kill" because we are terrified, and confused by
perverted love:

I thought I had outgrown my need for you,
getting the wife and kids,
an office door that named me,
but tonight I take you out.
Down this street, televisions look at one another
like a row of prison guards.
They say a red button can end the world,
a red telephone can save it.
The man between shakes with sexual desire.
But here we are alone.
We kiss at last.
(SS, 121)

Despite what seems inescapable in human nature, Woods has written
several poems in protest of war's wasteful capriciousness; "Some Martial
Thoughts" is especially bitter in its attack on our reasons for fighting. There
is dark humor at the beginning:

"Things are rough all over,"
we said as soldiers.
To think we fought Japan for apple pie,
Korea for the United Nations,
and the Viet Cong for a debate topic.
The way it's going, my sons will fight China
for abstract expressionism.
(SS, 128)

But the end of the poem lists, in a satirical tone, some of our official inhu-
manities, and concludes with a directness that almost, but not quite, topples
the poem:

The D.A.R. counts our rings.
Grosse Pointe, Michigan, listed several degrees
of "swarthiness" for their restricted tracts.
The American Legion goosed Chicago,
later doubted the patriotism
of the Campfire Girls. (Would it were so.)
There is no army against these things.
You can burn your birth certificate
and go on living. They have copies.

In 1918, my father was gassed.
I must ask him sometime what he coughs for.
(SS, 128)

But finally we are all caught up in the inescapable cycles; as Woods says in "Kill to Eat,"

In the green, strange eyes of lions
we turn to meat
as though the gray tusks of their paws
swung us through Chicago slaughterhouses.
(SS, 147)

Because Woods sees the human condition as a state only willfully disconnected from nature, yet connected to it in ways that many humans do not understand, he can invest the inanimate with weird but convincing "life," in a manner that is often surrealistic. Just as the recalled images of childhood and youth—machine parts, hand tools, edged pieces of iron and steel—invest their world with lively tension, the ordinary objects of contemporary life sometimes take on a curious ability to impinge on our consciousnesses, in a way that sometimes seems threatening. "The Room Under the Sink" is a short poem that merely states that these things occur, that

From the dust coils
of the refrigerator, the room
under the sink, a silence
enters the body.
Eyes plunge down the tunnels

of the pulse. The scalp twitches,
and ears hear backward
what has happened to everybody.
(SS, 185)

This convinces because the objects named are familiar; the things they do
here, though we may not have seen them before, are acts that we can follow.
But when a touch of narrative is added to this method, the effect is even
more compelling, as in "Knowledge," one of the poems from *The Valley of
Minor Animals*:

She does not know what called her out
to this dull field. Was it the small dog
broken by wheels, the husband
who put everything down
in the old snow, all the belongings,
the gifts, the albums, and then
lay down beside them?

She does not know
why the arm rose in the raddled woods,
why the finger turned in a bright fanning,
pointing out the olive tremble
of fall leaves, the seed hiss of snow,
her deep eyes in the water.

But the stream slowed, metaled,
and dreamed forever
the old face of the moon.[5]

The husband's astonishing yet archetypal behavior is reminiscent of
some passages in the work of James Wright, but the ambiguity of the second
stanza is Woods's own manner at its best. We cannot be sure whose arm,
whose finger, whirled and pointed in the woods; they could be the woman's,
or they could belong to a vision, like an angel. The use of *raddled* is both
precise and suggestive; it means "interwoven," and yet it sounds like *rattled*;

5. John Woods, *The Valley of Minor Animals* (Seattle, 1982), 35.

the thicket is both coherent and chaotic. The sound of snow on leaves is like the sound of seeds being sown, though snow marks the end of the season of germination. And so, in the final stanza, everything stops—everything, that is, except a general consciousness, dreaming.

The Salt Stone and The Valley of Minor Animals contain many more poems worth mentioning, or examining; I have slighted the blend of wild humor and mortal fear in poems like "Auction Day," and the reverence in such poems as "Striking the Earth." There is rich variety in the poems Woods now has in print, and in his most recent poems there is evidence of continuing exploration of ever deeper mysteries. Woods writes of the world's motions; he is sometimes a poet of change, but he goes beyond that to meditations on the evolutionary history of human urges, and on the unity of all life. He simultaneously loves and distrusts the human factor in earthly processes; through violence, treachery in love, or lack of care, the works of humans decline. And yet, through love, long attention, and sometimes even through violence, the human spirit often triumphs. It is Woods's great gift that, in language of rare and haunting durability, he can balance these opposing observations.

FRED CHAPPELL The World Was Plenty

I

When, in 1971, Fred Chappell published his first book of poems, *The World Between the Eyes*, he had already published three novels and completed a fourth. The first three—*It Is Time, Lord* (1963), *The Inkling* (1965), *Dagon* (1968)—revealed not only a thorough command of the ingredients and conventions of southern gothic fiction, but a view of the world shaped by wide-ranging and tireless reading. They are brilliant, brief, allusive, densely textured, and difficult. They found skilled translators, and came to be widely respected in France—a fact that Chappell acknowledged gratefully when Bob Edwards brought it up on "Morning Edition" a few years ago. Chappell added, "But it should be remembered that this is a people with admiration also for Jerry Lewis and snails." In an afterword to *The Fred Chappell Reader* (1987), Chappell points out the shortcomings of his early fiction (though without disavowing it), and says that his ambition has shifted away from excessively intellectual experiments with form: "I have got to where I should like for my work to be humane, and I do not much care if it even becomes sentimental. Perhaps it would be nice if a few artists in our time decided to rejoin the human race, and I think that I would be glad to do so, however much I disagree with its politics."[1]

1. Fred Chappell, *The Fred Chappell Reader* (New York, 1987), 486.

The humanity, clarity, and apparent directness of Chappell's more recent novels, *I Am One of You Forever* (1985) and *Brighten the Corner Where
You Are* (1989) would seem to bear out this statement, though one begins
with a narrator swimming through a teardrop, and the other begins with the
protagonist's theft of the moon.

If Chappell's fiction has undergone a noticeable transformation, his poetry has maintained a consistency of style and approach, even as its scope has
extended to the book-length *Midquest* (1981). The title poem of *The World
Between the Eyes* presents a speaker who, in various guises and at various ages,
continues to be the means of perception throughout much of Chappell's poetry. In this poem, he is a boy caught between the world his body inhabits
and the world he finds in books. More precisely, he lives in a larger world
that includes both:

The house is chill, he wanders room and room,
October is seething at the windows.

Hands lax in his pockets. He sees
Through it all. Man of the boring world,
He dangles his cigarette and his dangerous charm.
        "Ah, Comtesse, it's all too apparent,
            you know little of the ways of the Hindoo;"
Insouciant in jade cufflinks,
While the skyline flickers with the Big Guns.[2]

Here, he shifts the "real" world and his imagination, a little like Stephen
Dedalus wishing he were the Count of Monte Cristo. But as the poem proceeds, October works its magic not only on the house, but on the landscapes
drawn in the books; time is "Charged past endurance with the future," but
the poem ends with the boy "blest in his skins, an old stone / House, and a
sky eaten up with stars" (*WBE,* 15).

"February" and "Weird Tales" emerge more purely from the two realms
of rural childhood and literary fantasy, respectively. The first recounts a hog-
butchering from the boy's point of view; he is "dismayed / With delight,"

2. Fred Chappell, *The World Between the Eyes* (Baton Rouge, 1971), 12–13. Hereafter
cited in the text as *WBE,* followed by a page number.

"elated-drunk / With the horror," as the hog is killed, scalded, gutted, cloven. For a while the poem looks like something vegetarians might use to gain converts, but it takes in the brisk air, the joy of community ritual, and ends with a nostalgic tableau:

> And his bladder and his stomach sack! puffed
> Up and tied off and flung to the kids,
> Game balls, they bat them about,
> Running full tilt head down across the scattered yard.
> And then on a startled breeze
> The bladder's hoist, vaults high and gleams in the sunlight
> And reflects on its shiny globe
> The sky a white square
> And the figures beneath, earnest figures
> Gazing straight up.
> (*WBE*, 5)

Imagination and recollection combine here into something stronger than the experience itself; and in "Weird Tales," it is finally friendship that is the theme, rather than the fascination with the obscure writers of horror and fantasy who supplied that magazine with material. The poem begins with an evocation of Lovecraft and proceeds to a kind of honor roll of

> those who witnessed, away
> From the rant of commerce, the shriek of lying newsprint,
> The innocent intimate truths that gnaw the marrow.
> (*WBE*, 40)

But the poem ends with love and gratitude expressed to Richard Dillard, author of *News of the Nile* (1971), the title poem of which makes beautiful and elaborate connections among sites along the Nile, flowing north as a train runs north to Wisconsin,

> Where August Derleth prints the books
> Of Lovecraft. . . .
> . . . . . .

And east of this train, south of Virginia,
In western North Carolina, Fred Chappell
Has written a novel, *Dagon,* and all these things
Come together, turn together, and will pass on
To come again. The Nile flows sluggish
And is thick with mud. It bears the news.[3]

Chappell's poem, in turn, becomes a letter, signed "Fred," and makes
more connections; to add to them, I acknowledge here that Richard Dillard
provided me with the information that Farnsworth Wright (1888–1940) was
the editor of *Weird Tales:*

This news too the Nile bears, Richard Dillard,
Flowing past "Dongola, Kerma and Wawa;"
Past Karloff double features, Lugosi revivals,
The spiderwebbed offices of Farnsworth Wright:
That rather than injustices and generals,
We choose to live with vampires, demons, ghouls.
(*WBE,* 40–41)

Even the slighter poems in *The World Between the Eyes* are fine examples
of the delight to be taken in finding the right words, in the power of words
and literature to transform the everyday. Near the end of the book there are
five poems about baseball; their true subject is wit, and the similes available
to a person who has done some reading. The first of the five, "Third Base
Coach," begins and ends with literary comparisons:

He commands as mysteriously as
the ghost of Hamlet's father.
.   .   .   .

Like an Aeschylean tragedy he's static; baffling;
Boring; but.
                                        Urgent with import.
(*WBE,* 48)

3. R. H. W. Dillard, *News of the Nile* (Chapel Hill, 1971), 27.

Further into the sequence, as a quotation from Ty Cobb describes a fast ball, and invented similes and jokes combine with those that appear to have originated on the field ("Trying to hit Wednesday with a bb gun" ["Junk Ball, *WBE,* 51]), the poems begin to revel in their slightness, reminding us that "it's just a game" is about the most ignorant statement that can be made to someone who takes a game seriously. In other words: people who think it's just a game had better play among themselves.

II

In 1963, a few months before Chappell published his first novel, Duke University Press published *Under Twenty-five,* an anthology of "Duke Narrative and Verse" edited by the distinguished creative writing teacher William Blackburn. Chappell is represented by two prose pieces and ten poems, only two of which were later collected in *The World Between the Eyes.* Others are interesting primarily as evidence that Chappell was committed at an early age to using traditional forms, and sometimes interested in combining them with free verse or very loosely cadenced lines. "Familiar Poem," the meditation of a man lying awake beside his sleeping wife, is in many ways the most ambitious of these poems. The first of the four sections sets the scene, in a dark bedroom where "rain is sound"; the lines, moderately regular iambic pentameter, drift among rhyme schemes based on the quatrain, on five lines, and on seven. In midsentence, the section ends, and the form becomes looser iambic pentameter, unrhymed, and the speaker's thoughts wander more noticeably, from his love for his wife, through poetic ambition as alchemy, to the knowledge of the writer's struggle to find, against "The onyx mirror of history past and future," the "bitter poison of salvation."[4]

The third section is a sonnet; the octave addresses the sleeping wife and tries to characterize her dreams; the sestet addresses God, and prays "that I may / Not be insane":

> Let my love's dreams as spies
> Into that trackless wild. When I trace back

---

4. Fred Chappell, "Familiar Poem," in *Under Twenty-five,* ed. William Blackburn (Durham, 1963), 200. Hereafter cited in the text as *UT,* followed by a page number.

My life, thought seems the suffering, slack
Thread preserving my self from the gray, gay
Narcotic mazes and hysteric skies.
(*UT*, 200)

In the fourth section, dawn arrives, and "reality" overcomes "imagination." As objects become discernible, "light is sound," and free verse embodies random observations of the waking world:

The sunlight shapes all objects, destroying images to being.

I rise and turn and unravel
The ghost of myself from among the sheets.
(*UT*, 201)

"Familiar Poem" is sometimes self-consciously ambitious, and contains
more nearly "confessional" passages than Chappell has since allowed himself;
he may have admitted some youthful follies, and drawn upon autobiographical material, but he has done so without the self-importance that sometimes
reveals itself in this poem. Most of the time, inhabiting the worlds of imagination and of dailiness is a source of joy in Chappell's work.

The poem's chief interest now, aside from its demonstration of a twenty-
five-year-old poet's enormous promise, is that it is a clear forerunner of *Midquest* (1981), the superb long poem that first appeared as four separate volumes: *River* (1975), *Bloodfire* (1978), *Wind Mountain* (1979), and *Earthsleep*
(1980).

Like "Familiar Poem," each part of *Midquest* begins with a speaker awakening beside his sleeping wife; the phrase "light is sound" also appears at the
beginning of *Earthsleep*, in "Earth Emergent Drifts the Fire River." Furthermore, each of the waking poems rings some variation on the idea that in
waking, the speaker must lose, or abandon, some essential part of himself.
But the speaker of *Midquest* is ten years older than the author of "Familiar
Poem," and the author, most of the time, is older than that. At the Dantean
midpoint of his life, the speaker takes stock, and meditates: on his love for
his wife Susan, the selves he has been and is becoming, the significance of
place and family, of friendship, music, and literature.

As Chappell points out in a preface to the one-volume edition, each of the four parts of the poem consists of "eleven longish poems . . . covering four times the same twenty-four hours of the speaker's life."[5] The date is May 28, 1971, his thirty-fifth birthday. Chappell goes on to declare that the speaker, called "Fred," is no more or less Fred Chappell than any of his other fictional characters, and to explain a few of the principles according to which the poems are arranged. The organization allows the gradual unfolding of a life, a loose narrative, yet it also retains most of the advantages of a collection of shorter poems; there is little here that is not enriched by its context, but there is no single poem that could not stand outside the context. For this reason, the order imposed on the poems, though satisfying and persuasive, is not inevitable. Chappell's remarks set the reader up to notice certain large rhythms:

> And each of the volumes (except *Wind Mountain*) is organized as a balancing act. The first poem is mirrored by the last; the second by the next to last, and so on inward. But the sixth poem in each volume is companionless in that volume, and concerned with a garrulous old gentleman named Virgil Campbell, who is supposed to give to the whole its specifically regional, its Appalachian, context. The fifth poem in each is given to stream of consciousness and these interior monologues become discernibly more formal as the speaker begins to order his life. Each volume is dominated by a different element of the family, *River* by the grandparents, *Bloodfire* by the father, and there is a family reunion in *Earthsleep*, the part most shadowed by death. (In order to suggest the fluid and disordered nature of air, *Wind Mountain* was exempt from some of these requirements.) (M, ix–x)

It turns out that in *Bloodfire*, the second part, Virgil Campbell holds forth in the seventh poem, "Firewater." In the more loosely arranged *Wind Mountain*, he gets the eighth poem, as it happens; he does not settle back to the middle of a part until *Earthsleep*.

My point is not to show that there is a mistake in the order of the poems, or even in Chappell's description of it; it is rather to notice that it is just as effective to give Virgil poems VI, VII, VIII, and VI, as it is to give him VI every time. It is only the prefatory remark that brings attention to this matter. Other "mirrorings," and the consistently stream-of-consciousness fifth

---

5. Fred Chappell, *Midquest* (Baton Rouge, 1981), ix. Hereafter cited in the text as M, followed by a page number.

poems, are perhaps regular enough in their recurrence to evoke recognition, but a number of Chappell's self-imposed rules were more useful to him than apparent to his readers, in something like the way in which syllabic meter can be useful: it is in itself inaudible, but it gives the poet something to work with and against.

Many of the poems are in loose blank verse or free verse, but various traditional forms are also used, from the Anglo-Saxon strong-stress meter of "My Grandfather's Church Goes Up" to the elaborate chant royal of "My Mother's Hard Row to Hoe." The several voices in the poems, and the fully realized characters behind them, help to keep the formal variety from becoming obtrusive, but so does Chappell's command of meters that range from the stately to the rollicking, and his ability to work in many tones and genres.

The central "balancing act" in *Midquest* is the speaker's steady exploration of the tensions between his rural Appalachian childhood and his urban professional adulthood. His grandmother is perhaps the richest source of the earlier values and attitudes; she speaks most of four poems given to her, and Fred listens, occasionally asking questions or commenting; at times she seems conscious of her role as informant, but often she drifts from there into a spoken re-creation of a moment in the distant past; her strength and independence, and the ways in which she accommodates these to marriage and widowhood, provide some of the most moving passages in *Midquest*.

The anecdotes and recollections of Fred's parents are either wildly funny, or a sweet blend of nostalgia and a wish to be true to the difficult times. When his mother recalls their first meeting, she vacillates between the warmth of a funny story, and insistence that their early life was "hard, hard, hard, hard, / Hard." In "My Father's Hurricane," his father indulges himself in a tall tale of being blown around in a wind that had everything on earth airborne, but in "My Father Allergic to Fire," he tries to assume a heavy weight of guilt for a childish and ignorant initiation into the Ku Klux Klan.

Against the background of these poems, and the rowdier episodes involving Virgil Campbell, Fred addresses love poems to Susan, beholds the changing landscapes of his past and present, recalls his attempts to play the trombone, and, with graceful freedom from self-indulgence, explores the sources and nature of his literary ambitions. "Science Fiction Water Letter to Guy Lillian" begins as a thoughtful discussion of that genre's limitations, and ends with a précis of Fred's own unwritten sci-fi novel; "Rimbaud Fire Letter to Jim Applewhite" is a painfully humorous evocation of youthful pretensions arising from misapprehensions of Rimbaud's life and work. If these poems were required reading in creative writing workshops, student writers would have less trouble understanding what it really means to take one's work seriously.

Throughout the book there are echoes, sometimes respectful and sometimes parodic, of other writers—Wordsworth, Cummings, Eliot, Frost, and others come in for brief and witty allusions, and Dante, who stands behind the whole poem, is both translated and transformed in *Wind Mountain*. "In Parte Ove Non E Che Luca" begins as a somewhat colloquial but perfectly honorable rendering of Canto V of the *Inferno*, and holds its own against other translations for fifty-one lines. But when Dante begins to introduce individual victims of lust, building toward Francesca da Rimini, Chappell loosens his diction gradually as he introduces Casanova, Lord Byron, and James Dickey, before turning back inward to his own poem:

"Master, wait!" I said. "I recognize
  From childhood the round form, the red face
  Of Virgil Campbell, one of my father's cronies.

May I not hear what brought him such disgrace?"
"Of course," he said, "I'll bid him to this place."
(M, 123)

Among the best of the literary poems is "Hallowind," the tenth poem in *Wind Mountain*. It is a "playet," reminiscent of Yeats in length and meter, but set in Durham in 1961; the characters are Reynolds Price, Susan, Fred, the rain, and the wind. In an argument about the nature of fiction, Fred pushes for the paradigms and myths discoverable in stories, and Reynolds argues for each story's particularity, until Susan enters with tea and cakes; she shifts the conversation toward conclusion, but the rain and the wind interrupt them. The wind's closing speech is a surprising and moving argument for what might be called the humanities:

It's soon enough that we dissolve
Their names to dust, unmoving move
Against their animal powers to love
And weep and fear. It's all too soon

They grow as silent as the moon
And lie in earth as naked bone.
We'll let them sit and sip their tea
Till midnight; then I'll shake the tree
Outside their window, and drive the sea
Upon the land, the mountain toward the Pole,
The desert upon the glacier. And all
They ever knew or hoped will fall
To ash . . . Till then, though, let them speak
And lighten the long dim heartache,
And trifle, for sweet trifling's sake.
(M, 139)

This inclusive and loving recognition of the world we inhabit is the foundation on which *Midquest* stands. What this world is to us is touched on in a brief passage in *Brighten the Corner Where You Are*; the protagonist, Joe Robert Kirkman, is loosely based on Chappell's father; his son is the narrator. One full and fateful morning at the school where Joe Robert teaches science, he is visited by the parents of Lewis Dorson, a former student who returned from the Second World War unable to pick up his life, and at last committed suicide; Joe Robert has just learned this from Lewis' mother:

> It was over between them forever now, but my father felt the need to say something, knowing there was nothing to say, yet knowing, too, that she would listen. It came out lame and hoarse: "I thought the world of him. More than that."
>
> "More than the world." She looked into his face. "I count on more."
>
> But that wasn't what he meant, whatever he meant. The world was what my father knew, nothing more or less, better or worse. The world was plenty. "We all do," he said.[6]

III

In the ninth poem of *Bloodfire*, "Burning the Frankenstein Monster: Elegiac Letter to Richard Dillard," Fred acknowledges a perception of Dillard's, and

6. Fred Chappell, *Brighten the Corner Where You Are* (New York, 1989), 65–66.

adds, "But *The Inkling* is long out of print, bemuses not even my mother. / Let it smolder to ash on whatever forgotten shelf" (M, 85). My copy of *The Inkling*, however, is holding up very well. Between the front cover and the flyleaf, there is a paper napkin on which, in April of 1966 at the Pickwick in Greensboro, Fred Chappell scribbled these lines:

> When it's
> Ginsberg on the Ganges,
> Him with
> His hairy phalanges,
> I'll be back
> Again, sweetheart,
> In the following stanges.

None of the other writers there assembled could rise to that challenge, which is quoted here for the fun of it, as an indication of Chappell's restless interest in saying the world, and as an epigraph to the question how a poet, still in mid-career, might follow a book as strong and deep as *Midquest*.

Writers are often more interested in their recent work than in what they think of as older or earlier work. Young writers, on one hand, like the sensation of improvement, and sometimes add to their enjoyment by undervaluing their past work. On the other hand, writers in or beyond middle age can sometimes think with equanimity that their best work may already have been done. But gratitude for having done that work can be liberating: now it will be less troublesome to pursue idiosyncratic impulses, to take what others may call risks. By this time, they know that they must be interested before they can hope to be interesting.

These notions arise from contemplation of the startling oddity and the surprising success of *Castle Tzingal* (1984), a poem consisting of twenty-three dramatic poems, most of them monologues. The nine characters are occupants of a mythical principality, remote in unspecified time and place, ruled by a mad king. The imprecision of time, especially, is that of dream or of vaguely researched costume drama; the speakers use such words as *arras*, *florin*, *villeyn*, *catamite*, *scranny*, and *grutch*, but they also use words of more recent origin, as if to remind us that they are detached from real history.

As they certainly are. The first monologue is spoken by "The Homunculus," an eighteen-inch creature named Flyting, but called Tweak; his account of his origins is a fine humorous example of alchemical fantasy:

> I was born
> On a table bright with flame and glassware,
> And had no childhood except an ignorance
> Of politics and gossip. And what a boring year
> My childhood was. No company
> But the pottering alchemist, his cat
> Who wanted to gobble me up, and three
> Disgusting nodules of melting flesh
> That were earlier attempts at being me.[7]

Tweak is a gleefully wicked spy for the king, who suspects everybody of plotting against him. His queen pines for one Marco, a troubadour from a neighboring province, who has disappeared. Petrus, an envoy from Marco's father, gradually comes close to discovering that young man's grisly fate, and in three poems sends reports back home. The Astrologer, the Admiral, and a Page all take their turns exposing their fears and treacheries, and they are all disturbed at times by the disembodied voice of Marco, who still manages to sing from his place not far this side of the grave.

The poem is another balancing act, and the reader teeters on the line between standing well back, in arm's-length apprehension of the self-consciously literary language and allegory, and being drawn into the melodramatic story. Among the forces that draw the reader in is the skill with which Chappell sometimes echoes the sound of anonymous balladry:

> As the lone long wind unwinds
>   Her bobbin of white thread
> She sings a song rejoicing
>   That she never wed. (CT, 5)

But if this were a bedtime story, it would be saved for the nights when the children had been very wicked indeed; that is another of the forces that draw us into these seeming improbabilities. The disloyalty, self-interest, madness, and grief of Castle Tzingal are common enough in realms with which most of us are better acquainted. Marco's disembodied voice is that of poetry, or even truth; he wonders at the enormity of his punishment:

7. Fred Chappell, *Castle Tzingal* (Baton Rouge, 1984), 1. Hereafter cited in the text as CT, followed by a page number.

No crime against humanity or God has yet deserved
Such unimagined punishment, no black sin
Received such frozen penalty.

Until a mad king dabbled in chemistry.

.   .   .   .

So I live on, if live I do,
To wrinkle and pull tense the minds of those
Who have created me what I am now
Until a thorough justice arise.
(*CT*, 31)

In our time, such words produce a chill of recognition; our alchemy is
farther-fetched even than that of Tzingal, and it has rendered us more vul-
nerable to madness. Many a poet in such a world has reason to feel like a
disembodied voice, but Chappell tells his story with too much skill, and too
much pleasure in the resources of poetic form, to be accused of losing hope.

IV

Source (1985) is Chappell's first full-length collection of short poems since
his first book, though the publication history of individual poems shows that
many of them were composed by the way while he was working on *Midquest*
and *Castle Tzingal*. Furthermore, in 1979 he published *Awakening to Music*,
a chapbook of fifteen poems, and in 1981 *Driftlake: A Lieder Cycle*, an elegant
limited edition; *Source* contains five poems from *Awakening to Music*, but
Driftlake is left uncollected in favor of a second "lieder cycle," "The Transformed Twilight," similar in form and length to the first. Between the two
small books and the larger one there are some important differences of tone
and apparent intention; these are particularly evident in the revisions of the
five poems from *Awakening to Music*, and one, "Seated Figure," reprinted
from *The World Between the Eyes*.

   Awakening to Music is characterized by imaginative play carried toward
extremes of verbal ingenuity, startling similes, and weird situations. A few,
like "Delayed by Mongol Forces at National Airport," posit wonderful prem-

ises, but trail off into unsatisfying endings. However, the title poem, a recollection of the pleasures and trials of caring for cattle, and "Music as a
Woman Imperfectly Perceived," handsomely sustain their ambitious figures.

In one view, *Source* is concerned with such literary gains as may be ex-
tracted from various other kinds of losses. The first section of the book,
"Child in the Fog," evokes scenes from a mountain childhood, in poems
simultaneously regretting their disappearance and rejoicing in the power of
words to recall their shadows. Here, "Awakening to Music" has been enriched and simplified; between the following two versions of the same passage, a strained simile has been taken out, and the syntax eased. Here is the
earlier version:

> Or:
>   with hands frost-grained
> from the bucket bail I'd clutch the brood-warm
> teats and mother of God how
> a cow would kick.
>   The leg
> like a diving board snapping off on second bounce.
> As sudden as a door blown shut.
> (In August they'd lash out
> when thistle-thorns hid in the udders.)[8]

And this is the later:

> Sometimes:
>   with hands frost-grained
> from the bucket bail I'd clutch the brood-warm
> teats and God help us how she'd kick a shapely
> leg as sudden as a door blown shut.
> Or just as quick in August when
> thistle-thorns embedded in the udders.[9]

8. Fred Chappell, *Awakening to Music* (Davidson, N.C., 1979), 9. Hereafter cited in the
text as *ATM*, followed by a page number.
9. Fred Chappell, *Source* (Baton Rouge, 1985), 10. Hereafter cited in the text as *S*, followed by a page number.

It is at the end of the poem that the most thematically significant changes have been made. The first version's ending is explicit in stating the loss attendant on living past those days of herding and milking:

> And all those years I went clothed in this sleep,
> odor and heat of cows
> blanketed about my head,
> blear low fever I breathed passionately.
> How would I get it back? Go to blood
> again, sleep the light green sleep?
> How can anyone live truly, waking without cows?
>
> Then . . .
> no more music.
> (ATM, 10)

> And all those years I went clothed in this sleep,
> odor and warmth
> of cows blanketed about my head.
>
> How would I get it back? Go to blood
> again, sleep the light green sleep?
> How can I wake, not waking to music?
> (S, 11)

The new last line allows for a paraphrase like "How can I help waking to music?" The emphasis is caught hovering between what has gone forever and what has been retained.

In the second and third sections of this book, "Source" and "The Transformed Twilight," Chappell moves beyond instances of personal loss to portrayals of the kind of destruction our age has taught us to consider. "The Evening of the Second Day" reports the vague movements of a band of people who have reverted to tribalism among the ruins of a city blasted almost beyond recognition. The lieder cycle is a love poem, but the speaker "can imagine no brutal history that will not be born" (S, 43), and describes a few that already have been. Yet even the darkness of these poems is mitigated by the pleasure of "Recovery of Sexual Desire After a Bad Cold," or the wit of "The Story," which thrives and gathers detail among such people as a farmer's wife and children and a jolly merchant, but then falls drunkenly among poets; when it is thoroughly derelict, the novelists find it.

The poems in the final section, "Forever Mountain," find various kinds of consolation in the knowledge that death is an eternal separation. The poem from which the section takes its title ends "*This is a prayer*"; it is an affecting farewell to the poet's father, who is visualized moving in a leisurely way through a day and night on the mountainside until he is out of sight. "Urleid" revives Lucretius and his ideas of basic atoms free of supernatural will; the poem revels in anachronism, as Lucretius dismisses Olympus as a "drawing-room farce" and takes Rilke to task for his angels.

Lucretius is treated with more affection in *First and Last Words* (1989); in "How the Job Gets Done," subtitled "an epilogue to Lucretius," a real battlefield becomes a literary battlefield, and the soil of a garden becomes a page. After the corpses and bones and weapons are dust, there is still

> in his garden the poet who labors to line-end,
> turns back like a sweating plowman to fold
> another loamy furrow over the crumbled palaces.[10]

The title of the collection arises from what Chappell is about in the first and third sections, which are devoted, respectively, to prologues and to epilogues for various works of literature—*The Georgics* and *The Dynasts*, Livy and Lucretius, Goethe and Tolstoy, *The Wind in the Willows*. Chappell makes us at ease with what he is talking about, however familiar or unfamiliar the works he addresses. These poems are, for the most part, refreshingly accessible without being simple or simpleminded. Like most of the poems I have been looking at, they hover between the world of literature and the world we live in, as if it were sometimes hard to tell the difference.

The middle section of *First and Last Words*, "Entr'acte," contains a few miscellaneous poems—not closely related to the book's central concern, but too good to have left out—and a few poems that come at the life/literature dichotomy from the other direction. "Word," "Literature," "The Reader,"

---

10. Fred Chappell, *First and Last Words* (Baton Rouge, 1989), 52. Hereafter cited in the text as *FLW*, followed by a page number.

and "The Garden" are witty texts in which the world itself becomes a text. It would be tempting to say that the poems and the world become one, but Chappell seems to like that shimmering margin between them. The two propositions of "The Garden" are, first, that "The garden is a book about the gardener," and, second, that "The gardener is a book about her garden":

> She walks among these leaves as easy as morning
> Come to scatter its robins and tender noises.
> As the plants inhale the morning and its green light,
> The book is open once again that was never shut.
> What now we do not know we shall never know. (*FLW*, 30)

The apparent directness of that passage, and the casual paradox of the next-to-last line, indicate some of the qualities that keep these poems, with all their colloquy with other books, from being too literary to be believed. Chappell's intelligence has always been among the gifts he puts to most powerful use, because he knows how to keep it from being too showy. He learned this, as *Midquest* makes clear, from hanging around very bright but nonliterary people, who speak their complicated minds in memorable country words. "Dipperful" gives us an encounter with an old man on a porch, under which his hounds are "warm spotted lumps of doze and quiver." He speaks of walking for pleasure, and walking to work; then, echoing the wind at the end of "Hallowind," he says,

> "But if we didn't have the triflingness
> To think back on, nobody would come this far."
> (*FLW*, 35)

"Remodeling the Hermit's Cabin" presents the words of a builder named Reade, who has accepted a contract to desecrate an old cabin for the new owner, who likes certain modern amenities. This is the poem's conclusion:

> "It looks kind of sad and busted, what we've done,"
> I said.
>   "That Florida feller will tack up plastic,"
> He said, "and put him in an ice machine,
> And have him a radar carport and a poodle
> He's trained to count his money. These modern days

We're all a bunch of cowbirds, you know that?"
(*FLW*, 51)

This wonderful poem is presented as an epilogue to the Constitution of the United States. As with many of the other poems in *First and Last Words*, the connection is not forced, or required for understanding. But the connections, even when we do need to make them before the poem is clear, are rich with marvelous possibilities.

A certain occupational hazard troubles some poets; as Tony Connor once put it, they "find poems in everything," and fear the failure "to feed silence to death."[11] But Fred Chappell has long since learned that memorable poems, whatever perception or occasion gets them started, occupy a mysterious realm somewhere between where we are and what we speak. The difference between the trees among which he grew up and the trees in the sacred wood diminishes with each of his strong advances upon the wilderness.

11. Tony Connor, "Fashionable Poet Reading," in his *Lodgers: Poems* (London, 1965), 5.

ROBERT WATSON Everything We Cannot See Is Here

I

In *A Paper Horse* (1962) Robert Watson presented a first collection of poems that is unusually polished and mature. From the outset, he has displayed mastery of a style at once colloquial and densely textured, along with a fiction writer's gift for creating the speakers of his many soliloquies and dramatic monologues. His subsequent four collections have extended the range of his subject matter, but since the appearance of his first book, he has not needed to undergo profound voice changes.

Among the qualities of that voice is a density of texture that, paradoxically, is free of superficial difficulty. Watson achieves this by using what seems like the language of real speech, and by compressing his syntactical structures. For example, he often arranges repetitive parallel clauses so that essential grammatical elements can be omitted without loss of clarity. When this device is laid over an assertive meter, such as octosyllabics, the results include an idiosyncratic but completely plausible speech, and a rare energy, as in the opening lines of "The Judge Winds His Clock":

Each week I deal out years of jail.
Each year discard a life or two.
Each day for lunch a salad bowl.
(He sliced her head off in a fit;

She'd hid his shoes to keep him home)
Two bourbons evenings, never more.
I bathe at nine, I bed at ten,
I play croquet, cards, fish for trout.
(Law allows twelve fish in season)
The crimes men do. I see them all.
By now a million years of jail.[1]

The Judge arranges his life partly according to the chiming and the wind-
ing of his hall clock, which he calls "Grandfather," and partly according to
"ORDER, ORDER in the court," a phrase that appears as an irregular refrain in
the poem; as he moves toward bedtime, and experiences a few doubts, the
lockstep of the end-stopped lines begins to waver, though the meter is not
strikingly varied:

The clock ticks like a heart. My heart
Ticks like a clock. Ice in my glass
Of bourbon clicks like dice. I shake
My fortune, my head. Grandfather chimes.
It's ten. I lock doors, windows,
Shut opinions in a briefcase,
Wind up Grandfather for tomorrow's
Judgment day. All is in order.
(SP, 81)

The poem ends with the Judge in bed, drifting toward sleep, aware of his
dream in which the clock becomes the Chief Justice, chiming twelve:

"Twelve what?" I ask. "Twelve fish
In season?"
"Just twelve!" chimes the Judge
In his bathrobe and whacks the bench.
So it is. I roll in a ball.
The gavel strikes. My sentence dealt . . .
A million years and lives discarded.

1. Robert Watson, *Selected Poems* (New York, 1974), 80. Hereafter cited in the text as
SP, followed by a page number.

It rains outside the house, the jail,
And order, order in the court.
(*SP*, 82)

It is characteristic of many of Watson's poems that some threatening
force is first suggested and portrayed, and then accepted, even embraced. The
acceptance may sometimes be no more than tonal, as it is here. But Watson's
poetry makes an interesting commentary on the idea that, as Faulkner put it,
we have lived with fear "so long sustained by now that we can even bear it."
Some of Watson's characters cherish their dreads, as if they were essential to
their identities; others would shake them if they could; and a few are satirized
for the futility of their fears.

The satirical mode is well represented by "Callers," whose richness of
tone is achieved by a daring mixture of humor and melodramatic pathos. Miss
Burckhardt, the reclusive miser, is mercilessly lampooned:

"Silence! While I add infernal taxes up—
Federal, state, city grasp and grasp
What I have spent my lifetime saving.
Wolves at my door, callers, away, away!"
(*SP*, 98)

The callers are never clearly defined; the opening line, which appears
twice more with slightly altered phrasing, introduces the first curious ambiguity of their being: "May we visit you, Miss Burckhardt, my dear?" The odd
combination of plural and singular pronouns suggests either that the callers
have appointed a single speaker, or that the force behind the voice uses the
editorial "we." Either way, as the urgency of their errand increases ("We have
come for you" and "We must have you"), its precise nature becomes increasingly vague and threatening. The last line given to that voice quotes Revelation 3:20, the conclusion of the address to the well-off but lukewarm Laodi-
ceans: "*A thief? Behold, I stand at the door and knock.*" But the poem's final
stanza does not allow us to take much comfort in the notion that Miss Burckhardt has been overtaken by the Holy Spirit. The second line especially has
the flavor of an animated cartoon:

The knocking and ringing and calling at last
Shook up her head like a dynamite blast.

She limped to her dresser, to her sock for her keys.
She unbolted her door, but saw nothing there,
Not caller, not thief, not tree, dust, nor air.
(*SP*, 99)

The world has vanished from her sight. It would be easy and tempting
to say that this is because Miss Burckhardt has departed from the world by
the usual route, thereby illustrating the folly of avarice. The case can be
made, but it is unsatisfying. Miss Burckhardt's fears have emptied her life to
the point that no one can tell whether she is alive at the end of the poem,
which is on the same rewardingly mysterious plane as the beginning.

In many of Watson's poems, fear of the unknown is triggered by the
external world—especially, in *Christmas in Las Vegas* (1971), by inanimate
objects and nonhuman processes. The threat posed by such modern conve-
niences as jet planes, air conditioning, and artificial light is most palpable in
"The Glass Door," which is about walking through a glass door that was not
open. After being mended and told he should soon be the same as ever, the
speaker finds that he is in fact not the same—he is always on the lookout for
crystallized air,

For invisible curtains between what we see
    And what we think we see
On rainy nights staring beyond the windshield
    Or out the kitchen window
Washing glasses in the sink. Telescopes are useless.
Everything we cannot see is here.
(*SP*, 14)

It is the mind, of course, that makes inanimate objects seem to have
malevolent intelligence; this is more explicit in the title poem, "Christmas
in Las Vegas," where a widower finds himself becoming a machine as he faces
a one-armed bandit, in an atmosphere so bright and otherworldly that no one
ages. A chorus girl is "pretty as any juke box," the hours "shuffle by metalli-
cally." The "jackpot" the speaker wants to win is the return of his humanity.

The mind's tendency to personalize objects becomes more nearly abstract
in "Nostalgia of the Infinite," a short poem in which Watson's virtuosity with
sound is pushed to the limits of control:

Flags fly from a white tower's top in a green sky.
The dark couple at its base do not embrace,

> Look up or down. This is the nostalgia
> Of the infinite,
> Of the infinite set on the retina,
> On the base of the brain when the rain wipes clean
> The brain pan and the wind bangs the pan on its nail.
> (*SP*, 65)

In the last three lines, sound patterns become so crowded and repetitive that even the prose sense of the passage is somewhat elusive, plain as it is when grasped.

Watson returns often to the question whether love may be a refuge from such vague apprehensions. "The Night Fear," also from *Christmas in Las Vegas*, is one of his most direct treatments of the three-way relationship that develops between irrational fear and two people who live together for a long time. Though the topic is stated clearly enough in the title, the word *fear* does not appear in the first two of the poem's three sections. Instead, there is something, constantly referred to as "it," that "swoops and hisses over the dark room like a bat / Or pendulum." It inspires the couple at first to fiercer love-making, which in turn makes them think that their bed rises above the earth and then slides

> Down, down past the moon
> Through the French doors back into their room.
> The clock nods, a dog barks,
> The bathroom tile glows safely in the dark.
> (*SP*, 91)

The third section of the poem finds the couple still in the same room, accustomed to the idea that there will always be some "terror buzzing in their hearts or skies." They no longer "cling and bite"; the poem ends with an image of peaceful exhilaration:

> To sink in sleep each now pictures a skater,
> His face muffled, his long scarf ends streaming
> And snapping in the crystal air,
> His heart racing, swooping and hissing
> Over the frozen, star-pocked pond of night.
> (*SP*, 92)

The swooping and hissing of the first two stanzas do not go away, but they are no longer so troublesome as to suggest such disparate things as a bat and a pendulum. Watson does not come much closer than this to suggesting that love, when it endures, can keep people and the world together. "Winter Lovers," in which a man and a woman are sledding at night, makes somewhat less reassuring use of winter sport:

> And so on runners over ice and snow we lovers
> Of simple black and white hurtle through our nights,
> Avoiding black, holding to white; we never look to left or right.[2]

II

Throughout Watson's work, there are poems arising from the hope that there is redemptive power in love; many of them deal with the difficulty of distinguishing between love and momentary lust, and some portray relationships in various states of dissolution, or tenuous persistence. Many of these are satirical, or gently humorous; but a few arise from occasional realizations of something more substantial and enduring.

One of Watson's earliest explorations of this theme is still among his most complex and powerful. "Her Father Is Drunk in the Graveyard" (reprinted in *Selected Poems* as "Her Father Is Drunk in an Abandoned Graveyard") first appeared in *A Paper Horse*, where the specificity of its title seemed perfectly in keeping with the whole table of contents; Watson's titles turn out to be exact captions for the unusually specific people and situations he imagines and portrays. The first few lines of this poem get us past the oddity of the situation and show us the speaker's sympathy for her father, and her perception of what he shares with many of us. Having established the setting—a cemetery ravaged by age and vandalism—and shown us the man asleep near a broken marble hand and a dead dove, the speaker looks into her father's life:

> No middle for him: a beginning and end,
> An unending ending of his waking life,
> A shade drawn daily against the living world,
> A walk in blindfold to a borderland,

2. Robert Watson, *Advantages of Dark* (New York, 1966), 9.

Where this stateless man sees, or dreams he sees,
The soft, welcome shadow of his lover
Waiting, secret on the river's other bank,
Arms outstretched, beckoning him softly over.
(*SP*, 104)

She wonders briefly whether "all men stray to dark" and "fiddle with death," and wishes for a husband "Who will outrage the other life and leap in this," before she finds a way of expressing love and rejection at once:

Dear dreaming, wasted Father, floating
Further each day from my hardening memory,
I will let you slumber here, let you lie
While I move further from you tenderly.
O my dear dying, drunken Father, go floating
Softly to her dark, winged kingdom waiting.
(*SP*, 105)

The somewhat inflated emotion of the daughter, evident in such usages as *slumber* and *O,* is balanced by the background presence of the poet's voice, perhaps most audible in the phrase *hardening memory*. It is this delicacy of touch that enables Watson to draw out over two pages a situation that is potentially (if not unavoidably) melodramatic. The constant presence of his idiosyncratic voice is an unobtrusive reminder that the poet cannot withdraw too far from a scene and let us see it only through a created speaker's eyes, lest the speaker go unconvincingly to pieces.

When the speaker is not readily distinguishable from the poet, the problem is more commonplace, but no less difficult. "Years After the Death of Frances Gluck," from *Christmas in Las Vegas*, begins with two lines that immediately put the poem at risk:

I lie at night on a warm summer's grave
In Provincetown, a practice death.
(*SP*, 31)

With economy and directness, the poem recalls a woman of attractive eccentricity who died in a motorcycle accident, and lies buried not in Provincetown, but in North Carolina. That the speaker is not lying on her grave is a relief, of course; it not only restores poignancy to the recollection, but, as the recollection sharpens, it takes us away from any questions about the speaker's presence in the graveyard, or the occupant of the grave on which he lies. The rhymes at the end of the poem make it sound simpler than it is; it takes a moment to see who is not to be disturbed:

> What a swift arc from seat to curb.
> "Love" was your most popular verb.
> I'll place a sign around my neck
> For you, reading
> PLEASE DO NOT DISTURB.
> (SP, 31)

The swift arc of the world's unpredictability most often appears danger-ous in Watson's poems, but if it can bring fear and destruction, it can also bring good fortune, as he says in "God as Magician." This near-sonnet opens by presenting both possibilities:

> He yanks a whole Spring out of his top hat
> Of night: warm air, leaves, violets, daffodils.
> Or maybe wraps up the town in ice.[3]

The poem continues with a list of the magician's extravagant displays of appearance and disappearance, saving the actual topic of the poem for the last three lines:

> It beats me. You flew, a bouquet from his wand
>
> To me as I flew. I love you, I say
> Before he tucks us with his wand away.
> (NBC, 21)

Among the forces before which men seem helpless is the sudden attrac-tion to a woman whose attributes may be more imagined than actual. Wat-son's treatment of this attraction is most often satirical, though even within that mode his tone can range from gentle self-deprecation to angry regret. "A

---

3. Robert Watson, *Night Blooming Cactus* (New York, 1980), 21. Hereafter cited in the text as *NBC*, followed by a page number.

Valentine for a Drug Store Clerk" (*SP*, 21), first collected in *Christmas in Las Vegas*, addresses a young woman whose "lanky form" makes the speaker forget the pills he came for; he buys only cigarettes (*Lucky Strikes!*), and "all is well." But "Going Nowhere Alone at Night" (*SP*, 111), from *Advantages of Dark*, presents a man driving aimlessly around at night, willing to admit to a policeman that he is going "Nowhere. I can't sleep." One sentence, repeated with different line breaks, contains the cause of this drifting; it is like other stupidly repetitive things we say to ourselves: "It's wrong to fall in love / So many times, so many times."

Clearly, Watson can find macabre humor in the grimmest of situations, and solemn implications in slight occasions. This inclusiveness of vision enabled him to produce "Lines for a President" (first collected in *Advantages of Dark*), one of the most honest and powerful poems yet written about the assassination of President Kennedy. It is in two parts, "The Inauguration and Shortly After" and "At the Funeral." The first part is so immediate in its evocation of the inaugural ceremony, so dry and direct in its satire of life in the White House, that it might have been written while Kennedy was still living:

> Your wife's French chef breaks skulls
> Of eggs. Upstairs her dresser
> Gardens in her hair.
> A maid brings scented pearls,
> The world of Louis and Molière,
> Her conquest of Versailles
> And Athens. Downstairs
> You praise the Spartans.
> (*SP*, 143)

The second part begins with a recollection of Kennedy's rocking chair as a symbol, and then cuts, almost without transition, to the six grey horses drawing the hearse, and the seventh, "wild and black / And riderless." It is a deeply moving performance, free of the posturing that overtook so many poets who, in the aftermath of the murder, seemed to act more out of a sense that they really ought to write about it, than out of genuine poetic impulse. The end of the poem is a stunning convergence of the dreadful event and Watson's usual view of the world:

You could not stop the shells,
The drowning of your boat in war;
You could not stop the snow the sky dumped down,
The cold, the lectern smoking when your priest invoked
The Lord, your poet struck blind, the bullets in your head,
The six grey horses drawing you to where you are
Rocking and will always rock.

The seventh horse is riderless, wild and black.
(*SP*, 144)

III

Love and the apparent perversity of the external world are only two of the recurrent themes in Watson's shorter poems. Others, such as the seductiveness of self-delusion, the related conviction that elsewhere is better than here, or the difficulty of locating the boundary between life and death, turn up not only in the short poems, but in the several longer ones, ranging roughly between 80 and 240 lines, which have constituted an important part of each of Watson's separate collections.

"Voices from the Palace," which appeared in *A Paper Horse*, is a closely related sequence of five monologues, so nearly self-contained that Watson can select one or two for performance at a reading. But the sequence seems greater than the sum of its parts. Each monologue provides a particular point of view on the life of a bloodthirsty tyrant and his household; as we hear in turn from "The Deposed Prince from his Tower Prison," or "The Minstrel," for example, the specific details of the narrative gradually come to seem less important than the chilling intimation that one of the easiest values to inculcate is violence, and that acquiescence in violence may be an inescapable human burden.

More recently, Watson has extended some of his monologues and given them to more fully realized eccentrics than appear in earlier books. "J. Goldsborough Bruff," from *Christmas in Las Vegas*, is an astonishing *tour de force* spoken by an old man lost in California snow, thinking over the gold fever that brought him there:

I am J. Goldsborough Bruff, President
Of Washington City Mining Company
In my winter palace. Addressing my dog.
(*SP*, 146)

Tired, starving, lost, Bruff finally gets up and walks aimlessly, having considered his impending death. But when his pole strikes the frozen corpse of an ox, gold fever returns with this news of survival:

> I press my knife with all my weight and cut
> Into the golden flesh of ox. I will
> Return to Washington, rich, well, honored,
> J. Goldsborough Bruff, mapper of the unmapped
> West. The gold dust will fall like snow, my pup.
> (*SP*, 147)

Because he is thoroughly in control of tonal ambiguities, Watson manages simultaneously both a tribute to the human spirit and a caricature of it.

Christmas in Las Vegas also contains "The Last Wild Indian," one of two long monologues in Watson's work that were inspired by accounts of minor historical figures (the other is "Victoria Woodhull," from *Night Blooming Cactus*). The challenge in such poems is to find a voice that will not seem too bookish, too dependent on the known and researched facts. Watson achieves this in "The Last Wild Indian" partly by compressing into some 120 lines more facts about the Yani tribesman Ishi than are readily found outside Theodora Kroeber's *Ishi in Two Worlds*, and partly by imagining the central dilemma of Ishi's life after he became associated with a museum in San Francisco:

> Alone in the old world, alone in the new.
> Dead in the woods my body would rot unclean,
> My soul unclean. Here they promise to burn at death
> My body, unlock my soul to shoot back
> To heavenly fields of my tribe, my life.
> I see through glass of the showcase I polish
> The model huts, harpoons, baskets, arrows,
> The feather robes. It is snowing. I join
> Our father in a hunt for grizzly bear.
> My name is Ishi, and Ishi means man.
> (*SP*, 151)

"Victoria Woodhull," Watson's longest poem, appears in *Night Blooming Cactus;* it also has to do with more than one "world," or mode of existence. Victoria Claflin Woodhull (1838–1927) and her sister Tennessee, according to *The Oxford Companion to American Literature*, were for many years involved in various odd and unpopular activities. With their mother, they presented spiritualistic exhibitions, and then went to New York, where Cornelius Vanderbilt helped establish them as brokers. Soon they began publishing *Woodhull and Claflin's Weekly*, which advocated free love and socialism, and published the story of the Beecher-Tilton affair that launched the trial of Henry Ward Beecher. In 1872, Victoria ran for president under the banner of the Equal Rights party, which nominated Frederick Douglass for vice-president. The two sisters moved to England in 1877, where they both found husbands. All of Victoria's principal writings appear to have been published by 1892.

Watson's poem is in two sections, each preceded by a note on the setting. Part I is headed "*Cell 11. Ludlow Street Jail. New York City. 1872,*" and takes the form of a narrative written by Victoria "To ask if, / Because I am a woman, / I am to have no justice." It takes her through the presidential campaign, and may suffer here and there from the weight of the facts it contains; there are moments when her references to actual people—Beecher, Anthony Comstock, and so on—ring more of the library than of the character. But most of the time, this intrinsically interesting story is told energetically and economically; that it is prologue does not become obvious until part II, which recounts a less publicly tempestuous period in Woodhull's life. The poem is much more interesting here, partly because it seems to rely more on Watson's imagination than on biographical research, and partly because it is a renunciation or denial of many of the positions Woodhull had earlier espoused. Its heading sets the scene in England, a year before her death. She refers to her having published *The Human Body as the Temple of God*, and offers revisionist versions of her earlier doctrines. She is old, and sits in a chair or rides in a car, and looks back on a life almost ridiculously full; but reading the end of the poem, it is hard not to think of Miss Burckhardt greeting callers at her door:

> I have lived to get what I want.
> I won all but one,
> The Presidency, the White House.
>
> They saw to that: Tilton, Beecher, Comstock.
> All dead, all lies, all dead.
> And I? What next?
> (*NBC,* 34)

"The City of Passaic," a narrative poem in several voices (*Advantages of Dark*) is in certain ways more ambitious. The prologue sets a scene: apparently an old woman, gathering coal near a railway track, is raped. As the poem moves through its seven sections, the old woman's background is supplied, the rape is casually mentioned in Benny's bar, and a nearby factory catches fire. Two monologues make it clear that the rape of the old woman, and the rapist's conviction that she regained her youth at that moment, are both illusions: the old woman had sent her daughter to gather fuel in the old woman's haunts under the railway tracks. The coincidences of substitution, fire, and firebells are explained, even as the mysteries surrounding them are deepened; the poem's deft shifting between the exterior world of the city and the interior worlds of the characters creates a narrative rich in character and event.

At each end of Watson's career to this point, there is a long poem based primarily on a single consciousness that sometimes drifts into semiconsciousness. "Watson on the Beach" and "Island of Bones" conclude *A Paper Horse* and *Night Blooming Cactus*, respectively; both present speakers who seem to represent the poet, drifting from observation to introspection, and sometimes into dream, in vacation settings—Nauset Beach and Key West. Both are fragmentary, though the later poem is more obviously so.

"Watson on the Beach" is divided into a brief prologue and seven numbered sections, but within each section the leaps from observation to speculation are sometimes without transition. A middle-aged man and his family spend Independence Day at the beach; he has reached a time in his life when he notices that the beach and the ocean are littered with the dead, and that his own flesh has begun to sag a little. The young, in their perfect bodies, are mildly but unconsciously threatening, primarily because they inspire meditation on mortality; morbidity, however, is not in order here:

> In looking from their flesh to ours,
> I see we have a kind of beauty too:
> Ignore a line off plumb, a blur,
> My wife and I are as beautiful as they.
> The swimming mackerel cannot tell,
> I'm sure, one human swimmer from another.
> (SP, 166)

Despite occasional acknowledgments of mortality, of anonymity, and of the futility of trying to solve mysteries of origin and conclusion, the poem is a celebration of life, and of the dreams that sometimes mystify.

"Island of Bones" is a darker performance; the decadence and the fecundity of Key West are sometimes occasion for irony bordering on the
heavy-handed, as in this echo of a line from Wallace Stevens' more famous
poem in the same setting:

> She lies on her back in a pink bikini
> She removes the top
> He kneels rubbing Copper Tone
> Into her thighs.
> "What's your name?" she asks him.
> *She sings beyond the genius of the sea.*
> (*NBC*, 52)

The poem continues to throw up snatches of overheard conversation,
along with brief comments on the sights and on the speaker's thoughts; the
overwhelming impression is of sexuality, vulgarity, and even crime, but most
of the time the speaker is not outraged or even intolerant. There are passages
of almost pure fun:

> "Hiss, spaugh, squeak.
> Honey an effen tire's flat.
> Now the fish is in the fat.
> Jeez I've got to take a leak.
>
> .   .   .   .
>
> Blue light, blue light, blue light!
> Snap, crackle pop.
> Club, cuffs, squat, search.
> Hi ya cop."
> (*NBC*, 54)

Speeches like this are balanced by brief monologues spoken by a prosti-
tute who participated in a murder, and another whose language is shot through
with psychobabble. In between, the speaker complains that his mind seems
to be emptying; he says "*To live on memory is to live on tea and jello*" (*NBC*,
58), and "*I sit here wishing for wishes / In the Pier House bar*" (*NBC*, 59).

The impression grows subtly that the speaker is among nihilists. A recipe for Key lime pie is dropped almost arbitrarily onto the next-to-last page; then, at the end, the speaker describes the evening ritual of applauding the sunset, in terms that leave little doubt that he does not share the crowd's enthusiasm:

> Everyone clapped when the sun went down
> And the clouds went up in flame.
> (NBC, 59)

Watson has managed a rare accomplishment in recent poetry: he has simultaneously maintained a very high standard of excellence and demonstrated a restless curiosity and courage. His poems are constantly surprising for the grace with which they can include much that is far from conventionally poetic, even by contemporary standards. It is easy and fashionable to make ugly art out of unpromising materials; but Watson's vision, craft, and audacity transform such materials into poems of durable beauty.

GWENDOLYN BROOKS An Essential Sanity

Gwendolyn Brooks's emergence as an important poet has been less sche-matic, but not less impressive, than commentary upon it has suggested. It is difficult to isolate the poems themselves from the variety of reactions to them; these have been governed as much by prevailing or individual attitudes toward issues of race, class, and gender, as by serious attempts at dispassionate examination and evaluation. Furthermore, Brooks's activities in behalf of younger writers have demonstrated her generosity and largeness of spirit, and wide recognition of these qualities has led some critics away from the con-trolled but genuine anger in many of the poems. Brooks has contributed to this process; in interviews, and in her autobiographical *Report from Part One* (1972), she speaks engagingly and with apparent authority about her own work, and many of her judgments have become part of the majority view of her career. Nevertheless, it is worthwhile to consider whether there might be more unity in the body of her work than conventional divisions of her career suggest.

Brooks herself, as William H. Hansell has noted, indicated the divisions when, "in a 1976 interview at the University of Wisconsin–La Crosse, [she] said that her work falls into three periods that correspond to 'changes' in her perspective." Hansell's note: "Works of the first period are *A Street in Bronze-*

ville (1945), *Annie Allen* (1949) and *The Bean Eaters* (1960). The second period is represented by the 'New Poems' section of *Selected Poems* (1963) and by two uncollected poems, 'The Sight of the Horizon' (1963) and 'In the Time of Detachment, in the Time of Cold' (1965). The third phase of her development is marked by her most recent collections: *In the Mecca* (1969) [1968], *Riot* (1969), *Family Pictures* (1970) and *Beckonings* (1975)." [1]

Whether a writer's development involves improvement is highly questionable; but writers often think they are improving, because they are usually more interested in work in progress than they are in work long since completed. Since the mid-1960s, Brooks has revealed these attitudes in numerous comments on her awakening to the situation of the Black writer in America. On the other hand, when she ended her association with Harper & Row, and began to place her work with Black publishers, she retained the rights in her early work, and reprinted the bulk of it in a collected volume entitled *Blacks*. The stark inclusiveness of that one-word title suggests that Brooks perceives unity as well as variety in the range of her concerns and voices.

Report from Part One and, more recently, the late George Kent's *A Life of Gwendolyn Brooks* (1990) provide generous insight into the origins of Brooks's art. Her own work provides a livelier evocation of her early years than Kent manages in his first two chapters, but he has made a thorough examination of the young girl's notebooks, which she kept industriously. The child appears to have taken seriously her mother's prediction that she would grow up to be the "lady Paul Laurence Dunbar." Kent finds that she was a victim of an intraracial prejudice that put very dark girls at a social disadvantage among Black people of her age. (This theme recurs in Brooks's poetry through *In the Mecca*.) The energy that might have gone into a more active social life was instead poured into poems and stories that show promise more in their profusion than in their accomplishment.

Though she had been publishing poems in the Chicago *Defender* since her high school days, she was twenty-eight when *A Street in Bronzeville* (poems, 1945) appeared. Concerning what was "new" about it, Kent writes: "The poet had rejected the exotic vein of the Harlem Renaissance—the

---

1. William H. Hansell, "The Poet-Militant and Foreshadowings of a Black Mystique: Poems in the Second Period of Gwendolyn Brooks," in *A Life Distilled: Gwendolyn Brooks, Her Poetry and Fiction*, ed. Maria K. Mootry and Gary Smith (Urbana, 1987), 71, 80n.

celebration of unique racial values, such as defiance of social proscription through emphasis upon joy and soul. A few poems in A *Street* work close to this vein, allowing the reader the enjoyment of the old colorful images, but use one device or another to bring them to the court of critical intelligence. Thus 'patent leather' and other poems devalue the 'hipness' that the Harlem Renaissance would have celebrated."[2]

As have all American poets, Brooks inherited the old problem of language, which in the nineteenth century divided poets into rebels and loyalists—those who knew that the central problem was to establish independence in the language of the colonizing country, and those who were content with the poetic tradition of the colonizers. This dilemma is exponentially more difficult for a Black woman; a term like "the lady Paul Laurence Dunbar" hardly needs comment on the forms of oppression it implies and, implicitly, accepts.

Still, Brooks had applied herself assiduously to the absorption of a largely white male tradition, in the apparent belief that all great poetry in English had something of value to teach her. A *Street in Bronzeville* introduced a poet of more technical accomplishment than was usual even in the mid-1940s. Forty-five years later, the variety of forms and tones in the collection remains impressive; Donne, Robinson, Frost, Dickinson, and even Ogden Nash seem to have left occasional marks, as well as Hughes and the blues.

But what strikes most forcibly now is the sophistication, and the Dickinsonian way in which sophistication sometimes becomes a shield, from behind which almost invisible darts fly often and accurately. Throughout Brooks's poetry, delicate satire regularly breaks through a surface that is pretending in some way to be well behaved.

In twelve lines, for example, "the vacant lot" provides a richly populated scene, in tones modulating from apparent nostalgia and regret through sarcasm to controlled, satiric flatness:

Mrs. Coley's three-flat brick
Isn't here any more.
All done with seeing her fat little form
Burst out of the basement door;
And with seeing her African son-in-law

2. George E. Kent, A *Life of Gwendolyn Brooks* (Lexington, Ky., 1990), 66.

(Rightful heir to the throne)
With his great white strong cold squares of teeth
And his little eyes of stone;
And with seeing the squat fat daughter
Letting in the men
When majesty has gone for the day—
And letting them out again. [3]

Throughout *A Street*, individual poems have lowercase titles when they are grouped under a larger heading. Despite this consistency, however, the device occasionally creates a local effect; here the suggested insignificance of the lot is emphasized by an immediate and energetic portrayal of what is not there. Among the departures is the mysterious African son-in-law, who briefly dominates the poem, his teeth packing the seventh line with stressed monosyllables, but whose "majesty," by the end of the poem, is cruelly diminished.

The gulf between imagined majesty and hard reality is a frequent theme in *A Street*. Its most ambitious treatment is "The Sundays of Satin-Legs Smith," a narrative of just over 150 lines in which satire is deepened by compassion. The ironic contrasts begin with the title; the protagonist's name yokes the exotic and the ordinary. The polysyllabic opening introduces a narrator whose self-consciously elegant language is mock-heroic:

Inamoratas, with an approbation,
Bestowed his title. Blessed his inclination.

He wakes, unwinds, elaborately: a cat
Tawny, reluctant, royal. He is fat
And fine this morning. Definite. Reimbursed.
(43)

As Satin-Legs commences his morning ablutions, the speaker becomes an ironically patient lecturer, addressing a "you" who is presumed innocent of the life being unfolded here, and who may therefore be taken as white. In

3. Gwendolyn Brooks, *Blacks* (Chicago, 1987; fifth printing, 1991), 42. Hereafter cited by page number in the text. Previous printings of *Blacks* are differently paginated. See note 11.

the following excerpt, the sentence "Maybe so" ends a passage of fourteen lines, concerning the appropriateness of Satin-Legs's choice of scents and oils, which both recalls and quietly subverts the sonnet tradition:

> might his happiest
> Alternative (you muse) be, after all,
> A bit of gentle garden in the best
> Of taste and straight tradition? Maybe so.
> But you forget, or did you ever know,
> His heritage of cabbage and pigtails,
> Old intimacy with alleys, garbage pails,
> Down in the deep (but always beautiful) South
> Where roses blush their blithest (it is said)
> And sweet magnolias put Chanel to shame.
> (43–44)

Satin-Legs has only an artificial flower, made of feathers, for his lapel; in the first of two brief asides, the speaker says, "Ah, there is little hope." Satin-Legs will have "his lotion, lavender, and oil"

> Unless you care to set the world a-boil
> And do a lot of equalizing things,
> Remove a little ermine, say, from kings,
> Shake hands with paupers and appoint them men. . . .
> (44)

But the speaker decisively returns to an inspection of "The innards of this closet." More strongly than "Maybe so" above, "innards" underscores the speaker's dualistic sense of language and class; if Satin-Legs is being satirized, so is the addressee, whose ignorance is more broadly satirized in such later poems as "I love those little booths at Benvenuti's," "The Lovers of the Poor," and "Bronzeville Woman in a Red Hat."

The closet contains the gaudy accoutrements of such a dandy as Satin-Legs is, or aspires to be; colors are "sarcastic," tailoring is "cocky," ties are "hysterical." Following this exposition of his tastes, two lines in a second brief aside hover between solemnity and humor:

People are so in need, in need of help.
People want so much that they do not know.
(44)

True enough; but the idea is complicated by its placement, which suggests that Satin-Legs needs advice from a refined haberdasher. Creating himself "is all his sculpture, all his art." However, after he enters the street,
halfway through the poem, there is no further description of his appearance;
instead, we see how things appear to him. Through the narrator, we experience his surroundings more vividly than he does. "He hears and does not
hear" an alarm clock, children, a plane, voices, and the elevated train. "He
sees and does not see" broken windows patched with newspaper, children in
worn but decently patched clothes, and

                   men estranged
From music and from wonder and from joy
But far familiar with the guiding awe
Of foodlessness.
(46)

The music he hears is popular blues; the narrator notes the absence of
strains by Saint-Saëns, Grieg, Tschaikovsky, Brahms, and questions whether
he could love them if they were audible; one brings to music what one is:

The pasts of his ancestors lean against
Him. Crowd him. Fog out his identity.
Hundreds of hungers mingle with his own. . . .
(46)

From a movie, where he is reminded that "it is sin / For his eye to eat
of" the heroine's "ivory and yellow," he proceeds toward the goal of all his
efforts. In a line that tumbles anticlimactically from faint echoes of the
courtly tradition to a place where main courses are served on meat platters,
he "Squires his lady to dinner at Joe's Eats" (47). The "lady" is different every
Sunday, but there are constant characteristics, most of them supplied by the
overstated dress and makeup that Satin-Legs could be expected to admire.
The ending of the poem subtly suggests that this is a kind of death-in-life.

Remarking that the food is plentiful at Joe's Eats, the narrator interjects: "(The end is—isn't it?—all that really matters)." The poem concludes with the achievement of Satin-Legs's objective:

> Her body is like new brown bread
> Under the Woolworth mignonette.
> Her body is a honey bowl
> Whose waiting honey is deep and hot.
> Her body is like summer earth,
> Receptive, soft, and absolute. . . .
> (48)

The slant rhymes undercut the directness of the statements and draw attention to the "absolute" nature of receptive earth, where, in the old courtly usage, Satin-Legs Smith is about to die. Unlike the pool players in "We Real Cool," who "die soon" in many senses, Satin-Legs will survive; this Don Juan's version of hell is to repeat this cycle indefinitely, with "little hope" of redemption. The ignorant white observer is presumed to accept this ending as all that really matters.

Brooks wrote this accomplished poem toward the end of her work on A Street, probably in response to Richard Wright's evaluation of the manuscript she had sent to Harper & Brothers; he praised her skill and genuineness, but added that "most volumes of poems usually have one really long fine poem around which shorter ones are added or grouped."[4]

A Street concludes with a sequence of twelve sonnets, "Gay Chaps at the Bar," which is close enough to what Wright was asking for. "Gay Chaps" is among the stronger poetic responses we have to World War II, and deserves inclusion in anthologies devoted to that subject, along with "Negro Hero," the monologue of a Black mess attendant who took up a machine gun and used it effectively when his ship was attacked at Pearl Harbor, despite regulations of the strictly segregated navy of that era, in which Black personnel did not handle firearms.

Brooks adopts several points of view throughout "Gay Chaps at the Bar"—omniscient, first-person singular, first-person plural—and her speakers demonstrate that Black soldiers suffered the same terrors and hopes as any

4. Kent, A Life, 63.

other soldiers. But she is equally concerned to present the injustices of the Black warriors' situation, and reasonable doubts about what they might have been fighting for. The sonnets submit to convention in several ways, but Brooks uses slant rhyme in them more often than she had earlier; they extend the range of sonic choices, and help to emphasize the paradox that these men were fighting for a country that in many ways refused to claim them.

Brooks's interest in traditional technical virtuosity reaches an apex in *Annie Allen,* the collection for which she received the 1950 Pulitzer Prize. The book is arranged in three sections: "Notes from the Childhood and the Girlhood," "The Anniad" (which includes the long poem of that title and two short pieces as "Appendix to The Anniad"), and "The Womanhood." The eleven short poems in the first section establish Annie as a daydreamer, resentful of restrictions imposed by her parents and society, hopeful of some idealized rescuer.

"The Anniad" is a technical *tour de force:* 301 lines in forty-three seven-line stanzas, employing thirty different rhyme schemes, a compelling meter (trochaic tetrameter catalectic), and a diction that is elaborate, dense, and compressed. Paraphrase is often difficult, and it is also difficult to resist being carried along on the sound waves, heedless of incomprehension. There is a definite narrative; some of the details are obscure, though the poems in the first section of *Annie Allen* provide background for the entrance to the poem:

> Think of sweet and chocolate,
> Left to folly or to fate,
> Whom the higher gods forgot,
> Whom the lower gods berate;
> Physical and underfed
> Fancying on the featherbed
> What was never and is not.
>
> What is ever and is not.
> Pretty tatters blue and red,
> Buxom berries beyond rot,
> Western clouds and quarter-stars,
> Fairy-sweet of old guitars
> Littering the little head
> Light upon the featherbed.
>
> . . . .

Watching for the paladin
Which no woman ever had,
Paradisaical and sad
With a dimple in his chin
And the mountains in the mind;
Ruralist and rather bad,
Cosmopolitan and kind.
(97)

The imperative of the first line, repeated six more times throughout the poem, implies a reader or listener. This strategy, not as fully developed as in "The Sundays of Satin-Legs Smith," still gives the speaker awareness of an audience, and an inclination to perform. In various tones—affectionate tolerance, adult amusement, or sadness and anger, the speaker shows us the impossible romantic aspirations that fill Annie's "light" and "little" head. The paladin's virtues are impossibly contradictory; that he is not a person, but an imaginary being, is obvious enough, but emphasis is provided in the relative pronoun: "Which no woman ever had."

As she grows older, a "man of tan" courts Annie, and his qualities and her predilections arouse her:

What a hot theopathy
Roisters through her, gnaws the walls,
And consumes her where she falls
In her gilt humility.
(98)

They move to a "lowly room" that she tries to transform into a lovely love nest. There follows a passage that has been subject to more than one critical bias:

Doomer, though, crescendo-comes
Prophesying hecatombs.
Surrealist and cynical.
Garrulous and guttural.
Spits upon the silver leaves.

Denigrates the dainty eves
Dear dexterity achieves.

Names him. Tames him. Takes him off,
Throws to columns row on row.
Where he makes the rifles cough,
Stutter. Where the reveille
Is staccato majesty.
Then to marches. Then to know
The hunched hells across the sea.

Vaunting hands are now devoid.
Hieroglyphics of her eyes
Blink upon a paradise
Paralyzed and paranoid.
But idea and body too
Clamor "Skirmishes can do.
Then he will come back to you."
(99–100)

To the reader biased toward a belief in the occasional usefulness of paraphrase, "Doomer" presents difficulties; but the second of these three stanzas
helps to identify it as a power suggestive of Uncle Sam, the draft, and the
intrusion of war. Noisily, prophesying slaughter, speaking almost bestially, it
attacks the little home life Annie has with difficulty achieved. It calls "tan
man's" name, inducts him into armed service, sets him to drill with guns,
reveille, and marches, and ships him overseas. Annie, bereft, looks blankly
on her altered life, but wants to believe he will not be killed.

Hortense J. Spillers, however, offers a feminist reading of the passage:
"As it turns out, he is not the hot lover 'theopathy' would make him out to
be, but Annie denies it, fearing that to say so would be to evoke an already
imminent betrayal: [quotes first and third of above stanzas]. This scene of
'ruin,' brought on by sexual impotence, gains a dimension of pathos because
it anticipates the woman's ultimate loneliness, but this judgment is undercut
by the caricature of the male."[5]

5. Hortense J. Spillers, "Gwendolyn the Terrible: Propositions on Eleven Poems," in *A
Life Distilled*, ed. Mootry and Smith, 230.

This may constitute misreading for the sake of an overriding theme, but Spillers characterizes, with justice and unintended irony, the poem's "specific end: to expose the sadness and comedy of self-delusion in an equally deluded world."[6]

Upon his return, troubled by conflicting recollections of horror and of power, and by predilections imposed on him in a white-dominated society, "tan man" finds a mistress whose color is more honey than chocolate. The twenty-third stanza begins by repeating the first line of the poem, and launches an account of Annie's life alone, from winter through the following fall; she attempts social gaiety, esoteric learning, the high life, and then tries to settle toward her husband's return. The speaker turns to "tan man" and chastises him:

> Hence from scenic bacchanal,
> Preshrunk and droll prodigal!
> Smallness that you had to spend,
> Spent. Wench, whiskey and tail-end
> Of your overseas disease
> Rot and rout you by degrees.
> (104)

At home again, he wastes away, and at last leaves the world, and the two women, who are contrasted harshly in successive stanzas:

> Leaves his mistress to dismiss
> Memories of his kick and kiss,
> Grant her lips another smear,
> Adjust the posies at her ear,
> Quaff an extra pint of beer,
> Cross her legs upon the stool,
> Slit her eyes and find her fool.
>
> Leaves his devotee to bear
> Weight of passing by his chair
> And his tavern. Telephone
> Hoists her stomach to the air.

6. *Ibid.*, 231.

Who is starch or who is stone
Washes coffee-cups and hair,
Sweeps, determines what to wear.
(105)

The second of these stanzas, the fortieth in the poem, reflects Annie's
static helplessness; it is the only one in the poem with two rhymes instead of
three. She becomes the victim of nightmares and a harried resignation, but
the final stanza mutes the verbal flash:

Think of almost thoroughly
Derelict and dim and done.
Stroking swallows from the sweat.
Fingering faint violet.
Hugging old and Sunday sun.
Kissing in her kitchenette
The minuets of memory.
(106)

Though much of the satire in this poem seems to be directed at Annie's
innocent romanticism, and at the circumstances that have nourished it, the
tone of the last stanza turns toward sympathy. Annie's pathetic stillness,
the amatory participles describing small aimless gestures, are mitigated by the
"almost" in the first line, and by the iambic fullness of the last. Annie is now
twenty-four, and has endured a series of disillusionments and bereavements.
If she is to blame for some of them, so is the world.

Whereas the poems of the first two sections of Annie Allen speak of
Annie in the third person, the third section opens with a sequence of five
sonnets, "the children of the poor," in which the mother speaks in the first
person. The sequence quickly ranges over several questions arising from the
profoundly mixed blessings and curses of disadvantaged parenthood—how to
protect children, teach them, prepare them for the fact of death. The fourth
sonnet is a complex variation on the persistent American theme that art
could not flourish in the period when people of ability were occupied with
settling the country. Its punctilious adherence to Petrarchan conventions of
structure momentarily withholds the sarcasm that bursts through in the sestet. It begins with two short sentences occupying exactly half a line: "First

fight. Then fiddle." The remainder of the octave describes the fiddling, fraught with "feathery sorcery" and "silks and honey," yet covertly rebellious:

> muzzle the note
> With hurting love; the music that they wrote
> Bewitch, bewilder.

The sestet returns to the fighting:

> But first to arms, to armor. Carry hate
> In front of you and harmony behind.
> Be deaf to music and to beauty blind.
> Win war. Rise bloody, maybe not too late
> For having first to civilize a space
> Wherein to play your violin with grace.
> (114)

Enjambment and shifting caesuras lend energy to much of the poem, but in the final couplet the energy is "civilized" to excessive tameness, reinforcing the "maybe" in the preceding line. The poem hovers between satire and direct polemic, both attacking and appropriating the notion behind it.

The inclusive vision that results in such a poem finds a variety of more single-minded expressions in the remainder of the book; this section of *Annie Allen* contains a few underachieved poems, but on the whole it is a sustained illustration of Brooks's many virtues. There are straightforwardly affectionate sketches, satiric portrayals of Black characters and of ignorant or sheltered whites, seized moments in the manner of Emily Dickinson, love poems, polemical addresses. The book concludes with an untitled poem of considerable power, addressing "Men of careful turns, haters of forks in the road," and declaring the speaker's full humanity. Its characterization of establishment caution is icily exact:

> "What
> We are to hope is that intelligence
> Can sugar up our prejudice with politeness.
> Politeness will take care of what needs caring.
> For the line is there.
> And has a meaning. So our fathers said—

And they were wise—we think—At any rate,
They were older than ourselves. And the report is
What's old is wise. At any rate, the line is
Long and electric. Lean beyond and nod.
Be sprightly. Wave. Extend your hand and teeth.
But never forget it stretches there beneath."
(136)

The poem ends with a chilling recognition that things will not soon change, especially if polite requests are depended on. The last line memorably combines determination and pessimism:

Let us combine. There are no magics or elves
Or timely godmothers to guide us. We are lost, must
Wizard a track through our own screaming weed.
(136)

If there are sharp divisions in Brooks's career, one of them comes at this point. As George Kent puts it, "For both whites and blacks, Gwendolyn would from now on be tagged 'the first Negro to win a Pulitzer Prize,' and with that label would come the roles of spokeswoman and arbiter in the upper realms of her city's and her nation's cultural affairs."[7] We may be able to see whether Brooks's work changed noticeably after this, but the question is obfuscated by the churning assortment of critical responses to her new status. The problem of Brooks's place in a white literary establishment had in fact been thrown into relief by Paul Engle's review, in the Chicago *Tribune*, of *A Street in Bronzeville*. Especially in the 1940s, trying to declare Brooks's transcendence of racial differences was to fall into the nearly inescapable trap of simultaneously affirming and denying the importance of race in her work: "Miss Brooks is the first Negro poet to write wholly out of a deep and imaginative talent, without relying on the fact of color to draw sympathy and interest. . . . The finest praise that can be given to the book is that it would be a superb volume of poetry in any year by any person of any color."[8]

There is no reason to doubt Engle's sincere admiration of Brooks's work,

7. Kent, *A Life*, 102.
8. Paul Engle, "Chicago Can Take Pride in New, Young Voice in Poetry," Chicago *Tribune* Book Review Section, 1 (quoted in Kent, *A Life*, 74–75).

or the honesty of his conviction that race should not be the issue that it is; but it is hard to get away from the hint of exclusiveness, the suggestion that Brooks is a fine poet, not regardless of her color, but despite it. In later years, increasing numbers of Black writers would question the extent of Brooks's commitment to Blackness; but there were confusing earlier questions by less militant writers. J. Saunders Redding, for example, in a generally favorable review of *Annie Allen* in the *Saturday Review*, found references to intraracial color preferences too esoteric: "Who but another Negro can get the intimate feeling, the racially-particular acceptance and rejection, and the oblique bitterness of this? . . . The question is . . . whether it is not this penchant for coterie stuff—the special allusions, the highly special feeling derived from an even more special experience—that has brought poetry from the most highly regarded form of communication to the least regarded."[9]

Redding and Engle were saying remarkably similar things, and missing an important element of Brooks's art. She sought to make her Black characters as rounded as poetry permits; this necessarily involved treating aspects of the Black experience that are imposed by white society. Through her first two books, her anger at injustice is comparatively restrained, but several poems in *The Bean Eaters* greatly increase the pressure of rage against the control of mature technique.

In one or two instances, the pressure overcomes control. "A Bronzeville Mother Loiters in Mississippi. Meanwhile, a Mississippi Mother Burns Bacon" is a daring response to the murder of Emmett Till, a Chicago teenager who was beaten and killed in 1955, during a visit to Mississippi. Brooks adopts the point of view of the young white woman who accused the youth of making sexual advances toward her. The sympathetic portrayal of the woman is striking; the husband, however, is a flat symbol of murderous white male oppression. He deserves that status, but in the poem he fails to earn it; instead of a plausible and therefore frightening and disgusting human, we have something too much like a cartoonist's drawing of Bull Connor. On the other hand, the woman's romantic vision of southern womanhood collapses convincingly before her growing knowledge of the Dark Villain's innocent youth:

Had *she* been worth the blood, the cramped cries, the little stuttering
   bravado,

9. Kent, *A Life*, 79.

The gradual dulling of those Negro eyes,
The sudden, overwhelming *little-boyness* in that barn?
(276)

Flat portrayal of white characters is more effective in such satirical poems as "The Lovers of the Poor" and "Bronzeville Woman in a Red Hat," where reduction of characters to cartoons serves a dual function: it permits broad sarcasm and indulgence in playful diction, and it invites the white reader to feel excluded from the portrait until it is too late to escape inclusion in it. Both poems portray whites in the act of dehumanizing Blacks, though "Bronzeville Woman" is heavy-handed in this respect. A rich and overbearing woman has had to replace her Irish housemaid, and the agency has sent a Black woman, whom the employer calls "it" throughout the poem. The portrayal becomes more effective, if nearly sentimental, in contrasting the reactions of the employer and the employer's child, "Not wise enough to freeze or be afraid" (306).

The other major treatment of racial violence is "The Ballad of Rudolph Reed," a fiercely ironic narrative of what proceeds from a Black family's purchase of a house in a white neighborhood. Traditional ballad meter and language give the poem a strange atmosphere of remoteness:

Rudolph Reed was oaken.
His wife was oaken too.
And his two good girls and his good little man
Oakened as they grew.
(312)

Contemporary racist brutality breaks with great force into such a setting, but the poem is strong enough to contain the atrocity of Reed's death, which comes as he is defending his house against rock-throwers who have wounded one of his daughters. The end of the poem is a powerful tableau of grief and strength:

By the time he had hurt his fourth white man
Rudolph Reed was dead.
His neighbors gathered and kicked his corpse.
"Nigger—" his neighbors said.

Small Mabel whimpered all night long,
For calling herself the cause.
Her oak-eyed mother did no thing
But change the bloody gauze.
(314)

These somewhat extended poems concerned with racial injustice, white insensitivity, and violence are scattered through an unusually varied collection of shorter poems, from the brilliant miniature "We Real Cool" to such humorous pieces as "On the Occasion of the Open-air Formation of the Olde Tymers' Walking and Nature Club." It is this mixture, perhaps, more than the presence of the longer poems, that led some readers to regret the increased emphasis on social issues in *The Bean Eaters*—as if social issues were making their first appearance in Brooks's work. It is true that these longer poems are more explicit, and reveal anger more openly, than do most of Brooks's earlier poems; but most of the shorter poems aroused regret that Brooks could not be consistently polite.

The new poems in *Selected Poems* (1963) did little to change these impressions; "Riders to the Blood-red Wrath," with its evocations of African majesty, the squalor of slave ships, and the commitment of Freedom Riders, both extends and rejects the polemical manner. Its content is occasion for celebration and exhortation, but in style it reverts to a density Brooks had not used at length since "The Anniad." It crams a racial history into a single consciousness, which ranges without transition between individual and collective recollection, and gathers momentum toward the polemical ending: "To fail, to flourish, to wither or to win. / We lurch, distribute, we extend, begin" (327).

On the other hand, a number of the new poems are brief character sketches; these presage the ambitious and thickly populated *In the Mecca* (1968), the book that has been said to initiate the third period in Brooks's career. If it does mark a significant shift in Brooks's way of writing and of thinking about what she is doing, this is more evident in the shorter poems that follow the title poem. "In the Mecca" is, at just over eight hundred lines, Brooks's most ambitious single poem; but in strategy and style it is an extension, not a repudiation, of her earlier excellences.

Epigraphs provide the information that the Mecca building, an extravagant apartment complex erected in Chicago in 1891, degenerated into an overcrowded tenement. Kenny J. Williams adds the important fact that the building was razed in 1952.[10]

In bare outline, the narrative is grim: Mrs. Sallie Smith returns to her apartment from hard domestic labor, and begins to prepare dinner for her family of nine children; she notices suddenly that the youngest, Pepita, is missing. There is a fruitless search, police are called, and at last the child is found to have been murdered.

The poem begins with a single line on a page by itself: "Now the way of the Mecca was on this wise." It remains for the poem to unfold the wrathful irony in this echo of Matthew 1:18 ("Now the birth of Jesus Christ was on this wise."). The rest of the poem is based in the present tense; Mrs. Smith encounters four neighbors on the way to her apartment, and each is sketched briefly; Alfred, an English teacher and untalented would-be writer, comes to act as a choral commentator as the poem develops. The children have their distinctive ways of trying to defend themselves against the reality of their lives; Melodie Mary, for example, "likes roaches, / and pities the gray rat." She is dimly aware of headlines announcing strife and suffering in China, but

> What if they drop like the tumbling tears
> of the old and intelligent sky?
> Where are the frantic bulletins
> when other importances die?
> Trapped in his privacy of pain
> the worried rat expires,
> and smashed in the grind of a rapid heel
> last night's roaches lie.
> (348)

When the family goes in search of Pepita, they inquire of several neighbors, each of whom is given several lines of characterization. Great-great Gram, who recalls her childhood in slavery, reverts to childhood as she recalls popping little creatures that "creebled" in the dirt of the cabin floor, thus inverting Melodie Mary's treatment of the same subject. Aunt Dill,

---

10. Kenny J. Williams, "The World of Satin-Legs, Mrs. Sallie, and the Blackstone Rangers: The Restricted Chicago of Gwendolyn Brooks," in *A Life Distilled*, ed. Mootry and Smith, 60.

reveling in her report of a child's rape and murder the previous week, is a gruesome parody of unfeeling self-satisfaction.

Toward the end of this section, there are three portraits without reference to Pepita or her whereabouts. The first, concerning Don Lee, is similar to several other poems Brooks has written about notable Blacks; even in the context of this poem, it appears to portray the poet and activist now named Haki R. Madhubuti. Along with Alfred's references to Léopold Sédar Senghor, "Poet, muller, President of Senegal," this constitutes unobtrusive anachronism.[11] "In the Mecca" contains few references that can be dated precisely, but some of them, such as Senghor's presidency of Senegal (1960–1980), convey the impression that the Mecca existed in the 1960s. This effect is only slightly complicated for the reader in possession of such arcana as the year of its demolition; the building itself may have been infamous, but its destruction did not significantly change the lives with which the poem is concerned. Brooks's Mecca outlives its namesake, and becomes a perceptible metaphor as well as a symbol.

The increasing desperation of the search for Pepita is reflected in the rapidity with which new characters are introduced from this point on. In the whole poem, over fifty people are mentioned by name or characteristic label; more than half of them appear in the last two hundred lines. Because this large cast moves in quickly, sometimes at the rate of four people per line, there is room near the end of the poem for four strophes of between a dozen and two dozen lines each, the first two introducing new characters, the third and fourth returning to Aunt Dill and Alfred, respectively. The two new characters reinforce the balanced vision of the whole poem; Way-Out Morgan is collecting guns, imagining "Death-to-the-Hordes-of-the-White-Men!" (367); Marian is ironing, wishing for some disaster to befall her so she may be noticeable. Absorbed in their visions, they have no time to wonder where Pepita is. Aunt Dill reappears in a gooey cloud of self-satisfaction; the narrator calls her

> the kind of woman you
> peek at in passing and thank your God or zodiac you
> may never have to know. . . .
> (368)

11. *Blacks*, 422, fourth printing; 359, fifth printing. The passage as quoted appears in all printings of *In the Mecca*, except that in the fifth printing of *Blacks*, the phrase "President of Senegal" has been removed.

In this welter of selfishness, Alfred makes a final appearance, allowing Brooks a sly reference to the temporal limbo in which she has erected this cosmos:

> I hate it.
> Yet, murmurs Alfred—
>
> who is lean at the balcony, leaning—
> something, something in Mecca
> continues to call! Substanceless; yet like mountains,
> like rivers and oceans too; and like trees
> with wind whistling through them. And steadily
> an essential sanity, black and electric,
> builds to a reportage and redemption.
>   A hot estrangement.
>   A material collapse
> that is Construction.
> (369)

The next strophe begins with two lines that look back toward this reverie, and forward to the discovery of Pepita's body:

> Hateful things sometimes befall the hateful
> but the hateful are not rendered lovable thereby.
> The murderer of Pepita
> looks at the Law unlovably.
> (369–70)

Beneath Jamaican Edward's bed lies the body of Pepita, who "never learned that black is not beloved." Remembering a rhyme the child once made with "rose," her mother decides to "try for roses." The final four lines of the poem revert to what only Jamaican Edward could have seen, but the powerful image of horror is rendered in a style that can only be the narrator's:

> She whose little stomach fought the world had
> wriggled, like a robin!
> Odd were the little wrigglings
> and the chopped chirpings oddly rising.
> (370)

"In the Mecca" is a large and largely successful poem, a benchmark in Brooks's career. The poem draws its strength both from her increasing interest in the possibilities for polemic in poetry, and from her broad and deep familiarity with poetry's technical resources. Except in scope and achievement, it is not a radical departure from the work that preceded it. However, it was completed during a time of upheaval in Brooks's sense of herself as a poet, and the shorter poems collected with it are evidence of a major division in Brooks's career.

Much has already been made of the external forces that wrought important changes in Brooks's thinking about her life and work. At the Fisk University Writers' Conference in 1967, she encountered, more forcibly than she had before, the power of young Black writers committed to making a literature for Black people, and to liberating themselves and their people from white oppression. The experience energized her in new ways. She also worked briefly with the Blackstone Rangers, a street gang whose younger mentors, especially Walter Bradford and Don L. Lee, provided encouragement as she sought her "newish voice."[12]

"After Mecca" is a coherent sequence of separate poems; it gathers force by proceeding from individual portraits, through two "public occasion" poems and the three-part "Blackstone Rangers," to "The Sermon on the Warpland" and "The Second Sermon on the Warpland." As the field of vision expands from one poem to the next, the formal scope extends from brief and nearly metrical to more widely various free-verse lines. The diction, however, remains characteristically Brooksian, as in this conclusion to "The Leaders," the second part of "The Blackstone Rangers":

> The Blackstone bitter bureaus
> (bureaucracy is footloose) edit, fuse
> unfashionable damnations and descent;
> and exulting, monstrous hand on monstrous hand,
> construct, strangely, a monstrous pearl or grace.
> (383)

But along with certainty that she had much to learn from younger Black writers, there came a desire to reach audiences unaccustomed to hearing or

12. Kent, A Life, 180ff.

reading poetry. This arose partly from increasing doubt about dependence on the Eurocentric tradition she had so thoroughly commanded for most of her career; at this point, the language problem referred to early in this essay becomes extremely difficult, despite Anglo-American's flexibility and relative openness to other traditions. With a few notable exceptions such as "We Real Cool," Brooks's poetry has depended not only on fresh and unusual language, but on the varying degrees of surface difficulty that such wordplay often creates. Her attempts at a more accessible style have sometimes resulted in oversimplified moralizing, and in indecision about which poems or versions of poems to reprint.

Of the roughly fifty poems Brooks published between 1968 and 1987, a few have appeared only in periodicals, and only nineteen are collected in *Blacks*. A white reader might be tempted to think that some of this indecision arises from Brooks's having accepted, in 1985, her second major accolade from the literary establishment, when she became Poetry Consultant to the Library of Congress; but in interviews over the past twenty years, and in her tireless work for Black writers during her tenure at the Library, she has demonstrated unwavering commitment to the cause of freedom for oppressed people.

Brooks's wavering over certain poems is evidence of crisis, but it is important to remember that crisis is usually much more rewarding for artists than for politicians. In adjusting her accustomed tools to her new tasks, she has taken some directions that she seems later to have reconsidered, but occasional frustrations have not sent her back to techniques in which she has long been adept. Her most recent collection, *Gottschalk and the Grande Tarantelle* (1988), is cause for gratitude that she has not retreated from trying to perfect her new ways of working.

This handsome chapbook contains only four poems, but one of them is "Winnie," some 375 lines spoken by Winnie Mandela. The character is of course a literary creation, partaking of what Brooks knows of Mrs. Mandela, and of what she knows of herself and the world. There are passages where one might wish that more memorable language had been found for the urgent messages:

> we are all vulnerable—
> the midget, the Mighty,
> the richest, the poor.[13]

---

13. Gwendolyn Brooks, *Gottschalk and the Grande Tarantelle* (Chicago, 1988), 18. Hereafter cited in the text as *Gottschalk*, followed by a page number.

But Brooks has hold of something here. In her early work, personal history (not necessarily her own) was a dependable provider of material. She began to merge social and political history with that strain in poems like "The Ballad of Rudolph Reed" and "A Bronzeville Mother Loiters," and perfected that merging in "In the Mecca." Now, she is after larger historical scope, and appears to be on the brink of finding the means to achieve it without surrendering particularity. As she has Winnie Mandela say,

This is the time for Big Poems,
roaring up out of sleaze,
poems from ice, from vomit, and from tainted blood.
(*Gottschalk*, 19)

BREWSTER GHISELIN The Gift of the Waters

Brewster Ghiselin is one of those writers whose work has long been admired by an international group of fellow practitioners, but whose "public," in a broader sense, has only recently begun to expand. He is, of course, known to thousands of readers as the editor of a highly influential anthology, *The Creative Process;* in 1970 the American Academy and Institute of Arts and Letters presented him with a substantial award in recognition of his poetry, and in 1981 he received the William Carlos Williams Award of the Copernicus Foundation for *Windrose: Poems 1929–1979* (1980), for the best book of poems published the preceding year by a university or small press. It is clear that his work has made a steadily increasing impact on American letters since it first began to appear over fifty years ago.

Windrose brings together most of the work in Ghiselin's four earlier collections, and adds to them twenty-four new poems. Specifically, it contains most of the poems, now carefully rearranged, from *Against the Circle* (1946) and *The Nets* (1955), everything but a small group of poems in Italian from *Country of the Minotaur* (1970), and all of the poems printed in a handsome limited edition, *Light* (1978). The new poems, arranged in two groups, "Waters" and "Shapes, Vanishings," reveal a finely honed sensibility not yet content with the dazzling successes of earlier work.

His comparatively small output, and the surface difficulty of some of his poems, have no doubt conspired to keep Ghiselin's audience from growing rapidly. But the difficulty of the poems is only a matter of surfaces; the poems are not obscure in any hermetic sense of the word. Rather, they have a precision of diction that requires close attention, and a shifting consciousness, the thread of which is sometimes elusive, especially in the occasional passage where the poet has sacrificed for the sake of momentum a small clarification that additional punctuation might have supplied. Finally, the poems may seem somewhat unfashionable right now; their voice has a prophetic, definitive quality that is rare in the poetry of the past two decades. In tone, though not in style, the voice is somehow reminiscent of Ezra Pound's hard-edged recorded speaking voice; and the prophetic quality is sometimes reminiscent of Robinson Jeffers, though Ghiselin does not share Jeffers' misanthropy or his tendency to oversimplify. In short, the difficulty of these poems is the reader's problem, not Ghiselin's; and once past the superficial obstacles to understanding, the reader finds that the concerns of the poet are timely, humane, and enduring.

Over the past fifty years, American poetry has become increasingly preoccupied with the personal, manifested as confession or subjective vision. What this means, or whether it is good or bad, is not pertinent here; it is noted because in such a context, Ghiselin's poems are unusual in the vastness of their scope, and in the reticence of those few poems that seem to arise from the poet's close involvements with other people. Ghiselin's subject is most often the place of man in nature—nature in the broadest sense, as when a particle physicist says, "In theory, quarks exist in nature." Such an utterance takes readers some distance from the Nature of British verse or landscape painting; and Ghiselin's poems, too, are far from that world, encompassing the ocean, the western desert and mountains, the moon, stars, and comets, as well as humankind, purveyor of real estate and installer of streetlamps.

Ghiselin's explorations of seascape and desertscape often lead him to a largeness of statement that is earned through close attention to observed details—the precise shape of a rock or a bird's head, for example—and an attention to the sound of words that is extraordinary even for a poet. Ghiselin has thought long and productively about the motions and sensations of the human vocal apparatus, and writes lines and phrases consciously designed to produce specific movements of the tongue and throat that, as the reader finds upon executing them, are surprisingly appropriate to the moment of the poem in which they occur. As he wrote for the "Sidelights" section of his entry in *Contemporary Authors*, "Like music, poetry embodies tonalities and movements, not ideas of these but actual sensuous components effective directly, in immediate and sequential experience."

In his search for precision and memorable statement, however, Ghiselin does not forget that ceaseless change is integral to his subject; and so a certain fluidity is noticeable even in his most definitive-sounding lines. He produces nothing unfinished—far from it—but he does not give the impression that he wants his words carved in stone. His poems are always on the move. Ghiselin's poetry might be described as he himself describes the work of Jacques Derrida: "Simultaneously lucid and elusive, Derrida's discourse is difficult in that engaging way which a characteristic fragment of Heraclitus distinguishes: 'The lord whose oracle is at Delphi neither speaks nor conceals, but gives signs.'"[1]

It is perhaps this quality of movement that enables Ghiselin to work with stories and characters from classical mythology. Such material has become unfashionable, mostly for sound reasons; Robert Bly's statement, that a classical reference means instant death for the poem in which it occurs, is perhaps intemperate, but Bly has reason to be impatient: such material, as Donald Hall memorably demonstrated in his preface to the first edition of *Contemporary American Poetry* (Penguin, 1962), weighed heavily on most of the worst poetry of the 1950s. But Ghiselin invokes only those myths that have life for him, and which he has the skill to make live; and so in his hands they still speak to our condition. As he says in the title poem of his third book, "Only because a man is here / This is the country of the minotaur."[2]

Most of the aforementioned qualities and tendencies are evident in the first poem in *Windrose*, "The Vision of Adam." This, at about 150 lines, is by 100 lines the longest poem in either of Ghiselin's first two books; not until *Country of the Minotaur* would he again approach the long meditation. Adam—not literally the first man, but a man with the Namer's name—at the edge of the ocean, ponders his place in the tension between wind and

---

1. Brewster Ghiselin, "*Signéderrida:* Brief for Jacques Derrida," *Western Humanities Review*, XL (Spring, 1986), 1.

2. Brewster Ghiselin, *Windrose: Poems 1929–1979* (Salt Lake City, 1980), 104. Hereafter cited by page number in the text.

wave, land and sea, wondering how to satisfy his desire for something like truth. Near sundown he enters the ocean, and in the darkness feels the power of life in the sea, and achieves a recognition of the kind of vision he has sought. It is curiously unvisionary:

> "There is no need of image, for him who can hide himself perfectly
> Under the shield of darkness," he thought, "and with naked hands
> Touch the live God, unbewildered by the mind's light,
> Prismatic through concept, coloring the world.
> I need always in me the Power without shining or darkness
> Flowing from the fountains that nourish
> Serpent and bird, ocean, and sun and moon, and the strong earth.
> These babblings are truth and falsehood mingled.
> No man tells the truth."
> (8–9)

The conclusion of the poem acknowledges the human ability to possess secrets for which there is no language, but which are available to almost anyone with good eyesight: the sun, the sea, the beauty of vultures in flight. The poem describes no hallucinatory vision, but the more difficult realization that may come with the hard-won recognition of things as they are. Most of the short poems that comprise the rest of *Against the Circle* and *The Nets* are devoted to achieving such clarity.

An interesting example of Ghiselin's attention and precision is "Watercolor by Paul Nash: 'Folly Landscape, Creech, Dorset,'" which manages to transcend the pitfalls of that subgenre of poems about paintings, too many examples of which recall the proverb about the relative value of words and pictures. "Watercolor" becomes a poem about something else, departing almost immediately from a literalist look at the picture; the opening lines describe a "folly," one of those odd stone structures built on the English countryside by eccentric gentlemen:

> Piercing a length of wall a child could circle
> In three breaths running, three great doorways gaze
> Through stonework paled by blisters of high cloud.
> (82)

Presumably, the running child is not depicted in the painting. Readers see the child, however, and are led on to see an imagined landscape informed by a poem, rather than a report on a picture. The odd structures on the hills are "solitude / And absence, voices in an enormous hall" (82); the arches have no function, provide no shelter, but make of themselves a "Threshold leading from the wind into the wind" (82). "Watercolor" is a poem of only a dozen lines, but it moves quickly and majestically from the child to the gigantic absence at the end.

Similarly, "Rattlesnake" begins as a first-person speaker encounters a snake; the pronoun "I" appears four times in nine short lines. When the speaker kills the snake, however, a general withdrawal of life from the landscape seems to occur:

> I crushed him deep in dust,
> And heard the loud seethe of life
> In the dead beads of the tail
> Fade, as wind fades
> From the wild grain of the hill.
> (19)

The shift from "I" and "him" to "beads," "tail," "wind," and "hill" is absolute by the last line; it emphasizes, as do many of Ghiselin's poems, that the human notion of permanence is subject to revision among the hard but mutable mountains.

The one-sided nature of the human interaction with the nonhuman world is treated ironically in another short poem from *Against the Circle*, "The Indifferent Mountains":

> They stare above me, hard and bleak and strange
> After a thousand days as when I came,
> Looking beyond me, aware of one another,
> Mountains like faces in a foreign street.
> They have not seen my youth.
> (42)

The next several lines speculate on various romantic recollections of childhood, and on what difference it would have made if the mountains could have seen those moments. If they had, "They could not look with a mask-hollow stare. / They would remember as the southwind does" (42).

I go back to that last line from time to time, to see whether I think the southwind actually remembers anything or not. But the mountains have not seen anything, ever; if the speaker had spent his childhood among them, instead of the brief period of a thousand days, they might seem less removed from his world; but as Ghiselin says again and again, theirs is an old world into which humans have lately come.

This is the predominant approach to nonhuman nature throughout these poems. The theme achieves its finest expression in several poems from *Country of the Minotaur*, which, as Ghiselin says in the preface to *Windrose*,

> stands as first printed, except for the omission of the final section, poems written in Italian, accompanied by literal translations. These, no longer in the place of conclusion, seemed likely to impede passage of most readers to the poems of the fourth book, *Light*.

In fact, Ghiselin has made one slight change that he does not mention: he gives the title "Triptych" to the third and central section of the book, thereby making explicit what seemed implicit even when "Sea," "The Wheel," and "Aphrodite of the Return" were preceded, in *Country of the Minotaur*, only by a blank page bearing the numeral III.

The *Minotaur* section opens with the title poem, which is in two parts. The first recounts the myth of the Minotaur's birth, emphasizing the mystery and terror surrounding "the cradle where a rumor slept"; the second illustrates the myth's unwillingness to die:

> Alone in a high valley of flowers leaning
> To a turquoise triangle of sea,
> I think of Minos and Pasiphaë
>   Who gave the Minotaur to shame
> And made their palace dreadful to explore.
>
> No rough ruin is here, or sad olive
> Rooting memory in stone, or fumitory
> Blowing, as out of ash of the old story.
>   Only because a man is here
> This is the country of the Minotaur.
> (104)

Most of the poems in *Minotaur* are concerned, in one way or another, with the ideas these stanzas suggest. The second section consists of eight poems involving animals; in most of these the speaker's attitude toward the animals is one of deep respect, almost as if the animals were totems. "The Catch," for example, is a highly charged account of the capture of a badger, discovered during a snake-hunting expedition; the poem celebrates the badger's power, and his eventual escape:

> Burrowing bearclaws rattled in tin. He tasted wire all round.
> He bucked, he bruised the ceiling, lunged at a beam and was eating
>   oakwood.
>
> But for that ravening he lived unfed and unslaked. His stench was
>   immense,
> His dung was the curved needle ribs of reptiles. He never slept—
> Daylong, nightlong. His furious freedom resounded. At starlit dawn
> Jaws and claws rasping and thudding thump of his thunder drummed once.
>   Long
>
> Silences rang for him, cage-eater greedy of snakes, abroad in the dawn.
> (113)

The diction and tone of this passage give the badger the status of a mythical beast; reading this, I think of primitive poems, like prayers, in praise of wolves or bears, made to propitiate a Great Spirit displeased with our tendency to objectify nature.

Human commerce with nature and the unity of life are the thematic concerns of the third section, the "Triptych" sequence. The first two poems, "Sea" and "The Wheel," are long lyrical meditations touching on our deep involvement in processes that are vaster than our own concerns; the notion of the eternal return, to which these two poems come round at length, is more briefly embodied in the third poem, "Aphrodite of the Return."

"Sea," at some 260 lines, is Ghiselin's longest poem; it may also be his finest. Divided into eleven sections, the white space between them providing room for movement and reverberation, the poem is a vast lyrical meditation on the sea as source and repository of life, and on the permanent cycle of change. A central tension in the poem is introduced early:

But all are issue of the dust. The clear
Water here in my hand is full of dust,
Dissolvings of life and death: powder of fire
And sea-born earth returned to the using sea.
(123)

The dust that gathers from the unmaking of mountains is a surprising
choice for a central image in a poem called "Sea." Ghiselin's vision, however, is inclusive, his attention unwavering, and the constant interaction
between water and dust becomes a stunning portrayal of the movement inherent in apparent stillness. Two passages from the sixth part demonstrate
the poem's sustained compression; between these extracts there are seven
lines:

The body of the brown world is beautiful—
Idol out of the blue vague of the sea.
Prairies are under the oiled hooves of riders,
Morning breezes trample the scent of grain
To the red hills with the passes blue among them,
And clouds beyond are watching the unknown earth
Their shadows stain. And no wall of an ending,
Only the halt in the dusk by the poppy fires
And dawns of discovery under a setting star.
.   .   .   .

The dry sound of our hands shifts on the walls
At morning as we stroke the doorframe thought.

Beautiful to us therefore the winds' violence,
The lifted modulations of the dust,
The dry hills that are called everlasting
Vague in the veils of their mortality.
(128–29)

First of all, one notes the speaker's stance—his almost Olympian view of
land and sea, and of the everlasting changes their intercourse means. Then
the reader is struck by the sounds of the words themselves: by the apparent
effortlessness with which internal rhymes, and the subtler echoes of alliter-

ation and assonance, have been effected. Finally, the inclusive vision of the poem is involved with an inclusive diction that makes possible the natural utterance of such lines as "the lifted modulations of the dust," or that enables the poet to tie the passage together thematically by the repetition of the word "vague." The word's first appearance above is memorable because its context may remind the reader that the same letters spell the French word for "wave"; to carry that association to the last lines above will suggest how those "veils of . . . mortality" are part of the process by which the sea gathers the earth's dust to itself.

Statement of such scope and finality of tone is hard to follow, even in a long poem; Ghiselin's tactic is to focus on something smaller in section VII: a skull rolling in the shallows. He gives it speech, and it sighs its desire for life, even amidst pain and filth: "Now I am a clicking system of reminders" (129). Yet the section concludes with the recognition that the skull's words are those of the speaker of the poem, "detained by dreams" (129).

The concluding sections of this poem return to the cycle of change, and to the exhilarating impossibility of finding words for it, and end with a knowledge of "something past belief," "The changes of the water and the dust, / And silence under every syllable" (132).

"The Wheel" is sharper in tone, more critical of the human tendency to make things that outrun human power. The wheel is an artifact:

> The dark of my theme
> Gathers on the street corners—names no day . . . .
> The repetitions of the wheel ascend
> All high places, fill up with honey light
> At evening the target towers.
> (135)

This poem reminds us that we are part of the changing earth. The only animal cursed with knowledge of the extinction of species, humans yet fail to imagine, at least constructively, their own extinction.

All three of these poems exhibit this lengthy compression; this is the essence of the difficulty I mentioned at the beginning. But, though any passage of comparable length to the above would demand even more attention than I have given this one, it will also yield as much. On the dust jacket of this book, Allen Tate says: "I consider 'Sea' and 'The Wheel' his masterpieces." I consider this a valid evaluation of the poems.

The "Triptych" ends with a much shorter poem than either of the first two. Although it is only forty-two lines, "Aphrodite of the Return" achieves largeness of scope, and its "place of conclusion" in the sequence, by means of a shifting and wide-ranging consciousness in its speaker, who moves from direct observation to statement and back again with an almost bewildering swiftness. The speaker visualizes Aphrodite on the waves, in the person of the woman he loves, and sees the possibility of love as a force like other natural forces, which may have power enough to redeem us, as dolphins "[stitch] the sea, sheltering only in their act, / As a running needle clothes itself in the garment" (141).

The poems grouped in the fourth section describe, for the most part, inland landscapes, most of which suffer from human intrusion and misuse. To call them "ecological" would imply that they are topical; but the poems, and the term itself, are concerned with matter that must soon transcend faddishness, unless we are to look forward to the fulfillment of the prophecy of "Vantage":

When our age of glass is no more
Than glitter in dunes
Of detritus
The clouds will be here
In season, the water
Always.

The regret will be gone.

II
Ocean and air will lift
Shoring combers pluming
Over their leaning green
In landwind wings of spume.

If creatures astir on the cliffs
Have then the gift of light, let it
Be larger than ours, that lost
The world and took the moon.
(156–57)

The poems in section V of *Minotaur* are more personal in tone than those which come before, and they speak for qualities that could forestall the bleak prophecies that precede them. Love of the sea is explored again, but in ways that reveal more about the poet's personal attachment to it than is revealed directly in "Sea." "Answering a Letter from a Younger Poet" and "Learning the Language" provide insights into Ghiselin's particular approach to *le mot juste*; whereas the phrase often suggests esoteric vocabulary, here it stands for an ability to make even such a word as "mud" sound as if it may never before have been put to proper use. Finally, there are a few love poems that give distinctive expression to universal feelings.

Light and the new poems in *Windrose* seem to be of a piece, interestingly different in some ways from what has preceded them. There is more variety of tone in these poems; touches of humor, satirical and otherwise, mellow the whole assortment. "Let There Be Light" and "And There Was Light" are concerned with the installation of streetlamps in the speaker's neighborhood—not a subject that I would previously have expected to see in Ghiselin's work. The first poem notes the way light has of lifting or dulling one's sense of fear, and the way humans have of unwittingly plotting their own destruction. The second poem finds the neighborhood protected by "Four Thousand Lumen Mercury Vapor Ornamental Luminaires," but the extravagance of the satire in that line gives way to a moving conclusion:

> But I, in our endless light,
> Whirl like a bird blown down
> With its boughs in a blast of sparks
> To fly from fire at the heart
> Of a dark forest.
> (186)

In these most recent poems, however, Ghiselin continues to be at his best observing waves, birds, mountains, and other entities beyond the human scale of things. "Song at San Carlos Bay," for example, is among his very best poems, treating with breathtaking clarity and grace the question of life elsewhere in the universe, and the tension between emotion and logic that complicates thinking about it:

If there are other worlds (there may be—must be—amid the billion
     trillions,
And more, of the stars) they cannot be wholly as this one is: the torrent of
     the galaxy
Falling—as I saw it today before dawn—down the whole height of the
     dark to the ocean
Could not be as here, that momentary mist of a cataract so slowly floating
     it seems
Unchanged forever, the same after fifty years as I saw it when first its light
Untangled to curve and cluster in constellations, Scorpio, Sagittarius, sea
     stars
The crickets of a cliff long crumbled landward and blind with houselights
     cried under and are quiet.
(212)

The syntax of the last line may require a second look, because the grace of
its sound conceals the complexity with which it compresses into its sinuous
phrasing the permanence of the stars and the comparative impermanence of
cliffs.

Since the appearance of *Windrose* in 1980, Ghiselin has published over thirty
poems—many of them in *Poetry* and *Quarterly West,* and all collected in
Flame (1991)—which demonstrate that his most consistent attitude is that
of exploration and experiment.

For example, Ghiselin published in 1986 a sequence of seven poems,
under the title "Elemental." Taken separately, the poems embody many of
Ghiselin's most persistent approaches to his most rewarding themes; the sequence begins with "Labyrinth," a brilliant juxtaposition of two human
urges: the need to surround ourselves with walls, and the desire to get beyond
them. The tension between the permanent and the ephemeral is treated in
"Haven," "Granite," and "Vigil"; and the theme of motion, almost of the
wish to escape the patterns in which we enclose ourselves, is picked up from
"Labyrinth" to appear again in "Pelagic" and "Here." There are also scattered
in the poems various phrasings and usages that it is fair to think of as Ghiselin's signature. In "Labyrinth" there is a precisely right use of a word we
seldom see, in a wonderful description of a small island seen from a distance:

stub of a monolith lost to the clouds
yet held

in the vast of inference
whole,
iron-red, unspalled
term of a tract of dust preempting the sun,
still as the shaft of a gnomon over its scythe of shade. . . .[3]

"Unspalled" arouses in one familiar with southern speech a momentary and wicked misinterpretation, but its meaning here is straight from the best of dictionaries: "unbroken, as of ore." Ghiselin's pleasure in such unusual precision makes for one of ours in his poetry. And his pleasure in sound, which may rarely border on some readers' notions of excess, leads him into lines like this, from "Haven":

No: only harsh wood of helm in hand like a helve,
Behind you the toppling bells and foamlike waving farewell
On the false trace of the wake the failed maps
Wandering, spreading and folding,
And before you
Halcyon storm.
(*Flame*, 26)

There are moments when I wonder whether that first line is a touch overwrought; but then I try to think how it might be improved, and have to give up. On a larger scale, Ghiselin's vision, and the diction that allows us to share it, arouse a deep ambivalence. The wish never to die is basic to our thoughtless urges, and he knows that. At the same time, the placement of some of the darker poems in this sequence has been contrived to make of the whole an acceptance, even an affirmation, of processes that most of us fear. "Vigil" takes only four lines to encompass much that Ghiselin has suggested to us over the years; that it cannot quite be pinned down is one of its triumphs:

The mountains are falling.

And the foot of my love—or yours, or another's—

3. Brewster Ghiselin, *Flame* (Salt Lake City, 1991), 24–25. Hereafter cited in the text as *Flame*, followed by a page number.

In dew-cold night, before dawn,
Is touching a dusty path.
(*Flame*, 29)

"Elemental" has not the weight and force of "Triptych," but it is one of Ghiselin's most significant achievements.

By now Brewster Ghiselin has long since established the style that makes his poems quite distinctly his. But in "Flame" (*Poetry*, March, 1983), he submits that style to the restrictions of the sestina, a form in which he has not previously done published work; on the other hand, in the March, 1980, *Poetry* he had published "Apocalypse," whose use of indentation and extra white space recalls Mallarmé's experiments, as well as his own preference for the poem that will not be reduced to motionlessness. Others have made similar experiments, to be sure; but Ghiselin continues, late in a career of great distinction, to extend his range both technically and thematically. It is cause for celebration that one of America's finest poets is not ready to call *Windrose* his definitive collection.

WILLIAM STAFFORD Millions of Intricate Moves

I

In "Thinking for Berky," many of the qualities that make William Stafford's poetry what it is are at their best.

> In the late night listening from bed
> I have joined the ambulance or the patrol
> screaming toward some drama, the kind of end
> that Berky must have some day, if she isn't dead.
>
> The wildest of all, her father and mother cruel,
> farming out there beyond the old stone quarry
> where highschool lovers parked their lurching cars,
> Berky learned to love in that dark school.
>
> Early her face was turned away from home
> toward any hardworking place; but still her soul,
> with terrible things to do, was alive, looking out
> for the rescue that—surely, some day—would have to come.
>
> Windiest nights, Berky, I have thought for you,
> and no matter how lucky I've been I've touched wood.

There are things not solved in our town though tomorrow came:
there are things time passing can never make come true.

We live in an occupied country, misunderstood;
justice will take us millions of intricate moves.
Sirens will hunt down Berky, you survivors in your beds
listening through the night, so far and good.[1]

The meter, strictly speaking, is unstable; some of the lines are iambic pentameter, and others stray from that toward fourteen syllables, yet the rhythmical rightness of each line is firmly there, not to be quarreled with. Similarly, the rhyme is the very opposite of insistent; though the rhymes between
the first and fourth lines of each stanza are solid and true, there is enough
between the rhymes to keep them from being more than a gentle and mysterious reminder that this is utterance weighed and wrought. Within this
delicate scheme, the sentences move easily from immediate description to
generalization and back again, the tone never modulating beyond the conversational. And yet there is something close to bravura in the calm statements of large truths: "there are things time passing can never make come
true," "justice will take us millions of intricate moves."

Certain qualities of calmness and unpretentious gravity may create the
impression that this voice is not easily modulated, or inclusive of various
tones. But many of the qualities evident in "Thinking for Berky"—discur-
siveness, directness, delicacy of meter, specificity of description, definitive-
ness of general statement—are to be found in "Adults Only," a recollection
of an evening at the state fair, in the tent reserved for the striptease act. The
poem begins with a general statement: "Animals own a fur world; / people
own worlds that are variously, pleasingly, bare." The rest of the stanza recalls
how those worlds came clear to "us kids" the night they found themselves in
that tent. The poem ends:

Better women exist, no doubt, than that one,
and occasions more edifying, too, I suppose.
But we have to witness for ourselves what comes for us,
nor be distracted by barkers of irrelevant ware;

1. William Stafford, *Stories That Could Be True: New and Collected Poems* (New York, 1977), 64–65. Hereafter cited in the text as *Stories*, followed by a page number.

and a pretty good world, I say, arrived that night
when that woman came farming right out of her clothes,
by God,

At the state fair.
(*Stories*, 93)

Several lines in this stanza—the first two, the last four—are quite clearly different from anything in "Thinking for Berky"; they are looser, more conversational. But only a few of the words—"pretty good," for example—are foreign to the diction of the other poem. The use of the word *farming* in each poem is indicative of Stafford's unusual sensitivity to context: in "Thinking for Berky" the word's immediate context gives it a hard and desperate sound, as if the parents farmed mostly with sickles and whips:

The wildest of all, her father and mother cruel,
farming out there beyond the old stone quarry
where highschool lovers parked their lurching cars,
Berky learned to love in that dark school.
(*Stories*, 64)

In "Adults Only" the word is quirky but exact: the woman comes rolling out of her clothes like a combine out of a wheat field.

Along the spectrum from pure conversation to elaborate oratory, Stafford's poems occupy a relatively narrow range. But his acquaintance with that zone, and his sense of what context can yield, seem from the beginning to have been more than sufficient to the creation of explosions that many other poets would need far more energy to bring about.

Stafford's first collection, *West of Your City* (1960) was published in an elegant limited edition by a small press; except for a few poems that have been widely anthologized, and fourteen that were reprinted in *The Rescued Year*, the work in it was unavailable for several years, until the appearance of *Stories That Could Be True: New and Collected Poems* (1977), which reprints Stafford's first two books, and three others: *The Rescued Year* (1966), *Allegiances* (1970), and *Someday, Maybe* (1973). *West of Your City* turns out to be a first book of great maturity, distinctiveness, and understated power; Stafford, it seems, is among those rare poets who do not publish a book before they have hit their stride. We are in danger now of taking Stafford's particular stride for granted, but it must have been earned courageously; most of the noisier proponents of this or that way of writing poems in the 1950s would have been reluctant to embrace these quiet, sturdy poems. In meters that are never too insistent, yet never out of control, the poems in *West of Your City* record the observations of a questing spirit—evoking the past, revealing in the present many small but significant signs of where we are, and heading westward, into the future. The style is discursive, the diction conversational, but everywhere in these poems shines Stafford's amazing gift for arranging ordinary words into resonant truth and mystery: "Wherever we looked the land would hold us up."

Though *West of Your City* was out of print before it came to wide attention, *Traveling Through the Dark* (1962) immediately established Stafford as a poet of rare gifts and unusual productivity. As the citation of the poetry judges for the National Book Award put it, "William Stafford's poems are clean, direct and whole. They are both tough and gentle; their music knows the value of silence." True enough; and one is then awestruck to realize that these splendid poems—seventy-six of them, enough for two collections—were published only two years after *West of Your City*. As James Dickey once said, "Communicating in lines and images is not only the best way for [Stafford] to get things said; it is the easiest."[2] This may be an exaggeration, but it is true that even in the most casual of circumstances, Stafford's utterances can have the distinctive flavor of his poetry, as when he closes a letter, "So long—I look toward seeing you everywhere."

In *Traveling Through the Dark*, the major advance over the first book is in breadth of tone. Looking at the ways in which his poems can break into humor, I begin to think that Stafford has a talent, never quite indulged, for self-parody. He is so attuned to the effects he can create, and so sensitive to various modes of surprise, that even within a restricted range of word choices, he can be haunting, wistful, or slyly humorous.

In *The Rescued Year*, there are many poems that surprise only because they did not exist before; they are otherwise very much like Stafford's earlier work. As he says at the end of "Believer,"

2. James Dickey, *The Suspect in Poetry* (Madison, Minn., 1964), 112.

You don't hear me yell to test the quiet or try to shake
the wall, for I understand that the wrong sound weakens
what no sound could ever save, and I am the one
to live by the hum that shivers till the world can sing:—
May my voice hover and wait for fate,
     when the right note shakes everything.
(*Stories*, 123)

But if the poems continue to sound like the poems his earlier work led us to expect, there are among the subjects of these poems a few matters that Stafford had not previously staked out as his kind of territory. The title poem, longer and more leisurely than most of Stafford's earlier poems, is a fine evocation of a year of happiness lived in his youth, when his father had a job in another town, and moved the family there. In "Following the *Markings* of Dag Hammarskjöld: A Gathering of Poems in the Spirit of His Life and Writings," Stafford fashions a moving long sequence of related poems, the more valuable because they do not depend too heavily on the inspiration acknowledged in the title. And in "The Animal That Drank Up Sound," he creates a myth of remarkable freshness, which has yet the flavor of folklore that makes it sound ancient. The first part of the poem tells how the animal came down and swallowed the sounds of the earth, until at last all sound was gone, and he starved. In the second section, a cricket, who had been hiding when the animal came by, awoke to a heavy stillness, and with one tentative sound, brought everything back:

It all returned, our precious world with its life and sound,
where sometimes loud over the hill the moon,
wild again, looks for its animal to roam, still,
down out of the hills, any time.
But somewhere a cricket waits.

It listens now, and practices at night.
(*Stories*, 147)

The boldness of this poem and others in *The Rescued Year* is carried forward into *Allegiances* and *Someday, Maybe*. The strain of odd metaphor against conversational diction is rewardingly increased: "He talked like an old gun killing buffalo, / and in what he said a giant was trying to get out."

As always, any observation might start a poem, but in *Allegiances* Stafford seems freer either to let the observation go as far as necessary, or to let it stop when it should. Several of these poems are tiny, fragmentary, but complete, like "Note":

straw, feathers, dust—
little things

but if they all go one way,
that's the way the wind goes.
(*Stories*, 181)

Sometimes these small observations are gathered in bunches under one title, like "Brevities" or "Religion Back Home." In these clusters of short poems, the tension between their disparateness, and their being gathered under one title, reminds us of Stafford's sense of his vocation: "The world speaks everything to us. / It is our only friend."

More and more often in *Allegiances* and *Someday, Maybe*, Stafford evokes the spirits of those whose ancestors lived here before white people came. "People of the South Wind," for example, is a mythic explanation of where a person's breath goes after he dies; the tone is radically conversational, even for Stafford, but the effect is, magically, dignified. And the title poem of *Someday, Maybe*, "The Eskimo National Anthem," recalls a song, "Al-eena, Al-wona," that echoes often through the speaker's daily life. The phrase is translated as "Someday, Maybe." (A small misfortune has befallen the version of the poem in *Stories*: "Someday" is misprinted as "Somebody.") The poem ends with the observation that the song might be to blame if the speaker's life never amounts to anything, though it is a comforting keepsake. The paradox is gracefully concealed; it is hardly possible, in the poetic world of William Stafford, to notice so much, and still live a life that amounts to nothing.

The gathering of previously uncollected poems, *Stories That Could Be True*, extends the range of Stafford's apparently boundless empathy. Many of the speakers in these poems are not the observer, but the thing observed— wind, seeds, trees, ducks—and they speak of how things are with them, in a voice that is of course truly Stafford's, but which is profoundly convincing; it is a lively extension of the myth-making tendency that began to be displayed in *The Rescued Year*. It is also noteworthy that in these more recent poems, Stafford often permits himself a strictness of meter and rhyme that is rare in his earlier work. He has usually preferred to suggest a form rather than commit himself fully to it; but there are poems here whose simplicity, memorability, and charm are like the verses people who speak English have had in their heads from childhood. It takes a lifetime of thoughtful and wide-ranging work to arrive at the stage where one can write a miniature masterpiece like "At the Playground," which in its way can speak for what Stafford has been up to all along, and for what he has been looking for in the books he has published since:

> Away down deep and away up high,
> a swing drops you into the sky.
> Back, it drives you away down deep,
> forth, it flings you in a sweep
> all the way to the stars and back
> —Goodby, Jill; Goodby, Jack:
> shuddering climb wild and steep,
> away up high, away down deep.
> (*Stories*, 11)

II

In the past few years, Stafford has published a number of prose pieces about how his poems come to be. Many of these have been collected in *Writing the Australian Crawl* (1978) and *You Must Revise Your Life* (1986), both published in the University of Michigan's Poets on Poetry series. It is widely recognized by now that Stafford presents himself as a poet for whom the process is in many ways more important than the product. He wants an openness to any possibility during the initial stages of—I almost said *composition*. He is therefore suspicious of technique, especially if used for its own sake, or used to force a poem in a preconceived direction. His rhetorical stance toward these matters is exemplified in "Some Notes on Writing," a prose statement at the beginning of *An Oregon Message* (1987):

> My poems are organically grown, and it is my habit to allow language its own freedom and confidence. The results will sometimes bewilder conser-

vative readers and hearers, especially those who try to control all emergent elements in discourse for the service of predetermined ends.

Each poem is a miracle that has been invited to happen. But these words, after they come, you look at what's there. Why these? Why not some calculated careful contenders? Because these chosen ones must survive as they were made, by the reckless impulse of a fallible but susceptible person. I must be willingly fallible in order to deserve a place in the realm where miracles happen.

Writing poems is living in that realm. Each poem is a gift, a surprise that emerges as itself and is only later subjected to order and evaluation.[3]

Despite the apparent directness of these paragraphs, there are certain questions that they do not quite answer. Is Stafford describing a process like automatic writing? Language must have "its own freedom and confidence," and "after they come," by "reckless impulse," the words "must survive as they were made." This is certainly suggestive of a method that involves little in the way of revision. On the other hand, the poems are "later subjected to order and evaluation," whatever "order" might mean here.

In "A Way of Writing," one of the essays collected in *Writing the Australian Crawl,* Stafford notes that others "talk about 'skills' in writing." He goes on to explain his difficulty with the concept:

Without denying that I do have experience, wide reading, automatic orthodoxies and maneuvers of various kinds, I still must insist that I am often baffled about what "skill" has to do with the precious little area of confusion when I do not know what I am going to say and then I find out what I am going to say. That precious interval I am unable to bridge by skill. . . . Skill? If so, it is a skill we all have, something we learned before the age of three or four.[4]

It is statements like that last one, taken out of context—sometimes, admittedly, by Stafford himself—that have recently given rise to the notions that Stafford wants all poems to be equally valued, that writing teachers

---

3. William Stafford, *An Oregon Message* (New York, 1987), 10. Hereafter cited in the text as OM, followed by a page number.

4. William Stafford, *Writing the Australian Crawl* (Ann Arbor, 1978), 19. Hereafter cited in the text as *Writing,* followed by a page number.

should not evaluate student work, and that a kind of open basking in possibility is more important than any talk of how to make a poem better than it is. "Well," I hear the teacher saying, "this might show us something important. Next?" I ponder the Zen of workshopping, the guru as wise ignoramus.

Again. In an interview with Cynthia Lofsness (*Writing the Australian Crawl*) Stafford speaks suspiciously of technique: "It's not a technique, it's a kind of stance to take toward experience, or an attitude to take toward immediate feelings and thoughts while you're writing. That seems important to me, but technique is something I believe I would like to avoid" (*Writing*, 98).

In conversation on various occasions since that interview, which was first published in 1972, Stafford has said similar things; but in those contexts, the interviewer's definition of technique, included in her question, has not always been present as a background: "I would define technique as a belief on the part of the poet that there are certain rules or forms into which his ideas must be channeled for proper expression. A belief that there is a proper 'framework,' into which he must fit his specific feelings . . ." (*Writing*, 97–98).

It is instructive to note the extremism of the positions Stafford opposes when he talks about these issues. In one case, we have the desire to control absolutely every impulse, to work everything toward a predetermined effect or end; in another, we have a belief in rules, in a proper framework. The first method is obsessive, the second oversimplified and ignorant. Of course these ways of trying to write poems are doomed; and of course it is better to be ready for surprises. More conservative voices than Stafford's have been heard to say, for example, that a poem glides on its own melting, like a piece of ice on a hot stove, or that poetry should come as naturally as leaves to a tree.

Perhaps Stafford is increasingly concerned to address the notion that all one needs to be a poet is to learn the things that are taught in writing classes. It may be that his own extraordinarily prolific output has often brought him questioners who want to know exactly how he does it. It is certain that he falls rather easily into moods that inspire him to easily misunderstood pronouncements; he says what he means, most of the time, but the most audible part of what he says is the more radical part. In the passage about "skill" above, for example, he is careful to establish that he has "experience, wide reading, automatic orthodoxies and maneuvers of various kinds."

In a couple of passages from *You Must Revise Your Life* there are useful examples, first of the haste with which Stafford can sometimes say things that his poems contradict, and second, of the ease and friendliness with which he can discuss matters of great technical importance. In a short piece about a short poem, "Where 'Yellow Cars' Comes From," there are these sentences about sound:

> As for sound, I live in one great bell of sound when doing a poem; and I like how the syllables do-si-do along. I am not after rhyme—so limited, so mechanical. No, I want all the syllables to be in there like a school of fish, flashing, relating to other syllables in other words (even words not in this poem, of course), fluently carrying the reader by subliminal felicities all the way to the limber last line.[5]

The paragraph begins with the general and modulates toward the specific poem, but the dismissal of rhyme sounds general.

A few pages later, in another essay about the same poem, he writes:

> And line breaks, too, happen along. By now, in my writing, many considerations occur to me in jotting down even first hints of a poem. I like to feel patterns—number of stresses, multi-unstressed or few-unstressed sound units, lines that carry over and make a reader reach a bit, pauses in the line that come at varying, helpful places: early in the line, middle of the line, later in the line. But I make the lines be the way they are by welcoming opportunities that come to me, not by having a pattern in mind. (*Revise*, 47)

If we think of technique, not as some rigid belief in proper frameworks and rules, but as a partial and growing understanding of an enormous array of verbal effects and opportunities, some of them traditional and some of them more nearly unprecedented, then it becomes harder to entertain the idea that Stafford cares much less about it than Richard Wilbur does.

III

In the light of these remarks, it is useful to look more closely at "Thinking for Berky," and at one or two poems from Stafford's most recent collections.

5. William Stafford, *You Must Revise Your Life* (Ann Arbor, 1986), 44. Hereafter cited in the text as *Revise*, followed by a page number.

A sense of Stafford's skill, or technique, or outrageous good fortune, is barely suggested in the brief metrical description at the beginning of this essay.

For some readers, the metrical question will be difficult; for even more doctrinaire readers, it will be easy, or nonexistent. There are respectable people, in the school of J. V. Cunningham, who believe that lines either exemplify a strict meter or do not, and that a mixture of both kinds of line in one poem is some sort of default on the contract. But Stafford has arrived at the contract, if any, with nearly evasive tact: the meter is so far from firmly established in the first three lines that it is purely a matter of opinion where to place stresses among the syllables "must have some" in the fourth. Yet, even veering as they do between nine and twelve syllables, and between four and six stresses, the first four lines arrive satisfyingly at their ends, and at the rhyme. Much of the satisfaction emerges almost unnoticed from rhymes and echoes elsewhere than at the ends of lines: *joined-kind-end, screaming-drama,* the march of four *l* sounds proceeding from beginning to end of words in the first two lines.

This kind of local sonic richness continues throughout the poem, even as a larger net is also being cast, to make connections by means of end-words not included in the "official" rhyme scheme (*patrol-soul,* both connecting with the second stanza's rhymes; *quarry-cars; come-came; wood-misunderstood*), and over the whole poem by the echo between *bed* and *beds,* and the repetition of *listening* and *night* in the first and final lines.[6] Meanwhile, another aspect of the poem's rhythmical balance is maintained by the tension between lengthening lines and shortening sentences.

Stafford's prose remarks seem intended to forestall the conclusion that these kinds of things are always calculated. Very inexperienced readers often want to know how many of a poem's effects could have been planned, and most practitioners know that many are not. But most practitioners also know that thinking about such matters, in one's own poems and in others', is a useful way to deepen acquaintance with them, and to grow toward recognizing them when an unpressurized knowledge, disguised as good luck, brings them into the lines we are writing.

6. For a while in the early 1970s, Stafford read this poem aloud, and authorized reprinting it, with a slightly different last line: "While in the night you lie, so far and good." It has admirable qualities, but Stafford had reverted to the original ending by the time he assembled *Stories That Could Be True.*

The convergence of impulses—from the tradition and from the individual train of thought—can even result in a sonnet. The discovery that a sonnet is under way is usually made before all the rhymes are in place, so some searching and rephrasing must usually be done. During that process, I imagine, Stafford might constantly weigh the effects of either staying with tradition, or noticeably departing from it, perhaps to the point that strict readers might decide that the result is not a sonnet. Here, for example, is "Seeing and Perceiving," from *A Glass Face in the Rain* (1982):

> You learn to like the scene that everything
> in passing loans to you—a crooked tree
> syncopated upward branch by pre-
> established branch, its pattern suddening
> as you study it; or a piece of string
> forwarding itself, that straight knot so free
> you puzzle slowly at its form (you see
> intricate but fail at simple); or a wing,
> the lost birds trailing home.
> These random pieces begin to dance at night
> or when you look away. You cling to them
> for form, the only way that it will come
> to the fallible: little bits of light
> reflected by the sympathy of sight.[7]

I believe it is possible to be drawn deeply enough into this poem, to follow its sentences with enough absorption, not to notice rhyme until the final couplet. It is unusual to find a sonnet, or near-sonnet, in which the form itself does not constitute much in the way of a statement; these days, to elect the sonnet form is usually to make a gesture with something behind it. Here, the form seems gradually to evolve, as it might "come / to the fallible," so that the short ninth line has a rightness that outweighs its failure to meet rigid expectation.

Rhyme is infrequent in Stafford's more recent collection, *An Oregon Message* (1987). One of its more obtrusive manifestations is in "Brother," a mysterious poem that defies literal paraphrase:

7. William Stafford, *A Glass Face in the Rain* (New York, 1982), 46.

Somebody came to the door that night.
"Where is your son, the one with the scar?"
No moon has ever shone so bright.

A bridge, a dark figure, and then the train—
"My son went away. I can't help you."
Many a clear night since then. And rain.

I was the younger, the one with the blood.
"You better tell Lefty what his brother done."
They went off cursing down the road.

A boy in the loft watching a star.
"Son, your big brother has saved your life."
He never came back, the one with the scar.
(OM, 98)

The difficulty of assembling the details into coherence is emphasized by the self-contained lines, each of which is resonant with possibility. There is reference to what sounds like a threatening encounter, and possibly some catastrophe; but the details hang in the memory as they might in the mind of a traumatized victim of imperfect recall. Because it borders on the incomprehensible, in most prose senses of the term, the poem benefits immeasurably from the added mystery of regular rhyme. Lines such as the fourth, with its assortment of three images that could add up in several ways concluding in departure, death, or rescue, becomes one of twelve beads on a string, attractive in itself; the same is true of the seventh, in which the phrase "the one with the blood" could suggest several paraphrases. The poem is reminiscent of certain ballads, like "Sir Patrick Spens," from which such usual narrative elements as motivation are absent, so that the events take on a stark necessity.

Some readers have called Stafford's poetry "simple," as if it had failed to comprehend our civilization's great variety and complexity. But the simplicity exemplified in "Brother" is exactly the kind that reflects complexity in human life. None of us knows enough, it seems. William Stafford's many ways of reminding us of that, and of offering consolation, constitute one of the most secure and solid of recent poetic achievements.

GEORGE GARRETT   The Brutal Rush of Grace

I

George Garrett's first book, *The Reverend Ghost*, was a collection of poems that appeared in 1957; since then, he has published six full-length collections and a chapbook of poetry. Nevertheless, his much larger achievement and reputation as a writer of fiction seem at times to have obscured the fact that his poetry is among the treasures of contemporary literature. Perhaps because fiction has a wider audience than poetry, and because this is an era when most writers are severe specialists, Garrett's poetry has been slower to be widely recognized for the superb work that it is.

And perhaps there are other reasons. Garrett has been blessed with a sometimes defiant individualism; the prevailing trends of a particular time seem to inspire in him an urge to see how differently a thing might be done. This attitude, combined with a profound knowledge of what was accomplished in English poetry of earlier periods, enables him to work within a larger tradition than seems available to many poets. But it also helps him toward poems (and fiction and essays, too) that are richly and hilariously disrespectful of current fashions and of those who work within them.

Garrett's willingness to go against the grain has been a constant in his work, though it was not as immediately evident in *The Reverend Ghost* as it was later to become. That collection, which received praise from Louise

Bogan and Babette Deutsch, among others, introduced a poet already steeped in the rhythms and voices of the English tradition. Thirty of those poems are scattered through Garrett's *Collected Poems* (1984); their surfaces are generally quieter and more orderly than those of many later poems. But reading all of them together, one can see, in their prosody, tone, or thematic stance, a certain rebelliousness of spirit. In the light of the decade when they appeared, it is clear that Garrett was not working with rhyme and meter merely because most people were; his lines wrestle against their metrical forms with rare liveliness, and often flout such bits of conventional wisdom as "Avoid inversions and end-stopped lines." If Garrett had not found such dicta worth testing, he would have sounded like plenty of other poets of the fifties. Now, the earlier lyrics seem clearly to acknowledge their origins in the work of masters like Campion, Wyatt, and Ralegh.

In creative writing classes at the University of Virginia in the mid-1960s, it was Garrett's custom to use Ralegh's poems as examples of flexibility in tone and diction. What he admired, and wanted his students to see, was the confidence with which a poem could "shift gears" perilously near its end, only to reveal itself, upon rereading, as having been aimed toward whatever surprise might come.

For example, "Child Among Ancestors" begins with the proposition that the dead are irretrievably lost to those who never saw them, whatever relics they have left behind "for a small boy to fondle," whatever "tales / he hears without believing a word."

But the poem rapidly takes a strange, satirical turn, as the ancestors' exploits borrow from mythology:

> The facts he's heard,
>
> how this one, tamer of horses, fell
> in a flourish of flags and groping dust,
> and one who met a dragon on the road,
> and another, victim of his lust,
>
> changed into a pig with a ring tail,
> fail to convince or bear the burden of
> flesh and his struggle for identity.[1]

1. George Garrett, *Collected Poems* (Fayetteville, Ark., 1984), 16. Hereafter cited in the text as *CP*, followed by a page number.

"The facts . . . fail to convince." These extravagant legends can hardly be facts, but the boy, if not convinced, seems unwilling to think they are lies. He listens for a while, then goes out with an old sword (one of the relics) to terrorize the chickens, which his imagination momentarily transforms into "nothing less than kings." Not until the last stanza does the speaker refer to himself in the first person; up to this point, it has been tempting to see in the boy a recollection of the speaker's younger self. When the speaker declares himself as an observer, that earlier impression is only partly dispelled by the surprising bitterness of the ending:

                              His joy

    is all my sadness at the window
    where I watch, wishing I could warn.
    What can be said of the dead? They rise
    to make you curse the day that you were born.
    (CP, 16–17)

The idea that a poem should make its way through a series of difficult moves, some of them more or less tacitly proscribed among the safety-conscious, is of a piece with most of the subjects and themes with which Garrett has most persistently engaged. He is a Christian poet, in a broad rather than dogmatic sense, and certain biblical images and stories appear recurrently in his work. Among these are several in which grace, or the will and voice of God, take people by surprise—the burning bush, David and Goliath, Jacob wrestling the angel. "Holy Roller," a poem first collected in *Abraham's Knife* (1961), begins by characterizing a revival preacher as a knowing and successful lecher, and ends thus:

    I know this too:
    the ways of God are crazy, daze
    a skeptic mind like summer lightning.
    Others false and foolish as you (and I)
    have been chosen and, so chosen,
    babbled more wisely than they knew.
    You bow your handsome goathead and
    God springs from your lips like a snowy dove.
    (CP, 18)

One of Garrett's most complicated treatments of these themes is "Buzzard," a splendid poem from *The Sleeping Gypsy* (1958). Because it sharply contrasts an indirect observation of "saintly hermits" with direct observation of a buzzard, it might be read as an expression of doubt:

> I've heard that holy madness is a state
> not to be trifled with, not to be taken
> lightly by jest or vow, by lover's token
> or any green wreath for a public place. Flash
> in the eyes of madmen precious fountains,
> whose flesh is wholly thirst, insatiate.
>
> I see this graceful bird begin to wheel,
> glide in God's fingerprint, a whorl
> of night, in light a thing burnt black,
> unhurried. Somewhere something on its back
> has caught his eye. Wide-winged he descends
> like angels to the business of this world.
>
> I've heard that saintly hermits, frail, obscene
> in rags, slack-fleshed, eyes like jewels, kneel
> in dry sand among the tortured mountains, feel
> at last the tumult of their prayers take shape,
> take wings, assume the brutal rush of grace.
> This bird comes then and picks those thin bones clean.
> (CP, 24–25)

This is a careful balancing of hearsay and eyewitness evidence. The energy and directness of the first stanza at first give us no reason to doubt that the speaker agrees with what he has heard; moreover, the daring syntactical inversion of the second sentence gives it the sound of conviction. The second stanza explicitly reports things seen, admittedly by a speaker who perceives in the buzzard's flight patterns a likeness to "God's fingerprint" and angels. The third stanza reverts to hearsay, though the first two lines are remarkably sharp in visual terms. Hearsay and direct evidence converge in the pause before the last line; we can only hear how it felt to be a saintly hermit at a moment of transformation, after which the buzzard does his work, the "business of this world."

The tension between what the speaker has been told and what he has seen is complicated, first, by the tone of the first and third stanzas, in which the phrase "I've heard" is the strongest evidence of skepticism, and second, by the middle stanza's nearly offhand declarations of belief in God and angels. The poem is clearly not a dismissal of "holy madness" as something that ends only in destruction, because the buzzard comes to embody St. Paul's "evidence of things not seen," his "substance of things hoped for."

In tone and diction, "Buzzard" is more elevated than many of Garrett's poems, but it does display his amazing ability to shift rapidly, at times almost imperceptibly, between the colloquial and the elevated. The spectacularly artificial syntax of the second sentence is cast in the language of the skilled southern tent preacher, who can career dizzyingly between echoes of the King James Bible and earthly analogies drawn from the daily lives of his listeners. In this context, even such a phrase as "the business of this world" has a dual function: it insists on the presentness and necessity of the everyday, but it also reminds us that angels descend from another world to the business of this one.

"Buzzard" appears early in The Sleeping Gypsy—third in the first section, "The Music of This World." The section ends with "After Bad Dreams," which draws on many of the same images—skin and bones, holy saints, angels, the desert—but which is direct in its praise of the world we inhabit. The speaker, having been troubled by dreams of isolation, thirst, and loss of faith, wakes to a world of light where "every stone smells freshly baked." The last three lines of the poem are a deft acknowledgment that we always shuttle back and forth between nightmare and sweet life, or between beautiful dreams and hard realities:

> I drink the wine of morning for my shadow's sake,
> he who has suffered and must suffer once again,
> who now falls victim to a perfect day.
> (CP, 54)

II

In 1961, Garrett published not only Abraham's Knife, his third book of poems, but also his second novel and his second collection of short stories.

Though his best work in both poetry and fiction still lay ahead of him, hindsight suggests that this was the year when the reputation of his fiction began to overtake that of his poetry. That it did so is unfortunate, and not only because it might wrongly suggest that the fiction is necessarily better or more seriously intended than the poetry. As R. H. W. Dillard has convincingly demonstrated in his *Understanding George Garrett*, Garrett's work, for all its astonishing variety of tone, setting, method, and subject, is of a piece, and the fiction and poetry draw upon and nourish each other, to the benefit of both Garrett and his audience.

During a poetry reading at Virginia Commonwealth University on July 20, 1988, Garrett read a brief statement about his tendencies as a poet, and followed it with an informal remark about the relationship between his fiction and his poetry:

> I've been writing poems a good while—all my life, I guess—and I published my first poems in 1947. I've been writing off and on since then. I'm not the best judge of my own development, by any means, but I can say this about it, which I address to the writers here.
>
> > Something—not everything—is determined by the world that you wake into as a writer. The world of poetry I came into at that time, which included two generations of very fine American poets, had characteristics that I immediately rebelled against, and I guess still am. One was the idea of voice as including, in its definition, habitual forms and habitual subjects. My elders had very firm ideas about what was poetic. So all my life, as a poet, I have tried to work with the voice that I was given and have found as my own, within the widest possible variety of forms, from strictly formal to loosely casual, long and short, and indeed in many tones of voice, high, low, and middle. And another strategy was and remains to try to do my best to extend the limits of what can be considered poetic, not to neglect any subject whatsoever as inherently unfit and unworthy.
>
> One other thing that I discovered after writing those things down—which is a rather obvious thing, I don't know why I hadn't thought of it before— when you do both poetry and prose and other things as well, you end up reacting to what you're doing with the other things. And I noticed that the

more lyrical and formal poems, the higher voice, came at a time when I was writing realistic stories about the Army and about life in the South, and during a long period when I was trying to work with Elizabethan prose, echoes of Elizabethan prose, I found myself writing a very down-home kind of poetry.[2]

It should be noted that this view of things might make *Death of the Fox* and *The Succession* sound traditionally formal, when they are in fact as daring in form as anything published in the last twenty years. It is true, however, that *Abraham's Knife* is generally looser in prosody than Garrett's first two books of poetry, and his two other books of 1961, *In the Briar Patch* (stories) and *Which Ones Are the Enemy?* (novel) are tighter and more traditionally structured than some of his later fiction.

Though several of the poems in *Abraham's Knife* (for example, "Fat Man," "The Mower," "Pandora," "Bubbles," "Old Slavemarket: St. Augustine, Fla.," and "A Modern Fiction") continue to draw on the traditions of form that characterize many of the poems in his first two books, Garrett uses a conversational and colloquial style, deceptively suggestive of looseness, in several of the best poems in the collection.

"Egyptian Gold" is so casual in tone that one is reminded of a witty raconteur at a party, delightedly describing the proficiency of Roman pickpockets, who can "lift a wallet from your pocket / with less touch than the breeze." Even when the poem approaches its theme more directly, the style remains almost startlingly conversational; a few lines of circling the subject by saying what it is not lead to a conversational cliché, which is followed almost immediately by a direct address to the Lord:

> The point is:
> what happens when you fall among thieves?
> And who, Lord, is my neighbor?
> (CP, 70)

There follows a serious meditation on "an age when thievery / is so refined it calls itself / Success," countered by a recollection of St. Augustine's commentary on Exodus, which explains that God permitted Moses to take

---

2. My transcription from a tape recording provided by George Garrett.

gold from Egypt because everything is God's. The ways of poets seem to
follow from this:

> And if we're going to tell the truth,
> we'd better gut the pocketbooks
> of all the poets who tried and failed.
> As we pass by their honored biers,
> we'll pick the pennies from their eyes.
> (*CP*, 71)

Returning to the subject of the pickpockets, the poem draws more tightly the
parallel between aging poets and aging thieves, whose fingers "stiffen out of
subtlety / (just as sweet singers grow hoarse)."

The final stanza shifts the poem in yet another direction, deflating the
sense of the exotic that Rome and Egypt have supplied. In *Abraham's Knife*,
though there was room to end the poem on the same page with the passage
above, the reader had to turn the page to encounter these lines:

> But I don't want to leave the impression
> of an American overseas
> and overawed by all that's foreign.
> My grandfather lost his good gold watch
> on an elevator at the Waldorf.
> (*CP*, 71)

Though the tone of "Egyptian Gold" is unusually casual, the poem nevertheless proceeds with remarkable economy. Compression is evident not in
the style, but in the clarity with which a complex process of thought is elabo-
rated, and the subtlety with which an anecdotal and effortlessly learned meditation comments on contemporary attitudes.

To say this, however, is to approve of the poem according to such criteria
as might be applied by the very poets and critics Garrett sometimes seems to
want to irritate. Like "Buzzard," which makes fine use of strenuously inverted
syntax and ends with a line consisting of ten monosyllables, this poem exploits methods that many poets would disdain, as being too prosy.

A number of poets and painters in the past fifty years have demonstrated
that it is not necessary, after all, to follow the "rules" in order to break them

successfully. Excellent free verse can be composed by poets who have never written metrically, and valuable paintings of various kinds can be made by people who, as the saying goes, can't draw. Similarly, a person unacquainted with much in the English poetic tradition can read "Egyptian Gold" without difficulty.

On the other hand, a deep acquaintance with the English tradition informs this poem; seeing the various ways in which Garrett has gone against the grain requires of readers that they have spent some time going with the grain. It is almost as if he had set out to do most of the things Pope satirizes in "The Art of Sinking in Poetry," to see if he could stay afloat despite the presence of phrases like "As I said" and "I don't want to leave the impression," and despite a deliberately anticlimactic ending. One point that the poem makes, by both implication and example, is that the more one worries about making mistakes, the more difficult it becomes to do things right.

The mundane and the exotic meet again in "Crows at Paestum," in which a touring husband and wife visit the famous Greek ruins south of Naples, and find them populated with noisy crows and light-belled sheep. The speaker declares his unease among the ruins, being unable to populate them "with moral phantoms and ghostly celebrations." But another way of looking at Garrett's poetics appears in the life that is present there:

> "If sheep may safely stand
> for that which, shorn and dipped,
> is naked bleating soul, why then
>
> I take these crows, whose name
> is legion, for another of the same:
> the dark, the violent, the harsh
> lewd singers of the dream, scraps
> of the shattered early urn, cries
> cast out, lost and recovered, all
> the shards of night. Cold air
> strums the fretted columns and
> these are the anguished notes
> whose dissonance is half my harmony."
> (CP, 63)

The final stanza veers tumultuously from the metrical to the unmetrical and back again. The middle lines are metrically the loosest, and each has the caesura before one heavily enjambed monosyllable; but as harmony is reestablished, the caesuras move away from the ends of the last four lines, which settle toward more harmonious breaks.

It may not be going too far out on a limb to suggest that this poem is part of a continuing poetic conversation with Richard Wilbur, whom coincidence paired with Garrett at Wesleyan University, and during a fellowship stint at the Alley Theater in Houston. "Lacking / the laurel of nostalgia," a phrase that Garrett uses to explain the speaker's unwillingness to see ghosts among the ruins, may or may not be a conscious echo of the third line of Wilbur's "Tywater" ("Lacking the lily of our Lord"), but anyone will hear it who has read both poems a few times.

Wilbur's poetry, of course, is rightly praised for its euphony; it is easy to imagine the reservations he would have felt about some of the poems Garrett showed him in those days, and it is even easier to imagine Garrett saying, "Well, anyway, this is how *I* see and do it." Other poems in which Garrett seems to be responding to Wilbur include "Buzzard" (*cf.* "Still, Citizen Sparrow"), "Giant Killer" (*cf.* "Clearness" and "A Baroque Wall-Fountain in the Villa Sciarra"), and "Old Saws No. 2" (*cf.* "Epistemology," which Garrett's poem explicitly quotes). Garrett's apparent desire to do things very differently in no way diminishes his admiration for Wilbur; once, when I was his student, he told me with memorable conviction that Wilbur was the best poet we had. But the process of discovering a way of writing can often be fruitfully complicated by testing it severely against a different kind of excellence. Garrett's style seems peculiarly suited to his frequent reminders that life for various biblical figures could be as gritty and mundane as it is for us. His colloquial language is open to holy men who were often dirty and poor, with bad breath and teeth. To hyperhumanize such figures emphasizes the miraculous nature of their visions and their faith, even as it becomes more plausible. In Garrett's poems, the people of the old books speak to us, sometimes seemingly out of our own time.

The title poem of *Abraham's Knife*, for example, recounts the story of Abraham and Isaac, from a point of view that is at first strictly limited to Isaac, and later extends to a speaker contemporaneous with the poet. Abraham's unquestioning willingness to sacrifice Isaac is regarded with a combination of wonder bordering on incredulity, and deep reverence. In the second of the poem's three stanzas, the speaker tells how his life has changed since the day on Mount Moriah:

My own children, sons and daughter,
study my stranger's face. Their flesh,
bones frail as a small bird's,
is strange, too, in my hands.
What will become of us?
I read my murder in their eyes.
(CP, 4)

The mention of a daughter makes the speaker more like Garrett than
Isaac, and the poem begins to speak for all of us, in asking Abraham for
forgiveness and "a measure of [his] faith":

In naked country of no shadow
you raise your hand in shining arc.
And we are fountains of foolish tears
to flood and green the world again.
Strike for my heart. Your blade is light.
(CP, 4)

With equal stoicism and greater anger, "Fig Leaves" confronts the pain
of searching for truth in a world of lies—lies in which the speaker collabo-
rates, to the point of self-loathing. R. H. W. Dillard writes cogently of the
poem's conclusion:

But that disgust is finally resolved by a recourse to biblical truth and to a
clear-eyed recognition of what people are and must do:

Better our sole flag were fig leaves
at least to salute the mercy of God
when in the cool of the evening He came
(Adam and Eve on trembling shanks
squatted and hoped to be hidden)
and cursed us out of the garden.
But not before we learned
to wear our first costume
(seeing the truth was a naked shame),
to lie a little and live together.
(CP, 68)

The dream of individual purity must necessarily be rejected in order to live in the world of lies, enabling one then to recognize the importance even of the lie as a functional part of the truth of a world in which people must live together.[3]

III

"The dream of individual purity" to which Dillard refers is that of Salome, whose story has captured the imagination of many writers since her appearance in Matthew 14. Garrett's version, entitled "Salome" and spoken by her, first appeared in 1963, and was collected in *For a Bitter Season: New and Selected Poems* (1967). It is a boldly executed poem of exceptional power, and ranks among the very finest of Garrett's works in prose or verse.

The poem opens with a one-line sentence, set off by a stanza break: "I had a dream of purity." Salome proceeds to describe the dream, in which her body was burned away from "that part of me, the breath of God," which then was free of all earthly ties and suffering; but when she wakes and announces to those around her that she has had a dream of purity, they all laugh, and she joins in, pulled back into the web of desire and sin. She recounts two more dreams, "the ordinary ones"—nightmares that Garrett has crafted as Freudian clichés.

Up to this point, though the language is colloquial, there is little to dispel the illusion that the speaker of the poem is to be taken as the biblical figure. But having described the nightmares, Salome goes on in a more startling vein:

> I tell you all this
> not for the pennies of your pity.
> Save those coins to cover your eyes.
> Nor for your eyebrows
> to chevron my rank of shame.
> (CP, 6)

"Pennies" and "chevron" are anachronistic, but they indicate that Salome is speaking out of our time as well as hers: the voice makes Salome one

3. R. H. W. Dillard, *Understanding George Garrett* (Columbia, S.C., 1987), 19–20.

of our contemporaries. After describing the conflicting emotions and desires with which she confronted John the Baptist, she speaks in terms that Garrett has used before:

> The Dance?
> Believe what you care to.
> Picture it any way you want to.
> All the world knows
> truth is best revealed
> by gradual deception.
> My tongue cried for his head.
> But it was my mouth that kissed him
> and was damned.
>
> Then I was free and able to rejoice.
> (CP, 7)

In versions of the poem published before *Collected Poems,* another line appears between the sixth and seventh above: "It was a striptease pure and simple."[4] The tone is right, and the language is prepared for, but "pure and simple" is too easy and inaccurate a phrase for what Salome is talking about. "Old Saws No. 2," first collected in *The Sleeping Gypsy,* puts it this way:

> I say there's more than meets the eye
> when Salome, veil by veil, her fine
> clothes peels to the essential skin
>
> and bones.
> (CP, 94)

The revelation that has come to Salome is bitter, and has been slow in coming. The end of the poem has the earned sound of prophecy:

> We pursue ourselves,
> sniffing, nose to tail
> a comic parade of appetites.

4. George Garrett, *For a Bitter Season: New and Selected Poems* (Columbia, Mo., 1967), 15.

That is the truth,
but not the whole truth.
Do me a little justice.
I had a dream of purity.
And I have lived in the desert ever since.
(CP, 7)

Other important poems first collected in *For a Bitter Season* include "Rugby Road," a long meditation prompted by the death of the poet Hyam Plutzik, but taking the occasion to consider the various ways in which we let our manufactured surfaces enslave us. Garrett evokes the manicured lawns of the University of Virginia, where the professors (those who have not perished) busily publish, and the students' coats and ties are like the patina on the statue of Mr. Jefferson. We are imprisoned even by the words in which we say that "behind the words the song and dance is free" (CP, 67).

"Old Man Waking" is another monologue recounting a dream in which youth and beauty fall away almost instantaneously. The tone is unrelieved bitterness until very near the end, when the old man almost caricatures himself; there follows one of Garrett's wonderful demonstrations of control over the "unpoetic":

Now I will dress myself and go forth,
armed with a terrible temper and a walking cane.

Children,
children quicker than birds,
whose eyes are coins of light,
whose laughter is the source of music,
children, come taste my knuckles
and the hard shiny tips of my boots.
(CP, 22)

The variety of poems in *For a Bitter Season* is greatly enriched by two groups of somewhat slighter poems, "Some Women" and "Celebrity Verses." The latter group in particular comes closer to light verse than anything else in Garrett's work, though all of his books contain at least a few anecdotal "snapshots." "Celebrity Verses" satirizes the images projected by five sex goddesses of the 1960s—Ann-Margret, Twiggy, Kim Novak, Barbara Steele, and

Donna Michelle—in rollicking meters and obtrusive but witty rhymes. The speaker's lust for these figures also comes in for some pointed fun; one moral of these verses is that celebrity has become a commodity that can be marketed without regard for the people behind the images. Twenty years later, some readers will have trouble recognizing all five of these names; that the poems continue to give pleasure only emphasizes the emptiness of the myths and fantasies they satirize.

IV

After *For a Bitter Season,* eleven years passed before Garrett published another collection of verse, and that was a limited edition of twenty-seven poems, most of them fewer than six lines in length. Between 1967 and 1978 he spent most of his time on his vast Elizabethan novels, so it is not surprising, in view of his remarks at Virginia Commonwealth University, that the "flashcards" in *Welcome to the Medicine Show* (1978) are boldly informal and "antipoetic." After a series of attacks on such figures as "A Rival Poet," "A Certain Critic," and "Another Literary Wife," the title poem pronounces on the current poetic scene:

> What I have done here is simply to bottle
> some of the natural hatred and malice of poets for each other.
> I guarantee it will do nothing at all for you.
> But it will sure enough shame a hornet or a scorpion.
> It can make a rattlesnake laugh and roll over like a puppy dog.
> (*CP,* 100)

As in the "Celebrity Verses," the poet is not spared. "Portrait of the Artist as Cartoon" begins with the author's resolve to espouse "Silence, exile, cunning";

>   and then the phone rings
> and I trip and fall all over myself
> running for it, hoping it's for me,
> praying my luck has changed, my time has come.
> (*CP,* 99)

The few longer poems in this handsome little book are love poems. Throughout Garrett's work, among all the addresses to imaginary female figures, fables of lovers enmeshed in classic situations, and portraits of individual women, the poems addressed to his wife, Susan, grow deeper in their affection, more genuine in tone, and more inclusive of images and events that come to characterize a shared life. The presence of two or three such poems in *Welcome to the Medicine Show,* aside from their intrinsic value, conveys the poet's belief (or wish, at least and worst) that the joys and consolations of their life together mean more than the few triumphs and many disappointments that inevitably accompany a literary career.

This impression is even more forcefully conveyed in *Collected Poems,* because Garrett has placed a dozen of his strongest love poems at the end of the book. Six of them were first collected in *Luck's Shining Child* (1981). From self-deprecating humor ("Apology") through frank and humorous seduction ("Negotiations") to grave acknowledgment of aging and the pull exerted by shared tribulation ("Since It Is Valentine's Day," "The Bed"), these poems combine poetic compression and the novelist's t for character and narrative, to portray a rich and durable relationship.

Elsewhere in *Luck's Shining Child,* Garrett presents various versions of decline. One of the best of these poems is "Main Currents of American Political Thought," whose title at once seems to warn the reader away from seriousness; yet five of the poem's six stanzas offer a moving evocation of a vanished life—the gracious certainty of the life Grandfather lived, which led him to say once that free public schools and the petit jury would keep the democratic spirit of this country alive. The reader half expects some reversal of what has seemed a conservative outlook, but the concluding stanza contains a two-part surprise:

What became of all that energy and swagger?
At ninety you went out and campaigned for Adlai Stevenson
in South Carolina. Half that age and I have to force
myself to vote, choosing among scoundrels.
(CP, 9)

The idea of a ninety-year-old South Carolinian campaigning for Stevenson runs counter to most stereotypes of American politics; it seems that this very unpredictability is among the things being mourned in the poem.

"Mundane Metamorphosis" begins with a description of the speaker, waking to find himself dull and heavy as lead, to raise the window shade upon a brilliant day; he imagines Columbus being lifted from despair by discovery,

> Or stout Balboa rusty as an old woodstove
> sweat dripping beneath his dented helmet
> inching his bulky self up to another limb
> then inching his dented helmet above another
> whose leaves sigh with his weight and weariness
>
> To see suddenly and always the blue eye of God
> which greets his gasp with an enormous wink
> The river is burning and the gulls cry doom
> but the man of lead now smiles to discover
> that even his teeth are rich with silver and gold
> (CP, 49)

Quite aside from the fine ending, which has the ambiguity displayed in previous examples, it is an uplifting experience to encounter at last a wonderful line containing "stout Balboa," who may be English literature's leading symbol of the primacy of poetic effect over historical accuracy. The insistent avoidance of romance in that stanza, the portrayal of the great voyager as a kind of Don Quixote, is consistent with Garrett's concern always to try and render history as it must have felt, and not as readers have learned to visualize it through, say, the illustrations of Howard Pyle, whose Men of Iron never showed a speck of rust.

Garrett has not published much poetry since the appearance of Collected Poems, but in his most recent work he continues to take chances. One of his most audacious and successful poems is "Whistling In the Dark," which dares to remind us that Adolf Hitler was one of God's creatures. It begins with a creepy recollection:

> Not many may now remember.
> Fewer and fewer remember,
> most because they never knew
> in the first place, being lucky

and too young, and others
because they are too few, too old
already. But anyway I remember

the three reasons most often advanced
in those innocent days before the War
as strong and self-evident argument
that Adolf Hitler was crazy.
First, that he was a strict vegetarian.
Second that he did not smoke or permit
any smoking around him, being convinced
that smoking cigarettes was somehow
linked to lung cancer.
Third because he went around saying
that the Volkswagen, laughable beetle,
was the car of the future.
Maybe God, in all His power and majesty,
can still enjoy the irony of it.

Having said that it takes power and majesty to "enjoy the irony of it," the poem goes on to wonder at it—in the senses of pondering and of being awestruck. The middle of the poem recalls the speaker's visit to a *gasthaus* near Linz, where he stands at a bar listening to old men who remember the Austro-Hungarian Empire, and Hitler's father, and the boy himself, who used to come nightly to the bar for his father's evening bucket of beer, and then walk home, whistling with memorable skill. The speaker then tries to imagine that scene:

I lean back against the bar
to picture how he was then, lips puckered,
whistling tunes I do not know,
beer rich and foamy, sloshing in the pail,
smell of woodsmoke, cooking meat and cabbage.

And, invisible and implacable, always
the wide smile of God upon his creatures,
one and all, great and small,
among them, this one little palefaced boy
for whom he has arranged some enormous surprises

beyond any kind of imagining, even myself
drunk in this bar, years from home, imagining it.[5]

Another treatment of the scene in the *gasthaus* appears in the autobiographical essay Garrett wrote for the *Contemporary Authors Autobiography Series*. The essay alternates between two narratives. One is casual but direct,
and addresses most of the questions that come up in such an assignment; the
other is more nearly like a short story, and recounts a day in the lives of two
soldiers, a Corporal and a Sergeant, stationed near Linz in peacetime. "The
Sergeant, of course, is myself."[6]

There are several instances of Garrett's having used the same material in
both verse and prose, but here we have unusually strong evidence that the
poem is autobiographical. Yet, though the poem is based on fact, the constant and paradoxical tension between the present and the past, between
memory and imagination, is the source of its power. As he has done so often
in his poetry and fiction, Garrett here offers a celebration of our humanity,
and of the imagination, and of God. It is the great triumph of his work that
he can do this unmistakably and accessibly, while at the same time he pushes
energetically at the boundaries and limits of his art.

5. George Garrett, "Whistling In the Dark," *Wooster Review*, IX (1989), 15.
6. George Garrett, "George Palmer Garrett, Jr.," *Contemporary Authors Autobiography
Series*, V (Detroit, 1987), 72.

WILLIAM MEREDITH In Charge of Morale in a Morbid Time

The Wreck of the Thresher, published in 1964, was the book that most firmly established the nature and strength of William Meredith's poetry. It seems now to have been the culmination of a development in certain directions from which the poet has since swerved, though not unrewardingly. The poems in it reveal unobtrusive mastery of craft traditionally conceived; there are not many sonnets, villanelles, sestinas, or other insistent evidences that the poet is comfortable in formal cages; but beneath the steady, honest lines, with their sometimes unpredictable rhyme schemes, there is a sense of assurance that for Meredith, form is a method, not a barrier. In its range of subject, tone, and mode, the book consistently offers the voice of a civilized man, a man with good but not exclusive manners, engaged in encounters with matters of inexhaustible interest.

This style did not come quickly to Meredith—not that his debut was inauspicious: his first book, *Love Letter from an Impossible Land*, was chosen by Archibald MacLeish in his first year as editor of the Yale Series of Younger Poets. Here were a number of accomplished poems, including a few that spoke in the voice that would be firmly Meredith's by the time *The Wreck of the Thresher* appeared twenty years later. Much of the book is apprentice work, but in the "impossible land" of the Aleutians, of the Second World War, Meredith came to grips with strangeness for which no borrowed voice could suffice. So the book falls into two parts, whose relation MacLeish describes as "the way in which the literary vehicle (for it is nothing else) of the Princeton undergraduate turns into the live idiom of a poet's speech reaching for poetry." What is there, one wonders, to like about "the literary vehicle of the Princeton undergraduate"? A possible answer is that the earlier poems show us a young poet diligently studying his craft. In the brief lyrics that acknowledge various masters, there is little room for the voice of Meredith, but there is in them a serious and intelligent setting-forth after the tools that will give the voice, when it speaks, the distinctiveness and force of the later poems. Craft matters to the young poet: of the thirty-three poems in *Love Letter*, eight are traditional sonnets, and seven others are near-sonnets of twelve to fourteen lines. If some of these are predictable or flat, or if others are too insistent upon their experimentation with formal expansion (as in the packed internal rhymes and slant end-rhymes of "War Sonnet," for instance), practice has made nearly perfect by the time we come to "In Memoriam Stratton Christensen":

> Laughing young man and fiercest against sham,
>   Then you have stayed at sea, at feckless sea,
>   With a single angry curiosity
> Savoring fear and faith and speckled foam?
> A salt end to what was sweet begun:
>   Twenty-three years and your integrity
>   And already a certain number touched like me
> With a humor and a hardness from the sun.
>
> Without laughter we have spent your wit
>   In an unwitnessed fight at sea, perhaps not won,
>   And whether wisely we will never know;
> But like Milton's friend's, to them that hear of it
>   Your death is a puzzler that will tease them on
>   Reckless out on the thin, important floe.[1]

Here the experimentation with local sonic richness is muted, but not below the level of fruitful risk; for example, *Reckless* in the last line is right not only in itself, but because it echoes the second and fourth lines.

    1. Archibald MacLeish, Foreword to *Love Letter from an Impossible Land*, by William Meredith (New Haven, 1944); William Meredith, *Partial Accounts: New and Selected Poems* (New York, 1987), 6. Hereafter cited in the text as *PA*, followed by a page number.

In "Notes for an Elegy," a longer poem whose ambition and scope are larger than anything else in this book, Meredith sounds a note of modesty in the title, a note that he will sound again and again, even as his poems improve. This title, of course, means not to suggest that the poem is unfinished—it is quite brilliantly finished—but that in a time and place more distant from the war, it might have acquired more of the trappings of a formal elegy. Here, the first twenty-two lines, a meditation on flying and its relation to freedom, tyranny, and war, set the proper tone, verging toward an invocation to the muse. The death is that of an airman, but not one shot down in battle; for some mysterious reason, his plane has crashed in a wood. Having asked where the engine and the wings were at the crucial moment, the speaker concludes that

> the invitation
> Must have been sent to the aviator in person:
> Perhaps a sly suggestion of carelessness,
> A whispered invitation perhaps to death,
> Death.[2]

The quietness of this passage, while it emphasizes the distance of the crash from any battle, is at odds with the noisy violence of any plane's untimely coming down; it is as if the plane and its pilot had drifted silently to rest, like so many other things that fall in the forest when no one is there to hear them. This impression is confronted in the poem's remarkable conclusion, where the phrase "as it were in bed" lifts the tone out of solemnity toward something large enough to enclose great mystery:

> Note that he had not fought one public battle,
> Met any fascist with his skill, but died
> As it were in bed, the waste conspicuous . . .
>
> . . . .
> The morning came up foolish with pink clouds
> To say that God counts ours a cunning time,
> Our losses part of an old secret, somehow no loss.
> (EW, 34–35)

---

2. William Meredith, *Earth Walk: New and Selected Poems* (New York, 1970), 34. Hereafter cited in the text as *EW*, followed by a page number.

This ability to complicate tone by the subtle use of something close to humor has been important in much of Meredith's work, though it has been only recently that many of his serious poems have contained very wide streaks of humor. But fairly early, Meredith came to an inclusive control of tone that makes for greater strength than the owlish cultivation of high seriousness.

These qualities of strength and inclusiveness, however, are not much in evidence in Meredith's second book, *Ships and Other Figures*, which appeared in 1948, only four years after *Love Letter*. A note of acknowledgment states that "most of these poems were written and all of them collected while the writer was a Woodrow Wilson Fellow of Princeton University," and one feels keenly the absence of peril in these poems, the safety of academe. Under the pressure of his credentials as a promising young poet, Meredith seems not to be the aviator inspired to struggle with his craft and its relation to puzzles of much magnitude; he seems instead to be a Wilson Fellow who would like to have enough poems for a book. Under such circumstances, he turns his hand to various exercises in tradition and occasion, and is sometimes successful with slight poems where, the pressure being momentarily off, he can indulge his excellent sense of play without fear of momentous failure. Here, for example, is the first of "Two Figures from the Movies":

The papers that clear him tucked in his inside pocket
And the grip of the plucky blonde light on his bicep,
He holds the gang covered now, and backs for the door
That gives on the daylit street and the yare police.
But the regular customers know that before the end
With its kissing and money and adequate explanation,
He has still to back into the arms of the baldheaded man
With the huge signet-ring and the favorable odds of surprise,
Somehow to outface the impossible arrogant stare,
And will his luck hold, they wonder, and has he the skill?[3]

Meredith continues to be puzzled by my affection for this little poem; some years ago, when I sought to include "Two Figures" in an anthology, he

3. William Meredith, *Ships and Other Figures* (Princeton, 1948), 26.

granted his permission on the condition that my text not make fun of it or ask embarrassing study questions about it. True, its matter is more trivial than the matters that usually engage Meredith; but in its satirical arrangement of well-chosen cinematic clichés, and in its deft echo of classical heroic meters, it is a small but thorough success. The second of the "Two Figures" is less successful, as it lacks the particularity of the first, and is somewhat out-weighed by its epigraph from Shakespeare. Even so, these two poems have intrinsic interest, and reveal an impulse that is important in much of Mere-dith's later work.

This is not to suggest that, in his *New and Selected Poems* of 1970, Mere-dith saved from *Ships and Other Figures* all the wrong things; he saved the best six poems, but would not have tarnished his reputation by carrying for-ward a few more. The same could be said of his selection from *The Open Sea* (1958), a collection of nearly fifty poems of considerable range and effective-ness. Here Meredith continues his exploration of difficult fixed forms, not merely in order to submit himself to complex rules, but also to see how some of these rules may be pushed around. Aside from the half-dozen or so sonnets that one might expect to find, there are also two sestinas and a dedicatory villanelle. The usefulness of these explorations is perhaps most apparent in the title poem, which fits the definition of none of the fixed forms mentioned above, but which clearly takes advantage of their existence:

We say the sea is lonely; better say
Our selves are lonesome creatures whom the sea
Gives neither yes nor no for company.

Oh, there are people, all right, settled in the sea—
It is as populous as Maine today—
But no one who will give you the time of day.

A man who asks there of his family
Or a friend or teacher gets a cold reply
Or finds him dead against that vast majority.

Nor does it signify, that people who stay
Very long, bereaved or not, at the edge of the sea
Hear the drowned folk call: that is mere fancy,

They are speechless. And the famous noise of sea,
Which a poet has beautifully told us in our day,
Is hardly a sound to speak comfort to the lonely.

Although not yet a man given to prayer, I pray
For each creature lost since the start at sea,
And give thanks it was not I, nor yet one close to me.
(PA, 23)

The poem's debt to the formal repetitions of villanelle or sestina is clear enough; what is less clear is how the poet, in suggesting a form that already exists, walks the elusive line between failure to fulfill the contract and success in making something that is complete on its own terms. Here, the success is gained through a profound awareness of the subtle tensions that arise between hypothetical form and human utterance. The first stanza, with its second line reaching just above the sound of conversation, establishes a tone that is greatly broadened, but not obliterated, by the second stanza, which stays within the metrical bounds of the poem while it introduces a much looser diction. This thoughtful changing of voices is held in suspension through the final stanza, so that the speaker earns our belief in his prayer.

Another fine example of what comes of serious play is "The Illiterate," a poem whose structure is that of a Petrarchan sonnet, but repeated words appear at the ends of the lines, instead of rhymes. The octave begins by saying, "Touching your goodness, I am like a man / Who turns a letter over in his hand," and goes on to say that the man has never received a letter before, and is unable to read it, or to overcome his shame and ask someone to read it to him. The poem ends:

His uncle could have left the farm to him,
Or his parents died before he sent them word,
Or the dark girl changed and want him for beloved.
Afraid and letter-proud, he keeps it with him.
What would you call his feeling for the words
That keep him rich and orphaned and beloved?
(PA, 27)

The wit that chose recurring words instead of rhymes for a poem like this, and the craft that makes them work, have greatly matured since the

early sonneteering experiments; this poem transcends its quite noticeable pe-
culiarity, partly by drawing us away from the ends of the lines toward consid-
eration of the subtle use of *your* and *you*, in the first and thirteenth lines,
respectively: these words and lines are just enough to keep the simile and the
form from being self-conscious studies of themselves.

Of course such forms are, in some unself-conscious way, studies of themselves. By this time Meredith has wedded technique to meditation, so that
they are harder to separate, even for convenience in discussion, than they
were in his earlier work. Meredith finds several occasions in *The Open Sea* to
be explicit about the value of art; there are several poems about music, painting, sculpture, architecture, the ballet, and so on, and in all of these one
finds an admiration for formal restraint, especially when it is evident that
there is something beneath the form that is worth restraining, whose power
is worth conserving.

To this end, Meredith joins the urge to self-consciousness and a very
light touch with meter, to strike a precise balance of tones in the pleasant
but complicated "Thoughts on One's Head (IN PLASTER, WITH A BRONZE
WASH)." In a delicate alternation of masculine and feminine rhymes, and in
a meter of musical elasticity, these stanzas, like good heads, hold simultaneously a number of attitudes:

> A person is very self-conscious about his head.
> It makes one nervous just to know it is cast
> In enduring materials, and that when the real one is dead
> The cast one, if nobody drops it or melts it down, will last.

> We pay more attention to the front end, where the face is,
> Than to the interesting and involute interior:
> The Fissure of Rolando and such queer places
> Are parks for the passions and fears and mild hysteria.
> (*PA*, 37)

The slight confusion between the cast head and the real head, introduced by the unobtrusively vague *it* in the second line, modulates into clarity:
the head under discussion becomes the real head, with its Fissure of Rolando,
its judgment, and so on; but at the end, the poem seems to shift partly back
to the cast head for a moment, in the last line below:

This particular head, to my certain knowledge
Has been taught to read and write, make love and money,
Operate cars and airplanes, teach in a college,
And tell involved jokes, some few extremely funny.

It was further taught to know and to eschew
Error and sin, which it does erratically.
This is the place the soul calls home just now.
One dislikes it of course: it is the seat of Me.
(PA, 38)

"One dislikes it of course:" the cast head, occasion for an aesthetic judgment (however biased), has become the occasion for a meditation on its original, "the seat of Me"; and the cast head stays between the real head and the observing consciousness, a barrier against self-indulgence, a reminder that either head could be dropped or melted down.

The Wreck of the Thresher is both larger and smaller than The Open Sea. It contains fewer poems, and there is less variety of form and subject; but several of these poems are considerably more ambitious than anything preceding them. In somewhat narrowing the range of his attention, Meredith deepens his focus, producing a few poems that can stand with the best poems of his generation. (Often people write such phrases in their sleep; I am awake, and aware that I speak of the generation of Berryman, Bishop, Lowell, Nemerov, and Wilbur, among others.)

The title poem is a bold achievement, one of Meredith's rare "public" poems; its occasion was the destruction at sea of the nuclear submarine Thresher on April 10, 1963. Much has happened since that date to make that disaster recede from the public consciousness; one of this poem's strengths is that it has not been diminished by a fifteen-year torrent of public catastrophes. The poem deserves closer attention than it has received. Some reviewers have accused it of staginess; Richard Howard, to whose essay on Meredith I am in some ways indebted, does not mention it.[4]

The opening stanza, it is true, makes a few moves that seem suspicious; the first line arouses the fear that this may be just one more "I-am-standing" poem, a subgenre often exploited by poets who have nothing to say. And the description of the sea, with its zoömorphic similes, seems melodramatic:

4. Richard Howard, Alone with America (New York, 1969), 318–26.

> I stand on the ledge where rock runs into the river
> As the night turns brackish with morning, and mourn the drowned.
> Here the sea is diluted with river; I watch it slaver
> Like a dog curing of rabies. Its ravening over,
> Lickspittle ocean nuzzles the dry ground.
> (But the dream that woke me was worse than the sea's grey
> Slip-slap; there are no such sounds by day.)
> (*PA*, 46)

But it is the dream that has imposed this animistic vision on the speaker; it is, as "The Open Sea" has it, "mere fancy," to which the speaker will return as the poem shifts from the present to the dream, then to meditation derived from both:

> This crushing of people is something we live with.
> Daily, by unaccountable whim
> Or caught up in some harebrained scheme of death,
> Tangled in cars, dropped from the sky, in flame,
> Men and women break the pledge of breath:
> And now under water, gone all jetsam and small
> In the pressure of oceans collected, a squad of brave men in a hull.
> (*PA*, 46)

The only full rhyme in this stanza is one of the most predictable in our language, but the lines thus rhymed give the words freshness of context, and the rhyme's very obtrusiveness yokes "harebrained scheme" to "break the pledge," one of the many subtle juxtapositions that parallel the larger tensions between actuality and dream, land and sea, life and death. In dream, the speaker has met

> a monstrous self trapped in the black deep:
> *All these years*, he smiled, *I've drilled at sea*
> *For this crush of water.* Then he saved only me.
> (*PA*, 46)

The phrase "a monstrous self" suggests, at the same time, an other and a version of the speaker's own self; we are reminded, more subtly here than in some other poems, of Meredith's own war experience, the losses of friends, the perils survived. The poem moves again to the question of investing the inanimate with life, as in the tradition of naming ships "for ladies and queens,"

> Although by a wise superstition these are called
> After fish, the finned boats, silent and submarine.
> (PA, 47)

The complicated idea of a "wise superstition" carries one through the next stanza, where the sea is divested of emotion while the dead sailors, it seems, are given the capacity for it:

> I think of how sailors laugh, as if cold and wet
> And dark and lost were their private, funny derision
> And I can judge then what dark compression
> Astonishes them now, their sunken faces set
> Unsmiling, where the currents sluice to and fro
> And without humor, somewhere northeast of here and below.
> (PA, 47)

Astonishes, of course, turns out to be completely appropriate, as it means "renders insensate"; we are forced by the syntax, and by the word's placement at the head of the line, following a breathless enjambment, to examine it before passing on to the pun in "sunken faces." This vision of the sailors leads back to the dream again, in a stanza where impossible schemes of escape and heroism give way to the voices of the drowned: "Study something deeper than yourselves, / As, how the heart, when it turns diver, delves and saves." Earlier in the poem, the speaker asks, "Why can't our dreams be content with the terrible facts?" In the light of day, no one truly hears "the drowned folk call." The poem passes from the dream to a final stanza of great stateliness; in its treatment of the terrible facts, it shifts from the nearly conversational to the nearly prophetic, its movement genuinely suggestive of a musical coda:

> Whether we give assent to this or rage
> Is a question of temperament and does not matter.
> Some will has been done past our understanding,
> Past our guilt surely, equal to our fears.

Dullards, we are set again to the cryptic blank page
Where the sea schools us with terrible water.
The noise of a boat breaking up and its men is in our ears.
The bottom here is too far down for our sounding;
The ocean was salt before we crawled to tears.
(PA, 48)

In this poem, and in others in the collection, a quality of modesty asserts itself strongly; Meredith himself described it a few years later, in a foreword to Earth Walk: New and Selected Poems; he selected from earlier books, he says, "poems that try to say things I am still trying to find ways to say, poems that engage mysteries I still pluck at the hems of, poems that are devious in ways I still like better than plainspokenness." "The Wreck of the Thresher" only seems to be plainspoken; it engages and contains deep mystery, and makes it memorable.

Plucking at the hems of old mysteries sometimes compels a poet to go over ground he has visited before. "On Falling Asleep to Birdsong," the third poem in The Wreck of the Thresher, recalls the title of "On Falling Asleep by Firelight," from The Open Sea. The earlier poem is perhaps too tidy to be convincing; the later poem is much better made, and goes beyond tidiness, drifting with the consciousness of a man falling asleep, who hears a whippoor-will and thinks of his parents' and his own death. Trying to dream of nightin-gales, he is led on to Philomela, whose story appears gracefully in the poem, not as paraded learning, but as the unwilled reverie of a man who has read some books:

But I am in bed in the fall
And cannot arrest the dream
That unwinds a chase and a rape
And ends in Thracian pain.
(PA, 52)

The whippoorwill calls, and is not answered; his song becomes no more than itself, and no less: "When time has gone away / He calls to what he calls." And the speaker, thinking that "life is one," accepts both the written fable and the one the whippoorwill has helped him to invent:

I will grow old, as a man
Will read of a transformation:

Knowing it is a fable
Contrived to answer a question
Answered, if ever, in fables,
Yet all of a piece and clever
And at some level, true.
(PA, 53)

This idea, that unwilled or semiconscious rumination leads on to meditation and sometimes to fable, is taken up several times in The Wreck of the
Thresher, often in sequences or in poems separated into nearly self-contained
sections. "Fables About Error," "Five Accounts of a Monogamous Man," and
"Consequences" are all acts of a mind responding with attentive love to surfaces, but never being content with superficiality. The first of the "Fables
About Error" develops the amusing notion that "The mouse in the cupboard
repeats himself," being found dead every morning in the trap. On one level,
then, the idea that the mouse should know better after a while is preposter-
ous, but Meredith's conclusion is nonetheless apt:

Surely there is always that in experience
Which could warn us; and the worst
That can be said of any of us is:
He did not pay attention.
(EW, 82)

Meredith pays close attention, and finds even in our troubled age some
vindication of his tendency to praise, as he says in "of choice," the first
section of "Consequences":

More than I hoped to do, I do
And more than I deserve I get;
What little I attend, I know
And it argues order more than not.
(PA, 64)

This attitude of hopefulness comes through these poems tentatively, free
of the hectoring tone that often afflicts poems with something valuable to
say. They are "all of a piece," and let themselves come gradually to those
levels where they ring truest. At such levels, they are beyond cleverness.

In 1970, Meredith published *Earth Walk: New and Selected Poems*. I have already suggested that he was too stingy in making his selections from the four previous books, though he makes a handsome apology for this in a fore-word: "In making this selection from twenty-five years of work I have repre-sented my early books scantily, as I have come to feel they represented me. Juvenile gifts apart, it takes time to find out our real natures and purposes. But finally we have done so many things, good and bad, in character, that it is permissible to disown some of our other acts, at any rate the bad ones, as impersonations." He makes it clear in the next sentence, part of which is quoted earlier, that he is talking primarily about his first two books, and it is hard to quarrel much with his selection from those. But the slimness of the selection as a whole should have the effect, intended or not, of sending the reader back to the early work, especially to *The Open Sea*, where among the thirty-three "disowned" poems there are several that reward continued attention.

But one turns with greatest interest, of course, to the fourteen new poems in *Earth Walk*, and one is struck first by the variety of points of view. Poems spoken by fictional characters are not plentiful in Meredith's work, though on some occasions, as in "Five Accounts of a Monogamous Man," he has adopted, as Yeats often did, the device of applying third-person titles to first-person poems. *Earth Walk* opens with such a poem, "Winter Verse for His Sister," the speaker of which is not readily distinguishable from Meredith himself. Then in "Walter Jenks' Bath" the speaker is a young black boy thinking over what his teacher has said about the way everything is composed of atoms. The tension between the poet's level of sophistication and that of the speaker is first of all useful in setting the tone of the poem, the touching simplicity of the observations; but in the last six lines, what Walter Jenks says becomes larger in its grasp of things, so that in the final line, he seems to speak for the poet as well as for himself:

And when I stop the atoms go on knocking,
Even if I died the parts would go on spinning,
Alone, like the far stars, now knowing it,
Not knowing they are far apart, or running,
Or minding the black distances between.
This is me knowing, this is what I know.
(*PA*, 75)

That a child in the bathtub comes plausibly to thoughts like these is a tribute to the delicacy with which the tone is handled; the same delicacy sustains a tougher poem, "Effort at Speech," in which the speaker relates an encounter with a mugger. The speaker and the mugger wrestle briefly, the wallet parts "like a wishbone," the mugger flees with his ill-gotten half, and the speaker comes close to guilt at having retained the other half:

> Next time don't wrangle, give the boy the money,
> Call across chasms what the world you know is.
> Luckless and lied to, how can a child master
>   human decorum?
>
> Next time a switch-blade, somewhere he is thinking,
> I should have killed him and took the lousy wallet.
> Reading my cards he feels a surge of anger
>   blind as my shame.

(PA, 78)

The strength of the poet's control over these lines is felt in the prosody; this narrative of violence and guilt is cast in stanzas that come as close to Sapphics as idiomatic English can come. The classical echo puts a distance between the poet and the events described, but it also recalls the actual effort that real speech requires.

Colloquial language, contractions, and exclamations fall into regular stanzas in "Poem About Morning," a funny little lecture on waking up and facing the day. The suggestion of lecturing is made by casting the poem in the second person, though the "you" partakes of the speaker's experience, almost as if the speaker were addressing himself. And "Earth Walk" provides a final illustration of the experimentation with point of view that runs like a thread through these new poems. The title poem begins in the third person, as a man pulls off the highway and touches his seat belt. After the phrase "He thinks" the first stanza continues in the first-person plural, as it describes our habit of traveling in straps and helmets. The second stanza is in the first-person singular, but despite the stanza break, it all still follows from "He thinks." The man steps out of his car, parodying the careful steps of the men on the moon:

> I pick out small white stones. This is a safe walk.
> This turnpike is uninhabited. When I come back

I'll meet a trooper with a soft, wide hat
who will take away my Earth-rocks and debrief me.
(*EW*, 20)

The shift from third to first person, while it is perfectly within the bounds of
narrative logic, still gives the poem a scope of observation that a single point
of view might lack.

These new poems, with their restless personal pronouns, may now be
seen as forerunners of Meredith's next book, *Hazard, the Painter* (1975). This
collection of sixteen poems seems to have been designed to provoke a number
of reactions, not all of them charitable, and not all of them familiar to readers
of Meredith's previous books. One notices pure surface, a meticulous and
beautiful job of book production in which the cover and typography seem to
assert that the book amounts to more than its small bulk might suggest. Inside, there are poems composing a "characterization," as Meredith calls it in
a cagey note; he adds, "Resemblances between the life and character of
Hazard and those of the author are not disclaimed but are much fewer than
the author would like."

It comes to mind that in the work of William Meredith and John Berryman there are several references to their friendship; furthermore, as Meredith
has acknowledged in public readings, a line in the first of the *Hazard* poems
is taken from Berryman's conversation. The uncharitable speculation arises
that Hazard is too closely akin to Berryman's Henry, in strategy if not in size
and style. Clearly, though, Meredith cannot have conceived this book in any
competitive way, as Lowell seems to have conceived his *Notebooks*; the very
brevity of *Hazard* indicates that it is not useful to compare it with *The Dream
Songs*, even though that book continues to loom as a distant forebear.

Hazard is a middle-aged painter with a wife and two children. For two
years his subject has been a parachutist, but he is at the moment stalled in
his work; various pressures—family, uneasy friendships with other painters,
daydreams—take up more of his time than painting does. He has a fine eye
for detail, and a wry sense of the absurd; lying at the beach, where "they use
the clouds over & over / again, like the rented animals in *Aïda*," Hazard
nearly dozes as things impinge at random on his consciousness, making equal
claims on his curiosity:

The sand knocks like glass, struck by bare heels.
He tries to remember snow noise.

> Would powder snow ping like that?
> But you don't lie with your ear to powder snow.
> Why doesn't the girl who takes care
> of the children, a Yale girl without flaw,
> know the difference between *lay* and *lie?*
> (*PA*, 111)

The style of *Hazard* appears to be more casual, less concentrated, than anything Meredith has written before. One notices, for instance, that there is not a semicolon anywhere in these poems; instead, the independent clauses tumble along over their commas, contributing to the feeling of interior life, as in the second half of this stanza from "Politics," a poem about liberals gathering to hear jazz for McGovern:

> Hazard desires his wife, the way people
> on the trains to the death-camps were seized
> by irrational lust. She is the youngest woman
> in the room, he would like to be in bed
> with her now, he would like to be president.
> (*PA*, 100)

Gradually, as one rereads these poems, the accumulation of anecdote and detail provides the density that is missing from the style, and there arises the illusion of a life, a way of life, made difficult by a difficult time, but still enjoyable and cherished. "The culture is in late imperial decline," Hazard thinks in the line taken from Berryman; and in "Hazard's Optimism," considering his vision of the parachutist as he himself tries a parachute jump, Hazard concludes thus:

> They must have caught and spanked him
> like this when he first fell.
> He passes it along now, Hazard's vision.
> He is in charge of morale in a morbid time.
> He calls out to the sky, his voice
> the voice of an animal that makes not words
> but a happy incorrigible noise, not
> of this time.
> (*PA*, 96)

The mask of Hazard gives Meredith, at least for the duration of this deceptively brief book, the freedom to work out of ways in which he might think he was becoming set. In the chattiness that contains more than it at first seems to, beneath the detailed surfaces, there is room for satire as well as for a serious, loving exploration of a peculiar world.

But Hazard was not destined to take over Meredith's voice and life. He is an interesting character met along the way, and, having met him, Meredith was usefully diverted. In more recent work, the deceptively casual tone and form in Hazard's voice have been especially useful. The title poem of *The Cheer* (1980) says to the reader, "Frankly, I'd like to make you smile" (*PA*, 123), and speaks up for the cheer and courage in which words are born; but "Recollection of Bellagio" shows how far from humor such an optimistic aim can go. The first of the poem's two strophes describes the dance of pine needles against a night sky like a ballroom floor; here is the second:

> How long has this been going on, this *allemande*,
> before a man's thoughts climbed up to sit
> on the limestone knob and watch (briefly,
> as man's thoughts' eyes watch) the needles
> keeping time to the bells which the same wind rocks
> on the water below, marking the fishermen's nets—
> thoughts he would haul in later from the lake
> of time, feeling himself drawn clumsy
> back into time's figure, hand over hand,
> by the grace of pine boughs? And who
> is saying these words, now that that man
> is a shade, has become his own shade?
> I see the shade rise slow and ghostly from its seat
> on the soft, grainy stone, I watch it descend
> by the gravelled paths of the promontory,
> under a net of steady stars, in April,
> from the boughs' rite and the bells'—quiet,
> my shade, and long ago, and still going on.
> (*PA*, 129–30)

A number of the poems in this book elicit the deep and often unseen smile of pleasure at difficulty being negotiated with good cheer. Even in poems addressing a president guilty of "criminal folly," or friends—Lowell,

Berryman—who have died, love of the world often matters at least as much as the world's unwitting insistence on harboring wickedness, folly, and death.

Among the best poems in *The Cheer* are four unusually "literary" ones; three are responses to epigraphs at least as long as the poems, and one requires a prose preface of more than 150 words. This last is "Trelawny's Dream," in which Edward John Trelawny recalls—and, in dream, revises—the boating accident that took the life of his friend Shelley. A splendid poem taken alone, it also speaks to "The Wreck of the Thresher"; both poems are moving portrayals of our need to dream away our helplessness, and to wake to it.

Meredith's most recent book of poems, for which he received the Pulitzer Prize in Poetry, is *Partial Accounts: New and Selected Poems* (1987). Here, as in *Earth Walk*, he has represented his early work sparingly. I miss "Fables About Error," and like to think it took its small revenge at being dropped: its former neighbor "The Ballet," first collected in *The Wreck of the Thresher*, appears here among the poems selected from *The Open Sea*.

Partial Accounts adds a translation and ten new poems to the selections from earlier books; they meditate upon violence and love about equally, and often on the human ability to separate ourselves from the rest of nature. "The Jain Bird Hospital in Delhi" applies to its form the nonviolent attitudes of the Jains, who see all living things as brothers and sisters; the form is based on that of a sestina, but only one end-word is varied by so slight a device as shifting between singular and plural; others are replaced with homophones, synonyms, or associates; one appears as *pigeons, bird(s), creatures, pheasants,* and *flock*; another as *beings, men, women, laymen, poultrymen, women,* and *ourselves*. Few readers will ponder the adherence to traditional word-order long enough to discover that birds are creatures and people are beings; the poem wittily exemplifies nonviolent achievement of order.

In "Partial Accounts" a surprising juxtaposition makes a defense of optimism; the first part, titled "surgery," humorously remarks on the appropriateness of replacing a faulty valve with a pig's valve; the second part recalls the sympathy the speaker felt as he watched, or tried not to watch, an Arab woman in Morocco having a tooth pulled in the open-air market:

> The *chirurgien dentiste* was a small man,
> authoritative, Berber I think.
> His left foot was set gently on the woman's

shoulder, and when I last looked,
difficult, silent progress was being made.
(*PA*, 182–83)

Meredith continues to find fresh ways of reminding us that there is joy in plucking at the hems of even the darkest mysteries; as he says in "Among Ourselves," "Accountability / weighs on me, but so does happiness" (*PA*, 181).

MAY SARTON Home to a Place Beyond Exile

I

The retrospective exhibition of a poetic career may be either highly selective or generously inclusive; the choice the author makes between these two approaches has much to do with the poet's temperament. The highly selective poet, whose definitive collection contains, say, less than half of her published work, is likely to think of poetry as the production of separate finished pieces. The author of the more inclusive collection, on the other hand, is more forgiving of failure and false moves, on the grounds that poetry, as a way of perceiving and knowing, is a process in which one important thing is the trail of attempts, successful and otherwise. Diane Wakoski has sensibly pointed out that the difference between these kinds of poet is not that one is fastidious and the other sloppy; it is only that divergent but equally important aspects of the poetic life are attractive to them. And it should be obvious that no poet is exclusively one or the other of these hypothetical kinds. The product-oriented poet seeks a distinctive and unifying voice, and the process-oriented poet certainly welcomes isolated excellences.

May Sarton designed her *Collected Poems* (1974) with a lifelong process in view. Her aim was to reveal the development of a career and of a person, because the whole of her career is greater than the sum of its stages, despite the brilliance of many individual poems. She writes of the feminine condition, of art, love, landscape, travel, and the search for a lasting home, and of the inexplicable violence that can wreck even the mildest people. Her tone is often gently didactic. The largeness of her themes makes them worth returning to again and again; her didactic tone helps give her poetry its distinctiveness, for very few poets of this age seem willing to be purposeful about poetry's power to instruct. That didactic poetry can succeed in our day should come as no surprise, but somehow it does, probably because the word *didactic* has come to make people think not of Milton's sick sheep, but of John Dyer's bleaters. We have become accustomed to the idea that didactic poetry is not the real thing; in the process we must have forgotten that Eliot, Frost, and Yeats wrote many poems as consciously instructive as anything in this volume.

Sarton's concern to reveal human as well as literary development helps explain the presence in *Collected Poems* of some items that seem less successful than others. There are triumphs here, of form over chaos, delight over suffering, skill over intransigence, that must be seen in the context of the struggles they spring from, not because the struggles aggrandize the triumphs, but because these *Collected Poems* make a work of almost narrative continuity. What lies between the higher achievements comes to seem indispensable to the narrative.

II

This collection draws from each of Sarton's eleven previous books; only the first two, *Encounter in April* (1936) and *Inner Landscape* (1939), have been drastically pruned. In terms of thematic and technical development, the eleven books tend to fall into pairs; in each pair, the earlier book introduces themes and techniques that are extended and perfected in the later. The unpaired book in this scheme is not the eleventh, but the seventh, *Cloud, Stone, Sun, Vine* (1961), a new and selected collection that is the capstone to the earlier part of Sarton's career. The subsequent four books contain significant new departures, and again fall into pairs.

Many of Sarton's most persistent themes appear in her early work; for example, the second poem in this volume is a long free-verse exploration of the feminine condition; "She Shall Be Called Woman" first appeared over fifty years ago, but it is at least as pertinent now as it was then. Based on the biblical myth of creation, the poem portrays a gradual awakening to the apparent constancy of pain, then the mature coming to grips with the cycles that subordinate pain to a broader scheme. Between these developments falls a section describing a trancelike state of unconscious preparation for growth:

> And then one day
> all feeling
> slipped out from her skin
> until no finger's consciousness remained,
> no pain—
> and she all turned
> to earth
> like abstract gravity.
> She did not know
> how she had come
> to close her separate lids
> nor where she learned
> the gesture of her sleeping,
> yet something in her slept
> most deeply
> and something in her
> lay like stone
> under a folded dress—
> she could not tell how long.[1]

Following this, the woman wakes to a new self-awareness, a change of spirit wrought by menstrual and other creative cycles, until she can return to being part of the earth, "part of its turning, / as distinctly part / of the universe as a star" (26). She ends where she began, but with a knowledge of sources and of growth that will not leave her. The necessity of retaining contact with nature, often through consciousness of the natural processes within one's own body, is an abiding concern of Sarton's.

For this reason among many others, love is also a perennial theme in Sarton's work, and is behind the best of it. In her love poems, however, there seems to be a continual quest for what can never be found. Love is often

---

1. May Sarton, *Collected Poems* (New York, 1974), 23. Hereafter cited by page number in the text.

paralleled with suffering and struggle, because the poet and the woman seem sometimes at odds. "Summary," from *Inner Landscape,* is an early exposition of the dualities of love:

> In the end it is the dark for which all lovers pine.
> They cannot bear the light on their transparent faces,
> The light on nerves exposed like a design.
> They have a great need of sleep in foreign places,
> Of another country than the heart and another speech.
>
> . . . .
> [Lovers] are found to believe
> That love endures and their pain is infinite
> Who have not learned that each single touch they give,
> Every kiss, every word they speak holds death in it.
> (34)

The uneasy energy in the sound of this poem, which is in some respects not maturely crafted, still conveys the urgency that lies behind the statement. Sarton has always known that this kind of poetic energy is required, but it took her some time to achieve it consistently. However, a foreshadowing of the control that characterizes her later poetry appears in "A Letter to James Stephens," one of Sarton's earlier attempts to speak directly about her aims as a poet. It begins in winter, in a place far from a recollected conversation between Sarton and Stephens, in which some disagreement arose concerning the poet's task. Sarton asks, now that winter and distance lie between friends,

> What of this personal all,
> The little world these hands have tried to fashion
> Using a single theme for their material,
> Always a human heart, a human passion?
> You said "Seek for a sterner stuff than this,
> Look out of your closed spaces to the infinite.
>
> . . . .
> Forget your love, your little war, your ache;
> Forget that haunting so mysterious face
> And write for an abstracted beauty's sake."
> (42)

Of course Sarton must paraphrase for the sake of her form, and in doing so she makes Stephens sound perhaps more sententious than he was, because she cannot state his point of view with total sympathy. Her immediate response is to recall Stephens' heroic attempts to record "the ocean's rumor," then to state her own aesthetic:

> to write down these perishable songs for one,
> For one alone, and out of love, is not to grieve
> But to build on the quicksand of despair
> A house where every man may take his ease,
> May come to shelter from the outer air,
> A little house where he may find his peace.
> Dear James, if this fire seems only the strange
> Quick-burning fire of youth unfounded on the earth
> Then may it be transformed but never change.
> Let Him in whose hands lie death and birth
> Preserve its essence like that bush of flame
> That stood up in a path, and, fiery-plumed,
> Contained the angel who could speak God's name—
> The bush that burned and still was not consumed.
> (43)

The modesty is false that calls them "perishable songs." The first part of this passage lays the groundwork for a statement of poetic ambition no less vast than that attributed to Stephens; it is the tactical sense that is different. Not much really separates the poet who "writes for an abstracted beauty's sake" and one who seeks the energy of the angel in the burning bush.

Inner Landscape appeared in 1939, when Sarton was twenty-seven. Her next book of poems, The Lion and the Rose, did not appear until 1948; it was closely followed by The Leaves of the Tree (1950). Among the new themes introduced in these collections are the pleasures of travel and the fact of human brutality. But there are also strong poems here that continue to develop the themes of the teacher's commitment and the freedom of women. The Lion and the Rose contains a long five-part poem called "Poet in Residence," subtitled "Carbondale, Illinois." The first two sections, "The Students" and "Campus," set the scene and the mood: the writer-in-residence, an outsider, comes to a midwestern college to find that the students wander about apathetically, unaware that they inhabit the Waste Land:

Yes, I have been lonely, angry here,
Lonely on the suffocating walks under the trees
Where faces cross and recross bright with sweat,
And damp hands clutch the books unmarked by love.
· · · · · · · · · · · · · · · ·
And I, the stranger, often lit up by anger,
Waiting for someone to ask the simple question,
"Why have you come and who are you, stranger?"
And to say gladly, "Nothing but a voice,
Nothing but an angry joy, a protestation,
Nothing, a gift of nothing on the desolate air. . . ."
(62)

The poem covers a period of several weeks, during which the visitor's
attitudes undergo some changes. A foreshadowing of these changes occurs in
the third section, "Before Teaching," where the assurance and anger of the
visitor give way to humility and even fear in the face of each day's realization
that she "shall have to teach / When morning comes again." And yet the
night-sounds and the moon, which in the first stanza are associated with
the insomnia of stage fright, become at the end of the poem harbingers of the
skill the poet will somehow find:

These nights the frog grates and the firefly
Pricks the dense thickets of the gloomy heat
Have known the heart's will and its savage cry,
And too the delicate cool wind, the blessing on the air.
(63)

"After Teaching" continues this tone of renewed mission, if not of renewed confidence:

It takes a long time for words to become thought,
For thought, the slow burner, to burn through
Into life where it can scorch the palm of a hand;
· · · · · · · · · · · · · · · ·
Imagine a moment when student and teacher
(Long after the day and the lesson are over)
Will soar together to the pure immortal air.
(63–64)

The summer is redeemed by the knowledge that "It takes a long time to live what you learn." Sarton's view of poetry and of teaching has not changed much since this poem was written. What a poem records may sometimes matter more to her than the poem itself. This attitude may be more modest than is customary among poets, but paradoxically it is this very modesty that prevents Sarton from letting a poem stand if it falls far short of the experience that inspired it. Because of Sarton's didactic tendencies, the poem is often a record, not only of the experience behind it, but also of the struggle of the writing itself, the search for knowledge and skill. Again, with the accuracy of modesty, she reminds us that though knowledge and skill cannot be acquired without struggle, it is sometimes hard to see the causal connection between the nature of the struggle and the nature of their acquisition:

> So what you gave was given and what you taught was learned,
> Striking rock for water and the water falling from air,
> Opening a door to find someone in the room, already there.
> (65)

"Poet in Residence" records the gradual growth of strength and patience and love in an arid place; the subtitle is not a mere historical formality, because the name Carbondale is powerfully suggestive of an atmosphere, even a mentality, that Sarton wants us to bear in mind throughout the poem. Different places are different, a stranger is a stranger, and changing that requires some time. Many poems in *The Lion and the Rose* have this as their theme; they are travel poems, characterized by a sharpness of perception and a fine balance between bewilderment and familiarity. "In Texas," for example, one of several poems about the West, has a colloquial diction and a long, rambling line, as if the voice grew out of the place:

> In Texas the lid blew off the sky a long time ago
> So there's nothing to keep the wind from blowing
> And it blows all the time. Everywhere is far to go
> So there's no hurry at all, and no reason for going.
> (50)

This is surprisingly unlike Sarton's characteristic voice; one guesses at first that Sarton has attempted to create a Texan speaker. But gradually the poem moves toward observations that would probably not be made by a native: "(Nothing more startling here than sudden motion, / Everything is so still)." And by the end of the poem, the conclusions reached about the landscape and atmosphere of Texas, while they are fresh and convincing, seem also to be the same conclusions Sarton can reach when talking about art or love:

> What happens must be slow,
> Must go deeper even than hand's work or tongue's talk,
> Must rise out of the flesh like sweat after a hard day,
> Must come slowly, in its own time, in its own way.
> (50)

Good travel poems do not simply provide information about unfamiliar places. The encounter between the unfamiliar sensibility and that of the poet should produce poems that remind us of things we might have forgotten. All of Sarton's travel poems do this, whether they are set in America or elsewhere; this is partly because Sarton has had trouble being at home anywhere. She was born in Belgium, and her heart, according to "Homage to Flanders," will not give up that home, even though "the deliberate mind / Has yielded itself wholly to another land." The poem ends:

> I knew it when I was seven after the war and years of slumber:
> The Flemish self awoke as we entered the Scheldt, and suddenly
> The tears rushed to my eyes, though all we could see
> Was a low land under a huge sky that I did not remember.
> (85)

The many poems arising from European scenes, however, are still tinged with the stranger's point of view. However difficult it has been for Sarton personally to make a region for herself, the poems arising from that struggle gain from her sense of loss. The distance between speaker and landscape often cannot be reduced, and this heightens the value of whatever does cross the gap.

Over and over, Chartres has been a source of such poetry, because it signifies so much that has been lost: "The mastery of passion by belief, / With all its aspiration held in balance" (90). The remaining themes developed in *The Lion and the Rose* reinforce the sense that these qualities have been lost.

In another poem about the feminine experience, "My Sisters, O My Sisters,"
she says again, as she did in "She Shall Be Called Woman," that contact
with the earth itself must be restored before peace and balance may be restored to human life. But in poems like "Navigator," she offers evidence that
many people have no wish to reestablish connection with the earth:

> This lazy prince of tennis balls and lutes,
> Marvelous redhead who could eat and have his cake,
> Collector of hot jazz, Japanese prints, rare books,
> The charming winner who takes all for the game's sake,
> Is now disciplined, changed, and wrung into a man.
> For war's sake, in six months, this can be done.
> (88)

But *The Lion and the Rose,* though it sometimes seems grim and despairing, is
never quite without hope, no matter what modern monstrousness is being
examined. The poems seek answers to the questions monstrousness can pose;
if the answers are not forthcoming, that does not mean they are not there.
But this kind of search can often send the poet back to the self, in hopes of
finding the strength that will simply lead to better poems. *The Leaves of the
Tree* makes a kind of sequel to *The Lion and the Rose,* in that the poems settle
for the time being into more confidence about peace. This brief section of
the book contains one of Sarton's best poems, "The Second Spring." It begins "At the bottom of the green field she lies"; the first stanza portrays the
absorption of someone into the lanscape: "Has she been there for days, perhaps for weeks?" The poem continues:

> At the bottom of the green field she lies,
> Without moving, moves. She becomes a stream.
> Clouds pass in and out of her open eyes
> And no one knows the content of this dream.
> She has become a source, mysterious flow
> That is forever rooted and forever passes,
> The ripple of silence, infinitely slow.
> She lies as if asleep down in the grasses.
>
> When will the diviner be sent for, to strike
> The hidden source with his wand, and there the wand

Leap out of his hands as the waters wake,
She wake from her dream, alive and stunned,
The heart shape transparent in her breast,
And listen to its voice, buried so deep
She does not hear, nor know how far from sleep,
How far this intense growth is from rest.

At the bottom of the green field she lies
Deep in the spring, lost in its mysteries.
(102)

At first, the person in the field seems to have achieved a union with nature not unlike that called for in the poems about woman and war. The delicate paradoxes bring to mind the "bush that burned and still was not consumed." But who exactly is she? What happens in this poem could be happening to a woman of almost any age; the trancelike absorption into the landscape is like a girl's unknowing pause before the spring into womanhood, or a middle-aged woman's withdrawal from routine before writing a poem. In either case the third stanza anticipates a profound awakening, physical and spiritual, which might come to any of us; it is Sarton's hope that no one will fail to recognize it when it comes.

"Deep in the spring, lost in its mysteries"—that is where Sarton most often finds solace in *The Land of Silence* (1953) and *In Time Like Air* (1958). Her restlessness has not left her, but it no longer bewilders, because it is countered by a desire for a place where real roots may be put down. Having thrived on rapid growth and constant change of scene, she now reacts to a growing knowledge of death and a growing feeling of homelessness, by circling in search of a place to settle. She chooses New Hampshire, whose land and people will be important to her poetry from this point on.

Before making this discovery, she had recognized the lack signified by all her traveling, in a sestina called "From All Our Journeys":

I too have known the inward disturbance of exile,
The great peril of being at home nowhere.
(124)

As the knowledge of rootlessness grows, so does the urge to find a place, "A rock-bed for the elastic quickened love." At last, the place suggests its nature, if not its location:

There are no formulas for this allegiance.
I've had to push on to the end of parting,
To emerge clumsily from inward exile,

Try to come home to a place beyond exile,
Where love, that airy tree, is separate nowhere,
Greening impartial over every parting.
(125)

As if the traditional "woven" word-order for the sestina were insufficiently
suggestive of circular repetition, Sarton departs from the usual pattern and
devises one that is even more static: 1 2 3 4 5 6, 6 1 2 3 4 5, 5 6 1 2 3 4, and
so on, the last word moving to the head of the line only to begin a slow
progress down the stanzas.

In order for every parting to become a kind of arrival, Sarton consciously
feeds the center of her being with the images of permanence that suggest home:

Because what I want most is permanence,
What I do best is bury fire now,
To bank the blaze within, and out of sense,
Where hidden fires and rivers burn and flow,
Create a world that is still and intense.
I come to you with only the straight gaze.
These are not hours of fire but years of praise,
The glass full to the brim, completely full,
But held in balance so no drop can spill.
(137)

The gliding rhythms of this passage are suggestive of peace, but that is not
quite what Sarton is after. Permanence here is not changelessness, but a kind
of steadiness, a "rock-bed" for the heart's intensities, which are essential to
the growth of the poet.

The quiet intensity defined in "Because What I Want Most Is Permanence" is central to "These Images Remain," a sequence of nine sonnets
based on a love affair. Most of the time Sarton is successful in the extremely
difficult struggle to make contemporary sonnets that do not demand immediate comparison with every one of their predecessors. This sequence, less
important than the later "Divorce of Lovers," still contains some of Sarton's

richest work. It begins by expressing a longing for a usual, commonplace sort
of love, as opposed to the excessive intensity of the passion the speaker feels,
which is so strong that it necessitates frequent separations. Time at last wears
down the relationship, and only the speaker's imagination is free to revel in
the images that remain:

> Where we stood once, once free to stand and stare,
> Imagination wanders like a god.
> These images exist. They have not changed,
> Though we are caught by time, by time estranged.
> (147)

The final sonnet describes an idyll of peaceful, wordless cohabitation so
profound that "time, the river, flows gently below, / Having no false eterni-
ties to prove." But the fierceness of the lovers' feelings has made such a scene
impossible in this life: "Here is our peace at last, and we not there" (147).

Sarton devotes much attention to the dualities inherent in such experiences as this. For her, love is often complicated by the desire to discover the
masculine and feminine tendencies in each participant in the relationship.
"Dialogue," which appears in In Time Like Air, is a Yeatsian exchange between a teacher of logic and a poet, who argue the merits of reason and passion, the logician saying "'You sound like a woman,'" and the poet replying
"'You're just a machine'" (161). At the poem's end the teacher of logic says
"with passion" that he will stick to his reason; the sudden admission that
each speaker partakes of both qualities suggests that both speakers may represent opposing parts of the same person.

Such conflicts and tensions have produced most of Sarton's best poetry.
Among her finest works is "A Divorce of Lovers," a twenty-sonnet sequence
that appears in Cloud, Stone, Sun, Vine (1961). It recounts the evolving
reactions of the speaker to the bitter conclusion of a long love affair; it begins
with recrimination and satirical argument against the separation, which has
been effected by the person addressed; it ends in a genuine and convincing
acceptance of self, solitude, and things as they are. The richness of the sequence springs largely from the high tensions produced by ambiguities and
paradoxes that lie somewhat below the surface of the narrative. First of all,
it is not possible to be certain about the respective genders of the speaker and
the person addressed. This uncertainty is not particularly noticeable, since

most readers will bring to the sequence a set of preconceptions that will prevent their having any questions about the matter. But the unobtrusive ambiguity suggests one of the sequence's major themes: that people are inseparable, that peace comes easiest to those who have no fear of remembering, until they die, a person who has wounded them in love. The speaker of this narrative even begins to partake of the absent lover's qualities: "Nor time, nor absence breaks this world in two. / You hold me in your heart, as I hold you." The basic contrast between the lovers is that the speaker appeals to irrational and passionate forces, while the absent lover tries ruthlessly to apply reason to their situation, controlling emotions by force of will.

The speaker refuses to cauterize prematurely a self-inflicted wound, and chooses instead a process of regeneration involving the image of the absent lover as a constituent of the speaker's new and growing self. This regenerative process free the speaker, at least temporarily, from any dependence on human love, and makes possible an exploration of larger mysteries:

Take loneliness, take pain, and take it all!
Like some strong swimmer on the icy airs,
I glide and can survive the heart's own pitfall.
I tell you, I grow rich on these despairs:
For you I gladly yielded up my world,
Who now among enormous skies am hurled.
(208)

In the final sonnet, the speaker makes this observation: "Against our will now we are forced to grow / And push out from all safety into song" (209). Here the word *we* is more inclusive than at any earlier point in the sequence. It refers to the expanded, multiplied spirit of the speaker, who sees that growth may be partly an accretion of disparate selves still held in the heart, though no longer actively loved. As the ending of "Der Abschied" puts it,

What stays? Perhaps some autumn tenderness,
A different strength that forbids youthful sighing.
Though frost has broken summer like a glass,
Know, as we hear the thudding apples fall,
Not ripeness but the suffering change is all.
(219)

III

The struggle that produced "A Divorce of Lovers" produced also the impulses toward new poetic directions, taken in *A Private Mythology* (1966) and *As Does New Hampshire* (1967). Returning to consistent use of free verse for the first time in several years, Sarton makes *A Private Mythology* a journal of physical and spiritual travel from the Orient back through Europe to New Hampshire—from willed, Zen-like peace to the actual peace of home.

If some of Sarton's earlier travel poems carried an undertone of desperation, as if any travel were the same thing as fleeing, the free-verse poems about Japan that open the volume are serenely interested. Their tone is a combination of nostalgia and curiosity, as if some part of the poet felt at home in Japan, while another recalled the home she made in New Hampshire. She learns, for example, the transitionless presentation of images that characterizes some Japanese poetry:

> A sampler of fields,
> Those leaning pagodas,
> The haystacks,
> A water wheel
> And the white feet of the women,
> Like rabbits.
> ("Japanese Prints," 231)

At Ryoan-ji, the stone garden provides a fresh image for the energy that works without being consumed:

> All things are suspended
> In shifting light and shades—
>
> All but the theme itself:
> Fifteen rocks and sand
>
> Weaving a silent fugue
> Down through the centuries,
>
> So changeless and changing
> It is never exhausted.
> ("The Stone Garden," 238–39)

Such observations lead Sarton toward a condition of knowledge and recognition of gods and irrational forces; as she crosses from Japan to India and
on to Greece, in time to spend her fiftieth birthday on the Acropolis, images
and voices gather in her to form the private mythology. "At Delphi" finds
her consulting the oracle almost despite herself:

Everyone stands here
And listens. Listens.
Everyone stands here alone.

I tell you the gods are still alive
And they are not consoling.
(259)

The second half of the book is given over primarily to poems about New
England, but even here the images and ideas from abroad provide a new
background for local events. "Learning About Water" and "An Artesian
Well" describe an unusually long summer drought and the drilling of a well
on Sarton's property; the noisy violence of the drilling, followed by the flow
of water, lifts Sarton out of herself so that she can be credible at the end of
"An Artesian Well" when she says "I felt like the earth" (275).

Her sense of having found roots deepens in "Second Thoughts on the
Abstract Gardens of Japan," for she finds in retrospect a barrenness in the
rationality of excessive control:

Having sent memory to scan
The famous garden, it came back
Troubled from a too-formalized Japan
To take a look

At quaint New England wilderness.
Rocky, and twisted by harsh wind,
Nearer to Hell than Heaven though it is,
It rests the mind.
(278–79)

The seven new poems from As Does New Hampshire recall this restful-
ness; by turns serene, playful, and uneasy, they make a loving coda to the

movements of *A Private Mythology*. But even here, Sarton has moments when she feels exiled, an outsider, unsafe.

> Perhaps someone will pass this house one day
> To drink, and be restored, and go his way,
> Someone in dark confusion as I was
> When I drank down cold water in a glass,
> Drank a transparent health to keep me sane,
> After the bitter mood had gone again.
> ("A Glass of Water," 307)

A Grain of Mustard Seed (1971) marks another shift in theme and tone; much of it deals with the world's violence and with the hope that some force, perhaps religious, can help mankind toward peace. Sometimes marred by self-consciousness, this book is nevertheless an important step in Sarton's career, for it is the first time since *The Lion and the Rose* that she has devoted much energy to "public" themes. The most ambitious of the meditations on violence is "The Invocation to Kali," a five-part poem addressed to that goddess described in the epigraph from Joseph Campbell as "the terrible one of many names, 'difficult of approach,' whose stomach is a void and so can never be filled, and whose womb is giving birth forever to all things." Sarton describes the modern incarnation of this force:

> What Hell have we made of the subtle weaving
> Of nerve with brain, that all centers tear?
> We live in a dark complex of rage and grieving.
> The machine grates, grates, whatever we are.
> (316)

Then, following a sestina that recalls the horror of the concentration camps, the poem moves to the conclusion that violence must be confronted, almost embraced, because before it is seen as an indispensable part of the cycle of creation, it cannot be brought under control.

Near the end of the book, "Once More At Chartres" makes a similar suggestion by means of a delicate contrast:

> Chartres, you are here who never will not be,
> Ever becoming what you always are.

So, lifted by our human eyes, each hour,
The arch is breathed alive into its power,
Still being builded for us who still see
Hands lifting stone into the perilous air.
(349)

The last part of this book is the section devoted to *A Durable Fire* (1972).
It opens and closes with poems of psychological import— "Gestalt at Sixty"
and "Letters to a Psychiatrist." In these, Sarton examines with almost prosaic
directness her motives for living alone, the forces that lead her toward impossible loves, and the impulse to write. If these two poems are somewhat
too flatly direct, they still provide a necessary framework for the more elegantly finished poems in the collection; they illuminate in particular "The
Autumn Sonnets," the third and most hopeful of Sarton's sonnet sequences
about the changes wrought by love and solitude. "Who wakes in a house
alone / Wakes to inertia sometimes," she says in "Gestalt at Sixty" (361),
and in the seventh sonnet she amplifies this by showing how the demands of
solitude can shrink one's world dangerously:

I came here first for haven from despair
And found a deeper root than passionate love,
A wilder inscape and a safer lair
Where the intrinsic being kept alive.
Home is a granite rock and two sparse trees
As light and shadow may inhabit these.
(387)

From the public concerns of "The Invocation to Kali" to the intense
privacy of *A Durable Fire* is a dramatic shift, unless it is seen in the broader
pattern of Sarton's career; seen that way, it becomes clear that such shifts are
part of a cycle, and that Sarton will soon strike out in some other difficult
direction. Her craftsmanship has become so confident that it is hard to imagine a productive psychic danger that she would consciously avoid.

JOHN HALL WHEELOCK Letting the Darkness In

I

The career of John Hall Wheelock abounds with contradictions; the tensions between his prose criticism and his poetry, his employment as an editor and his life's work as a poet, his romantic temperament and this ironic age, at the same time produced in his poetry its most persistent weaknesses and its most permanent strengths. The year of his birth, 1886, falls between those of Pound and Eliot, and he graduated from Harvard only two years ahead of Eliot's remarkable class; yet his work was never characterized by modernism. His style continues to seem dated at times, and his approach to broad abstractions is most unmodernistically direct and free of irony. On the other hand, as editor of Scribner's *Poets of Today* series, he selected and introduced the first book-length collections of such poets as James Dickey, George Garrett, Louis Simpson, David Slavitt, and May Swenson, and his introductions to those volumes demonstrate his clear understanding of what those poets were doing.

In 1963, however, Wheelock published *What is Poetry?*, a collection of essays that included revised and less specific versions of his introductions; in these, where he is writing about poetry in general, he gives us a closer look at some of the almost anti-modernist attitudes that have shaped his poetry:

A charge less often, and more justly, brought than that of obscurity will be the complaint that the contemporary poem is cerebral, accomplished, erudite, and empty of feeling. . . . Emotion is not permitted to get through except in disguise, wit being the mask most favored for this purpose. Our age, like the Augustan age of Queen Anne, is ashamed and afraid of emotion. A poet is praised for being "tough"—"a tough thinker," "a tough-minded lyricist"—though just what he's supposed to be so tough about it's hard to determine.[1]

Merely from the tone of this passage, the reader skilled in wit and irony will deduce that Wheelock's poems will be too romantic and old-fashioned; and, for a prolific period longer than many poets' working lifetimes, they were. Between 1905 and 1936 he published eight books, only the first of which was proverbially slim; this immense body of work contains fewer than a dozen of the poems responsible for his present reputation, which was earned by the work he did after *Poems 1911–1936*. During the twenty years between that book and the first of the six books he published later, he seems to have honed the instrument that makes his later work capable of speaking gravely and gracefully of what Faulkner called "the old verities and truths of the heart." It is worth remarking, in a spirit of gratitude, that a poet could survive so many years and so many mediocre poems, and come to write, in his seventies and eighties, work that constitutes one of the notable achievements in our literature.

II

By Daylight and In Dream (1970) includes poems from all of Wheelock's earlier books, as well as twelve new poems completed after the publication of *Dear Men and Women* (1966); the collection provides some answers to questions arising from the contradictions I have mentioned.

Though most of the poems published before 1936 suffer from nineteenth-century stylistic influences and from a failure to focus on the unique aspects of an experience, there are hints in them of the voice Wheelock mastered in his later years. Some of these qualities are evident in "Lancelot to Guinevere," which was first collected in *The Belovèd Adventure* (1912):

1. John Hall Wheelock, *What Is Poetry?* (New York, 1963), 25–26.

Now all the east is tired of the twilight,
And the world's borders blossom like a rose,
And the world's tapers tremble and grow dim;
Under the cloud-line, under the gray twilight,
Under the pale, cold arch of heaven's rim,
The low, white fire of the morning glows,

And a clear wind is wandering in the meadows—
O queenly heart, never again, again,
Shall this thing be, or this sweet wonder be!
I take my way through the unending meadows,
Through the long fields beside the sunless sea
I take my way, I pass from your domain.

The spirit's fire, more fiery than the morning,
The inner flame, followed through night and day,
Burns to a purer light the old blind love;
Under the infinite arches of the morning
I move with a new gladness—high above,
The last stars fade, and I am far away.

I have found one thing more fair than the old heaven,
More sweet than all sad things to think upon—
Yes, and more sweet than your two folded hands.
Sleep, and forget; the opening gates of heaven
Flood with a sudden pain the empty lands,
And the old wonder wakes—but I am gone.[2]

The romantic excesses of language and imagery that mar this poem are evident and plentiful enough; but even where the words are uninteresting, the artfully varied meter contributes to the effectiveness of the poem's movement. The third line of the final stanza, for instance, is not very interesting in itself; but in the context of the whole stanza, it makes a humanizing descent from "the old heaven" to more earthly and private matters. The progress from the middle to the end of the stanza is similar, though in the last line it is right verbal texture, rather than imagery, that closes the movement.

2. John Hall Wheelock, By Daylight and In Dream (New York, 1970), 47–48. Hereafter cited by page number in the text.

None of this does much to rescue the poem, for if the poem's movement is more arresting than its language or imagery, it is still too easily predictable. But whereas a poem like Kilmer's "Trees" is almost mathematically predictable, the movement of this poem, because of the metrical variations, is foreseen more in the way one perceives an intricate physical action, like a school figure on ice skates: the continued flow of the movement arouses suspense, so that its graceful conclusion gives pleasure.

This ability to enliven the texture even of mediocre language seems to have marked Wheelock's poetry from the beginning, and may have helped blind him to his language's ineffectiveness, so that it was not until the middle 1930s that he began to simplify and strengthen his diction, as in "Silence," first collected in *Poems 1911–1936*:

There is a mystery too deep for words;
The silence of the dead comes nearer to it,
Being wisest in the end. What word shall hold
The sorrow sitting at the heart of things,
The majesty and patience of the truth!
Silence will serve; it is an older tongue:
The empty room, the moonlight on the wall,
Speak for the unreturning traveller.
(148)

Later on, in *The Gardener* (1961), Wheelock's language becomes supple enough to accommodate two voices, as in "Mr. X (——— State Hospital)":

He dreamt he was sleeping, he said, and when he awoke
Found he still was. Then he got all excited,
And had to tell it again—how, for a moment,
He could remember the future, and everything
Turned sad, like music: the timid sound mice
Made on the attic floor, moonlight,
The smile upon her borrowed face.
(226)

These poems show more confidence than is evident in the earlier work, and they even exemplify the toughness Wheelock derided: these poems stand up to greater forces than those that often collapsed the earlier ones.

The poems in this book, then, seem to have been chosen not only on the basis of quality, but also in order to give a clear picture of the poet's development, to compose a kind of poetic autobiography. (It should be noted, however, that from any given period, Wheelock has chosen his best: of the nearly 260 poems in *Poems 1911–1936*, which was itself a selection, he has retained here only 91.) In recording the whole career, *By Daylight and In Dream* also records what Winfield Townley Scott, writing of *The Gardener*, called a rare triumph: "John Hall Wheelock has published his best book of poems. As a practitioner in the field, I cannot think of any success so enviable and, as a common reader, of any that should make his readers feel quite so warm and happy. For of course the triumphs of such older poets are rare [Wheelock published *The Gardener* on his seventy-fifth birthday]. But they happen . . . and make younger poetry, no matter how ecstatic or brilliant or beautiful, certainly seem less."[3]

III

The eight sections of *By Daylight and In Dream* are arranged chronologically except for the first section, which contains the twelve new poems, and the sixth, "Scherzo," a group of lighter poems selected from the whole body of work. Before 1936, Wheelock's poems, besides being vague and derivative in language, were somewhat limited by the single-mindedness with which they made direct attacks on broad abstractions. In section II, for example, most of the poems are repetitive struggles with the mysteries of love unattained; but the young poet rendered his situation in vague terms, and so was unable to lift his poem out of the ordinary. In the third section, he emerges from himself and broadens his scope to include observations of the world about him; and in the fourth, lost love and the daily world conspire to produce poems of dejection, such as "In the Dark City," first collected in *The Black Panther:*

There is a harper plays
Through the long watches of the lonely night

3. Winfield Townley Scott, "A Late Flowering" (review of *The Gardener and Other Poems*), *New York Times Book Review*, October 22, 1961, p. 38.

When, like a cemetery,
Sleeps the dark city, with her millions lying each in his tomb.
I feel it in my dream, but when I wake—
Suddenly, like some secret thing not to be overheard,
It ceases,
And the gray night grows dumb. Only in memory
Linger those veiled adagios, fading, fading . . .
Till, with the morning, they are lost.

What door was opened then?
What worlds, undreamed of, lie around us in our sleep,
That yet we may not know?
Where is it one sat playing,
Over and over, with such high and dreadful peace,
The passion and sorrow of the eternal doom?
(98–99)

Wheelock asks old questions that poets have always asked, because the answers are elusive; but here the statement is too direct, and leaves no room for the reverberations of the mystery. However, the persistence of these questions, and a continuing failure to confront them profitably, at last led Wheelock to cast a wider net, in long meditative poems that increased in flexibility and power as he grew older. Most often, these poems begin with dreams, or with associations aroused by the house Wheelock's father built in East Hampton, Long Island, where the poet spent some part of every summer for more than eighty years. The technique of these meditations is foreshadowed in "The Divine Fantasy," which was first collected in *The Black Panther* (1922) and then, revised, in *Dear Men and Women* (1966); in the present collection, it appears in section IV, in still further revised form:

                    the hunted mouse
Timidly hurries through the lane, his eye
Turned up in terror as the owl goes by:
On softest feathers of silence overhead
Flits the dim shadow of the ancient dread,
Hooded and huge, the cruelty of his beak
Bent on old lustful mysteries. A squeak!
A scuffle! Beating of wings—and in the lane,

Silence! and the old wrong is done again,
That was before Adam—the triumphant heart
And the defeated, each one doomed to his part,
They play it through, the old tragedy, where one
Presence still wars and is warred upon,
Slays and is slain . . .
                                  on dark shores
Beats the insistent passion, that implores
The one dear breast of pity or disdain,
To be reborn, to be reborn again . . .
                                  Forever flows
The dreadful drama to its stately close
And endless ending, the fierce carnival
Of death and passion, wherein each and all
Mix, and are mingled, slaughter, blend, and pass
Each into other—the high poem that has
No end and no beginning, which the one
Self in all living forms beneath the sun,
And on all worlds around it and above,
Weaves with the strands of hunger, death, and love.
(111–12)

The whole poem exhibits the controlled movement of these passages, though the language is still marred by the accustomed difficulties; and the development of the theme is hampered by what Helene Mullins, reviewing *The Bright Doom*, called "a too-overwhelming desire to compress the whole of the universe into one poem. This is something that he tries again and again to accomplish, until one can imagine his becoming, at last, impatient of the limitations of words and utterly silenced by the unreasonableness of his own ambition."[4]

Something of this sort may have happened, for after *Poems 1911–1936* it was twenty years before another of Wheelock's books appeared. During this period, however, Wheelock was far from inactive; he had become an editor at Scribner's in 1926, and from 1932 until his retirement in 1957 his responsibilities were considerable—treasurer, secretary, director, senior editor—

4. Helene Mullins, Review of *The Bright Doom*, in New York *World*, December 11, 1927, Sec. M, p. 11. Quoted in *Book Review Digest* (New York, 1928), 800.

and, in 1940, he at last married the woman to whom many of his earliest love-lyrics had been addressed.

A study of this period in Wheelock's life could doubtless demonstrate that the editor's increasing involvement with contemporary literature helped the poet to shed some of his stylistic mannerisms; Wheelock was closely involved with such authors as Thomas Wolfe and Scott Fitzgerald, as well as with nearly every poet Scribner's published. In any case, the rhythmic control of "The Divine Fantasy" was sharpened during the relatively silent years; and in his later years, Wheelock made the long meditation his most versatile mode of writing. In it, he could venture on time-worn themes, in language that has previously had its uses, and could still bring renewed faith and understanding to himself and to his readers.

IV

"Scherzo," the section of this book that contains the lighter poems, precedes the two sections made up of recent work, and so serves as a kind of intermission, emphasizing the reduction of activity between 1936 and 1956. The humor of most of these poems is understated and polite, seldom resorting to the kind of verbal jollity normally associated with light verse.

Affection tempers satire without dulling it in most of these poems, of which the most interesting is a recent "frolic—with apologies to Wallace Stevens." In a little over a hundred lines, "The Plumber as the Missing Letter" combines a parody of Stevens with a humorous poem on the hopelessness of getting a plumber to do anything. Having summoned the plumber and his assistant, only to have them inspect the premises and depart for more tools, the householder, while awaiting the return of "the fictive pair," falls asleep over a volume by Wallace Stevens:

> Of what swank paradiso shall he dream,
> Land of swart dames seductive, the cohesive
> Feminine, woman the universal glue;
> Land of chubbed grapes and peaches, land of prime
> Poets, de jure some, some few de facto—
> Shall not the pumpkins on the pensive boughs
> Hang heavier there than here, the birds employ

A brisker breast-stroke, be more nude than here;
More pleasing to the sense, nimbler than here,
The sea's blue thunder, the curved smell of the sea?
(181–82)

Some things here are intrinsically attractive, and found their way into Wheelock's serious work, as in this passage from "Anima," first collected in *The Gardener* (1961):

> The silence there
> Had a certain thing to say could not be said
> By harp or oboe, flute or violoncello
> Or by the lesser strings; it could not be said
> By the human voice; but in sea-sounds you heard it
> Perhaps, or in the water-dripping jargon
> Of summer birds: endless reiteration
> Of chat or vireo, the woodcock's call,
> Chirrup and squeegee, larrup, squirt and trill
> Of liquid syrinxes—bright drops of song
> Spangling the silence.
> (217)

The energy and metrical variety of this passage convey, more clearly than could any direct statement in the earlier poems, Wheelock's love of the universe. His eye, despite the ingenious lists, is more narrowly focused on its primary object, and he is able to imply a great deal more than he states. One source of this confidence and renewed responsibility is advancing age; and with that came a focal point for some of Wheelock's finest poems; he returns again and again to his father's house in Bonac, which, with its lifelong associations, becomes a point of departure for meditations of depth and powerful serenity.

If age often brings the desire to recapture the past, it also brings, in Wheelock's case, an ability to capture what eluded the younger poet: patience, and a steady eye on the words themselves, as well as what they stand for. These qualities were widely recognized in *The Gardener* (1961), which was co-winner of the Bollingen Prize in Poetry, and which exhibits what Allen Tate later called "that 'middle style' which circumvents fashion and never is out of fashion." And here, too, fresh tensions arise from what is less

directly stated; music, movement, and statement combine to transcend the
nominal subject of the poem, as in the last stanzas of the title poem, addressed to the poet's father:

> The truth is on me now that was with you:
> How life is sweet, even its very pain,
> The years how fleeting and the days how few.
>
> Truly, your labors have not been in vain;
> These woods, these walks, these gardens—everywhere
> I look, the glories of your love remain.
>
> Therefore, for you, now beyond praise or prayer,
> Before the night falls that shall make us one,
> In which neither of us will know or care,
>
> This kiss, father, from him who was your son.
> (212)

The central tension here is not merely that between youth and age, or
past and present; it arises gradually from the speaker's realization that he
would not recapture his youth even if he could. He comes first to accept the
unifying process that ends in death, and then to celebrate it.

If *The Gardener* was the work of a man who had found his true voice in
age, *Dear Men and Women* (1966) was the work of a man to whom age had
given a new way of treating an old theme. The lost love of the youthful lyrics
has been regained, and informs several remarkable poems, notably "Eight
Sonnets," a sequence in which Wheelock not only redeems what a young
poet might find an unpromising subject—serene love and happiness between
two aged people—but in which he also unifies the various sources of his
feeling—love, the old house, and the perpetual sound of the sea:

> Great trees encircle her; her praise shall be
> The thrush's song; the sea-wind for delight
> Buffets her cheek while, massive in its might,
> Around these island solitudes the sea,
> Chanting, like voices from eternity,
> Will shake the shore with thunders, day and night.
> ("A Garden and a Face," 261–62)

These poems pulsate with a kind of knowledge rare in love poetry: we cannot quite respond with the shock of recognition, but must instead take it on faith that such deep, abiding love is like this; but our faith is strengthened by the conviction of the poems:

Outside, the darkness deepens, and I guess
What darker things the years may hold in store—
Watching your face, even lovelier than before
Age had given it this grave tenderness
Love stretches hands toward, that would shield and bless
A face, once young, in age loved all the more.
("Slow Summer Twilight," 263)

And in "The Sea's Voice," the expanded vision of age results in an inclusive emotion which had seemed forced in the earlier poems, but which is natural and convincing here:

Our talk has been all banter, to-and-fro
Of raillery, the bland mischief of your smile
Still leads me on, with nonsense we beguile
An empty hour: we speak of So-and-So,
Of Eliot and Michelangelo,
And of James Jones, his high, pedantic style,
And touch, by chance, after a little while,
Upon some sadness suffered years ago.

Now your eyes darken, turning serious,
As thoughts of the long past, by memory stirred,
Waken—life's venture, tragic and absurd,
How strange it is, how brief, how hazardous.
Far-off, the sea's voice says it all for us,
Saying one thing forever, barely heard.
(263)

Beside the main threads—love and the place where it has deepened—which are the basis of this sequence, there are interwoven other strands of thought that develop and subside almost imperceptibly. The sound of the sea, knowledge of mortality, and, finally, celebration of all these, enable

Wheelock to confront the universe, in the final sonnet, with this statement of earned belief:

> The old inexorable mysteries
> Transcend our sorrow; no mere discord jars
> That music, which no lesser music mars—
> It was enough to have made peace with these:
> To have kept high hearts among the galaxies,
> Love's faith amid this wilderness of stars.
> ("In This Green Nook," 265)

The earlier poems of resignation and acceptance suffered from a lack of irony, and seemed too abject; but here, irony is not needed, for the tone of resignation is strengthened by the tone of celebration, which in turn lends force to the aging poet's speculations on death. In "The Part Called Age," an extended reverie on the past, and on the sudden realization that age has come, Wheelock recalls part of an earlier poem, "House in Bonac," and turns from recollection toward the future:

> The house he had once compared to "a great ship foundered
> At the bottom of green sea-water" now seemed to him,
> As it lay there lonely in the sad evening light,
> More like a ship on some vast voyage bound
> Into the unknown seas of space and time. . . .
>   Far over, a waking star
> Glimmered in the west of heaven. He opened the door,
> And entered the house, the ship, where so many others
> Had embarked as passengers, where one passenger now,
> The dearest of all, awaited him. Quietly
> He turned the key in the lock, and gave the good ship
> To night and darkness and the oncoming stars.
> (284–85)

So Wheelock ends where he began—with love—but with this major difference: in its private fulfillment, his love has broadened, and encompasses more than the woman addressed in "Eight Sonnets"; she animates the house in Bonac, which Wheelock called "cradle and grave" of his poems, and from that house, with its myriad associations, the poet's love extends toward everything. Even fear and dejection, which once seemed too actively courted, are given their rightful place in his poetic universe; the aging spirit does what it can by taking everything as it comes.

This inclusiveness marks the new poems that open *By Daylight and In Dream;* the title poem, for example, is one of Wheelock's longest and most ambitious poems, and it is one of the most successful. It is in three parts; the first, "Monday," is a meditation arising from the speaker's view through his window of his "loved, familiar country," and is chiefly concerned with the knowledge of impending death. The idea is approached indirectly at first, in almost surrealistic images of the union between the man and his world:

birds

Fly in and out of his eyes . . .
              blue sea-odors inhabit him,
Waves crash in his head.
(3)

When direct confrontation comes, the speaker finds his terrors and desires inexpressible, and drifts into a tentative resignation to an old idea:

We must yield place to those who will come after,
As those before us yielded. Confusedly
He hears, deep in himself, yet far away,
Oceanic voices.
(5)

"Tuesday," the long second section, begins in the early evening; the old man stands at a west window, seeing his father's eye in a blue patch of the sunset, and he remembers an old debate between father and son, involving questions of conscious and unconscious forces in the universe; the young man argues for the former. But as the memory fades, the speaker accepts the latter view; almost consoled, he turns toward his bed:

Why, the whole earth

Is holy ground, hallowed by love and pain—
The graveyard of the self-effacing dead,
Crowded with sacrificial absences!
(9)

As he prepares for sleep, he almost finds contentment in the idea of oblivion:

> Opening the window,
> The cry of a whip-poor-will out of the darkness
> Seems to him now the sound of his own voice crying
> Back to him out of the darkness. For a few moments,
> He stands there, listening. He turns off the light,
> Letting the darkness in.
> (9)

In the final section, "Tuesday Night: His Dream," the exploration of these contradictory attitudes is strongly concluded, though not resolved. The old man dreams of sleeping under a tree, listening to three voices: a mysterious child, the sea, and a thrush. The child assures him that birth and death are part of a cycle that will return all lost things to him; the sea urges him to give over to the past, which is oblivion; and the thrush speaks of a youthful future. Near the close of the poem, the old man dreams he is ensnared in the tree's roots, and he cries out for help:

> And the tree,
> That is more silent than is the grave, for answer
> Rains down upon him all her bounty of bloom,
> Her springtime burden, her glory of teeming blossoms;
> And he looks up, startled, sensing in sudden joy,
> 'I am no longer afraid'; and the tree releases him . . .
>   and he wakes from dream,
> To hear, far off, the sea's lamentation
> Along these desolate coasts of night and day;
> And still the thrush sings on.
> (11–12)

It is a commonplace that to approach broad abstractions directly is rarely successful in poetry; as Wheelock himself said, during a television interview, "You have to sort of pretend you aren't really trying to do it; sort of walking around it, thinking of something else; because if you go at it too quickly and too hard, it gets away from you." Youthful impatience kept Wheelock from working this way for many years; but the old ideas in "By Daylight and In

Dream" live again because they have been allowed, rather than forced, to live: they have been carried by the music and the characterization, to which most of Wheelock's energy was devoted.

V

Shortly before his death in March of 1978, Wheelock completed work on two short collections that, taken together, might serve as prolegomena to a future selection of his best poetry. *Afternoon: Amagansett Beach* is a limited edition, produced with elegance by The Eakins Press Foundation and the Dandelion Press. It contains twenty poems selected from fifty years of work; but all the poems are chosen for their basis in Bonac. Because of this some-what narrowed focus, the book is a collector's item for those interested in the literature of a place, as well as for those interested in Wheelock's poetry. But because all the poems in this beautiful volume have appeared before, and all but one—"Solitudes"—are available in *By Daylight and In Dream*, a wider audience may find it somewhat less interesting than *This Blessèd Earth: New and Selected Poems, 1927–1977* (1978). To a very slender selection from more than fifty-five years of work, this, the last collection assembled by the poet himself, adds thirteen new poems, including what may be the finest short poem of his career.

For some reason, the subtitle of this book is not quite accurate; of the fourteen poems selected from earlier volumes, two are taken from *The Black Panther*, which appeared in 1922. This small matter may perhaps be blamed on an impulse—the publisher's or the poet's—to favor the good roundness of fifty years. It is astonishing that as late as 1978, we had in Wheelock a living poet of consequence whose career had begun with the century.

This Blessèd Earth, like many of Wheelock's previous books, is somewhat uneven. Of the fourteen selected poems, only six are undoubtedly as good as any he could have chosen; the other eight are probably among the hundred best, but they are not among the fourteen best. For the poet himself, the problems of selection must have been difficult, because he had somehow to walk a line between inclination toward old favorites of a sort he had not lately written, and acceptance of the remarkable fact that most of his best work was done in his seventies and eighties. These difficulties are of course less apparent in *Afternoon: Amagansett Beach*, since attachment to locality seems sometimes to have been a stronger criterion than excellence; however, most of Wheelock's best poems arise from Bonac, so that principle of selection is bound to have some good results.

In the new poems in *This Blessèd Earth,* awareness of impending death is a recurring theme. Though it occurs most often in poems that continue to be celebrations of life, there are moments, as at the end of "Address to Existence," when the idea of death is welcome, as if the speaker were ready at last for rest. And sometimes annihilation is presented factually, without overtones of revulsion or desire; "Intimations of Mortality" is such a poem, though its paradoxical conception gives it a complexity that the diction belies. The "intimation" is the sound of absence, which one hears all one's life, and which will grow "so faint it overwhelms everything." [5]

"Address to Existence" and "Intimations of Mortality" are both in free verse, which Wheelock used from time to time throughout his career. But these two poems share a minor technical feature unique in Wheelock's work: the heads of lines are capitalized only when prose usage calls for capitals. This practice is increasingly common among younger poets, but Wheelock had stayed with the old-fashioned use of initial capitals until he came to the last few poems of his life. The effect, in the context of this book, is to give the poem an air of freedom from artifice, as well as a sense of speed. These effects, of course, would be negligible if Wheelock had long been consistent in this respect; but since he had always been consistent in the opposite mode, and since he mixes his modes in this section of *This Blessèd Earth,* he subtly draws attention to what he is doing.

Though there are here, as in most of Wheelock's books, a few poems that are below the standard for which he deserves to be remembered, there is cause for poignant joy in the recognition that *This Blessèd Earth* contains what may be Wheelock's best short poem. It cannot be compared with his long meditations, but in seventeen lines of blank verse, "Melancholia" evokes a state of mind with particularity and memorable power. As a tribute to a long career, and in celebration of a life's work deepening toward its close, I want to give John Hall Wheelock the last word:

There is a place that yet is not a place,
And you have been there. In an empty room,

5. John Hall Wheelock, *This Blessèd Earth: New and Selected Poems, 1927–1977* (New York, 1978), 22. Hereafter cited in the text as *NSP,* followed by a page number.

Walled high and windowless, twin urns of light,
Under the ceiling, cast a somber glow,
And always, somewhere, a lone flute is warbling
Its desultory music. Also always,
From the high shelf along the western wall,
Those effigies look out, of carven stone
Or molded plaster, blessèd artifacts,
Exempt from breathing's harried to-and-fro,
The hounded heart's compulsive laboring—
In bloodless ease at rest, calm, sad, secure,
They wait upon the future, and the eerie
Enchantment of the music lends them there
A strange nobility, a mimic peace,
Such peace as comes after forgotten sorrow,
Dread peace, that follows unremembered joy.
(*NSP*, 20)

DAVID R. SLAVITT The Fun of the End of the World

It has been twenty-five years since David R. Slavitt invented Henry Sutton and embarked on a series of schlock novels under that pseudonym, but it is still fun to recall people's outrage when they learned that *The Exhibitionist* was the work of someone who had also written more serious fiction, and even poetry. On one hand, people of Jacqueline Susann's ilk were irritated because someone had done easily and laughingly what they worked hard to do; on the other hand, purveyors of solemn literature were offended at the success of this prostitution of talent. Even Tom Wolfe, who had no reason to feel either envious or superior, took a cheap shot at Slavitt's next serious novel, saying in a review that it was not as good as *The Exhibitionist.*

Meanwhile, having found a way to excuse himself from grantsmanship and literary politics, Slavitt kept on working. By 1975, when he published *Vital Signs: New and Selected Poems,* he had behind him sixteen books: four Sutton novels, six Slavitt novels, and six books of poems. *Vital Signs* established Slavitt as one of the most interesting poets in the country.

From the beginning, Slavitt's poetry has been characterized by profound wit, neoclassical attention to form, and generous erudition. Slavitt is also a master of tonal variety; within the same poem he can make shifts of tone that most poets would find too risky. Up through *Vital Signs,* which added eighty-five new poems to the selection from his previous volumes, Slavitt's poetry was fairly consistent: often cast in forms of sufficient difficulty that the poems were a celebration of the art itself, they meditated with a calm, almost cynical tone on the repetitions of history, the touching folly of people's relationships with one another and with the objects they are doomed to accumulate, and, more recently, on the pain of diminishing love.

A poem short enough to quote, and still substantial enough to represent the interested and interesting voice, is "Swoboda," which takes its epigraph from a set of program notes to *La Traviata*: "Wilhelm Kuhe 'remembers that as a boy in Prague he met Wenzel Swoboda, a double bass player, who had been a member of the orchestra on the first night of *Don Giovanni* in 1787, conducted by Mozart himself.'"

> Kuhe reports that Swoboda remembers . . .
> but what could he remember? I have been
> serif to the ELI's L, have marched,
> strapped to the big, blue bulldog's thoompa-thoom,
> and have heard the fweedle of the clarinets
> dribbling down my ears. The trumpet's tune
> was yards away, fluttering the flags
> at the end of the bowl. We marched down the field
> as letters we could not read, were ourselves the words.
> And Swoboda heard nothing, and saw nothing,
> remembered nothing but that his bow had moved
> with a baton as twigs of the same tree
> moving in a wind. What was there to tell
> but his double bass's zormm-zormm-zormm?[1]

Here, as in many of Slavitt's poems, there is an insistence not only on sharp observation, but also on the limits to the knowledge we may gain by it.

"Precautions" begins with an amusing account of having readied a boat for a hurricane, all the while looking forward to what would happen to the boats left unprepared; but the storm does not come. The poem concludes:

---

1. David R. Slavitt, *Vital Signs: New and Selected Poems* (New York, 1975), 284. Hereafter cited in the text as *VS*, followed by a page number. This book contains selections from Slavitt's first four collections: *Suits for the Dead* (1961), *The Carnivore* (1965), *Day Sailing* (1969), and *Child's Play* (1972).

Take Noah, with the ark all built, the hold
an incredible zoo, waiting, waiting for rain
which is predicted but never quite appears
and instead follows a low pressure trough, or a cold
front to the Persian Gulf. Or take Lot,
packing, quitting the cities of the plain
to which nothing at all happens. The careers
of these men are dreadful—rage at the world for not
ending at noon for its wickedness as it should.
The wicked are comforted. It corrupts the good.

There's no sense to it. I remember a tree,
a dead pine that a gust of wind blew over
and the way it hit, just a few feet away
from my children. It was out of sight of the sea
but it was the same wind, the same whim
of the wind, and we could feel the earth quiver
as if it were water. The children stopped their play
a moment, then balanced, danced upon the grim
dead threat, delighted. Lord, let me
keep that balance, that equanimity.
                    (VS, 158)

Slavitt keeps that balance, that equanimity, as his intelligence and imagination lead him gracefully through difficult transitions. Part of his success lies in his ability to deal with formal restrictions that are too much for most poets; though his stanza forms are often intricate, they never prevent, or even impede, the explorations of a mind that takes suggestions as they come, weaving them into the pattern.

Slavitt's most ambitious earlier poems are perhaps "Elegy for Walter Stone," from *The Carnivore* (1965), and "Another Letter to Lord Byron" and "Exhortation to an Arab Friend (1965)," from *Day Sailing* (1969). All three are extended, risky, shifty in tone, and finally quite moving, with the feel of performance. The background for "Elegy for Walter Stone" is given in a headnote: "In August of 1959, I interviewed John Hall Wheelock at his home in Easthampton, N.Y., on the occasion of the publication of *Poets of Today* VI, which Mr. Wheelock edited and which included the poetry of Messrs. Gene Baro, Donald Finkel, and Walter Stone" (VS, 185). By the time of the book's publication, Stone had committed suicide. The first section of the poem sets the scene, sketches in a few facts, and establishes Finkel as a living foil to the dead Stone; Slavitt's Finkel transcends the actual Donald Finkel to become, by contrast, all that Stone rejected. The second section speculates on the manner of Stone's death—hanging—and on his motives and final destination. The final section moves between the conversation with Wheelock and statements about death:

> All death is nature's,
> whether by germ in the blood or idea in the head,
> or sudden mischance in the wasteful order of things.
> Gaze fixedly at it, and the distinctions
> disappear.
> (VS, 189)

In 1967, Slavitt and I read with George Garrett at Washington University in St. Louis. As we approached the building in which we would make our first appearance, our student host turned and said, "Mr. Slavitt, there is someone here who looks forward to meeting you." "Oh? Who's that?" "Donald Finkel." There was a moment of real apprehensiveness; but during that afternoon gathering, Slavitt read "Elegy for Walter Stone," and Finkel said, loud enough for the group to hear, "That's why I forgive you."

It is Slavitt's custom to gaze fixedly at things, notions, and ideas, until he can summon precise ways of stating their essence, or the essence of his reaction to them. Even when the formal gamesmanship is of a very complicated sort, as it is in "Another Letter to Lord Byron," there is wisdom in the spectacularly rhymed stanzas. The first word of the title reminds us that Auden addressed a letter from Iceland to Lord Byron; but Slavitt mentions Auden only in order to establish his own place in what might become a tradition. The poem's actual subject is contemporary literature's low seriousness, and the vacuum that Byron's "hock and soda water" might fill. After a gloomy vision of dead authors as "volumes of blank pages, buckram bound," the poem focuses on Byron's liveliness:

> You come through whole, and live, and are not merely
>   a name on the spine of your book and its index card.
> The gestures you make in your poems, the jokes, are clearly
>   those of a man who's trying very hard

—and willing to pay the price, even pay dearly—
  not only not to be boring, but not to be bored
himself. Yourself. Myself. I know how it is.
It's always tough in the Quality Lit. Biz.
(VS, 315)

"Exhortation to an Arab Friend (1965)" seems to draw on all the peculiar resources Slavitt has demonstrated—passion and skill, to begin with,
but, more pertinent to this poem perhaps, an interest in history, and in the
music strange words and names can make. The message of the exhortation is
simple—let there be peace between us. The poem recounts the ancient history of the conflict, concentrating on those things that both tribes have in
common; it ends,

There is faith enough to finish us both. We have swarmed
the earth, have died like flies. Exiles or rulers,
it makes no difference. But coming back here, now,
after all those years, should Ishmael and Isaac
repeat, complete, what Cain and Abel started?
(VS, 184)

A somber quality in Slavitt's earlier work is tempered, in Day Sailing, by
the joy that is more recently in evidence; Slavitt's is a truly affirmative spirit,
rendering things as he sees them, clearly and compassionately, and in a spirit
of hope without which no one could make poems such as these.

The new poems in Vital Signs are arranged in three sections; the first,
"Vital Signs," contains a number of poems having to do with the ecstasies
and disappointments of love and marriage. However painful some episodes
might be, the poems, like the lovers in "A Parting," are "correct, restrained."
The poems are the more affecting for their restraint, their refusal to specify
their autobiographical origins, whatever those may be. "A Parting" is concerned with the healing of those deep wounds that we try to keep open, out
of a sense of obligation to the episodes that dealt them:

Tenderness turns to tough
scar tissue. We lose the nerve,

can suffer no more than we loved. It's never enough,
but it's what we deserve.
(VS, 15)

The second section, "At Home, In the World," takes advantage of the
ambiguity the comma gives the phrase, and ranges with humor and tenderness from the death of a family pet to a shop in Jerusalem. Beneath many of
the poems is the idea that we pay for what we get, whether we intend to or
not. "Airfield Rabbits," for instance, is a grim sonnet about rabbits who in-
vade airfields for their lush grass and high fences, only to be deafened by jet
roar, so that they cannot return to the wild where owls swoop down unheard.
Slavitt's elegant use of the sonnet form for such a subject is one of my favorites among his many tactics; I have often wished that he had collected in
Vital Signs a poem from *The Carnivore* called "Grenade Fishing," which argues in favor of this illegal method of killing fish by the dozen: "Morning's at
seven / and the fastest is the best death you can get."[2]

"Tough Characters," the third group of new poems in *Vital Signs*, takes
up the lessons of history, which have occupied Slavitt for years; the poems
dwell sometimes on extravagant revenge, sometimes on the mystery of fragmentary classical writings. "Tough Characters" are, for the most part, men
like Nebuchadnezzar, Hadrian, or Hitler; but the title poem is about written
characters—the alphabet:

> On the Sixth Day,
> late, as if in afterthought to His will,
> the Lord brought forth written characters: they
> are savage, with the reek of Chaos still.
> (VS, 124)

Slavitt's productivity since *Vital Signs* has been, through 1987, about
equal to that which preceded it: five pseudonymous novels, seven novels
under his own name, two books of nonfiction, and six collections of poetry,
two of those being adaptations from the Latin. A recurring theme or tone in
Slavitt's recent work appears to arise from the poet's perception of the wors-
ening of our times, as seen by an observer aware of his own increasing near-

2. David R. Slavitt, *The Carnivore* (Chapel Hill, 1965), 37.

ness to death. However, the bleakness of such a view is mitigated by the attention the poems have received during their making, and by the poems that draw parallels between our time and the bad times of ancient history. In writing alone, there is something consoling; at best, there may be more than consolation. In a brief poem called "Youth, Age, Life, and Art," first collected in *Rounding the Horn* (1978), it comes down to this:

> Innocent, young, I wove syntactical nets
> to snare moments of joy, but when one gets
> older, the trick is reversed, and, late at night,
> to fend the beasts off—fear, rage, and despair—
> that prowl the dark or hover in the air,
> I sit in my circle of lamplight and I write.[3]

There is considerable pleasure in finding the right lines above which to hang a ponderous and abstract title. Thinking of the tradition and the poet's stance toward it, I notice that this poem is a sestet, and ponder the knowledge and luck that kept the poem from ballooning into a sonnet. Such thoughts are prompted not by this poem alone, but also by several other poems in this book that take various stances toward the tradition and the techniques of sonneteering.

In the first several poems in *Rounding the Horn* the theme is generally that of physical decay and moral disintegration; in this part of the book, there are four poems with various clear relations to the sonnet. "Revolutionaries," the first of these, is close enough. Set in an imaginary country that could be our own, it describes the growing anarchy of the workers from the viewpoint of someone higher on the social scale. The vagueness of the location gives the poem the sound of a fable, but in the last sentence the sense of doom is brought close:

> The only question is when the regime will fall
> from the cancer. It is not a metaphor.
> (*RH*, 5)

The poem's rhyme scheme, wittily enough, is upside-down: a sestet precedes two quatrains.

---

3. David R. Slavitt, *Rounding the Horn* (Baton Rouge, 1978), 40. Hereafter cited in the text as *RH*, followed by a page number.

Similarly, "The Korsakoff Syndrome" consists of a sestet, a three-rhyme octave, and a sestet, in that order: a sonnet that does not know which way is up. It describes an advanced state of forgetfulness achieved by some alcoholics, who remember "their names, the brands / of cheap whiskeys—no more." And, as in "Revolutionaries," we are warned away from figurative interpretations: "The brain pickles—it is no conceit / but happens" (*RH*, 8). But in both poems, the denial of metaphor and the form act with paradoxical power, to lend the poems metaphorical force. The Korsakoff Syndrome is clearly described as an affliction that strikes only the most accomplished and dedicated of drunks; but the poem still frightens us as the disease frightened Dr. Sergei Korsakoff. Somehow, safe as most of us are, the poem suggests that something like this could strike us at any moment.

And in "ENGL. 498–C," an unrhymed sonnet (true, there is no such thing; but in the context of a tradition, or of a well-made book, such things can seem to be) about teaching, the speaker leaves the classroom when he has finished for the day, misses his train, and returns to the classroom, where all the students are still gathered. But now they are naked, drunk, disposed about the room in sexual postures of varying degrees of intricacy,

> and I perform
> my usual office, suggesting it might help some
> if this leg were moved there, or that conjunction
> somehow strengthened. Nobody pays any attention.
> I'm not surprised. Finesse will come later.
> Their crude energies serve them. I wish them well.
> (*RH*, 13)

Absence of rhyme prevents the poem from commenting on itself in a distracting fashion, diverting attention from its subtler, unrhymed statement about contemporary mores and literacy.

Finally, near the end of the first part of *Rounding the Horn*, "Landscape Artists" strikes another balanced attitude by deviating slightly from the usual sonnet form. Describing the lawns and gardens of insane asylums, deciding that orderly prospects might be therapeutic, the speaker says that, out in his "jungle," those clean visions have sometimes tempted him to go mad; but he knows that he needs his jungle to hide in:

> The sun
> sets, the cat prowls, the owl blinks,

and under the close-clipped bushes, blood and hair
punctuate what those gardeners have done.
(*RH*, 20)

The octave of this otherwise regular sonnet is rhymed *a b c a d b d c,* the *d*
rhymes thrown like stumbling blocks in between the repetitions of the first
three rhymes.

The second section of *Rounding the Horn* begins with several poems that
owe their excellence largely to Slavitt's detailed knowledge of history. He is
so at home in this mode now, and his readers so at home with him, that we
can foresee from the title alone that "The Later Ptolemies" will be, at least
in part, a meditation on our present decline.

But Slavitt has not lost his ability to surprise us, even when we are with
him on familiar ground. "Glaucus" takes as its epigraph a few lines from
Fitzgerald's translation of the *Iliad;* it is said that Glaucus had traded his gold
armor for bronze, because Zeus had deprived him of his wits. The poem
argues Glaucus' sagacity, gold being less useful than bronze when what is
wanted is a sharp spear point. Glaucus bought some time in this life, the
poem says, and that is worth more gold than anyone has. In the end, it makes
little difference; at the wall, Glaucus listens to Sarpedon, who in his quest
for glory delivers a pep talk:

> Biddledeegoo giddledeebah diddledeebee
> Honor giddledeeboo vines and fields
> Biddledeegah duty biddledeegee
> Wives children giddledeebah glory
> Deathless biddledeegoo we will attack!
> So Sarpedon spake, the morning sun
> kindling fire behind him, and on the wall
> Menestheus, hearing it, scared shitless, hollered
> for help, any help he could get—Tall Ajax,
> Little Ajax, any Ajax, Teucros,
> anybody, but quick . . .
>   but held the position
> as long as he had to, waiting for help to come.
> (*RH,* 29)

Slavitt's audacious control of his medium is such that the sharp contrast
between the first five lines above and the rest of the poem is not enough to

drown out the modulation in the second part of the passage, from epic echo to slang and back again. The satiric comment on Sarpedon's speech is not merely literary in its effect; we are enabled to see these soldiers as real people.

Such clear knowledge of the poet's connection with us is what makes Slavitt's translations as interesting as his historical anecdotes and meditations. In the early 1970s, he produced versions of Vergil's *Eclogues* (1971) and *Georgics* (1972) that were startlingly free by traditional standards, but which made the central concerns of those poems more interesting than they often are in the versions produced by professional classicists. His few "adaptations" in *Rounding the Horn* continue to make a successful connection between the living language and the cultural remoteness of the original, as in the shift toward classical distance in this first sentence of "Adaptation from Callimachus":

> Book club selections, interstate four-lane
> roads, school-hall fountains, and fall
> homecoming queens . . . any public thing
> disgusts me.
> (*RH*, 38)

Much more recently, Slavitt has published his versions of poems by Ovid, and by Tibullus, of whom Ovid, in Slavitt's version, said, "I knew Tibullus, but he died / young—there are poems of his that I admire / but can hardly bear to read, missing my friend."[4] *The Elegies To Delia Of Albius Tibullus* (1985), are, in outline, conventional enough: Tibullus loves a married woman, she loves him, then ceases to; he ceases momentarily to love her, then addresses a final elegy to Eros, trying to make the best of it. But the energy and quickness of Slavitt's translation make these poems immediate and engaging.

The Tristia of Ovid (1987) is in a class with the best verse translations of the century. Ovid began these long, self-pitying poems in the hope that they might help cut short his exile. As years passed and he saw that this would not occur, he lapsed more deeply into anguish; this is one of the most elegantly sustained whines in literature. Removed from the society he loved,

---

4. David R. Slavitt, Preface to *The Elegies To Delia Of Albius Tibullus* (Cleveland, 1985), unpaginated.

from his wife, even from other speakers of his language, Ovid is by turns praiseful, cajoling, satirical, bitter, and never quite resigned. This book has more narrative strength than most fiction, and a flexibility in the use of an accentual elegiac couplet—six stresses, five stresses, unrhymed—that seems as close to the Latin version as we can get in the American language.

In one of the best poems in *Rounding the Horn*, "Reunion Elegiacs," Slavitt loosely adapts the classical meter to the subject of his twentieth reunion at Yale, where men come briefly to grips with what they and the world have failed to become, or worse, what they have begun to see falling away from them. It is a moving poem, the more so when one recalls that Slavitt's first book contains "Class Poem," written for his graduation in 1956. That poem ended,

> My valediction then: 'It's understood
> Yale men do well; may some of you do good.'[5]

Twenty years later, he writes

> Battered as we may seem, we're the golden boys,
> still fortune's darlings, who once roistered here,
>   blessed: it is up to us in turn to bless.
> (*RH*, 55)

It is a note of hope and perseverance, perhaps called for by the occasion; but, unlike the earlier poem, this one transcends its occasion, and earns its stated conviction that the main thing is survival.

That survival is hard, and certain to fail eventually, is the theme of many of these poems; perhaps it is most powerfully handled in the final section of the book. "Garbage," "Dickens' Inkwell, Etc.," "Mess," and "Poison" are all concerned with the things we clutter our lives with, thinking that the things may speak to us or for us; and, if they sometimes do, the poems ask what they might say to someone else after we are gone. But the most sustained and thorough evocation of our trip through bundles of baggage is the title poem.

"Rounding the Horn" is composed of twenty-five numbered stanzas. The

5. David R. Slavitt, *Suits for the Dead*, in *Poets of Today VIII*, ed. John Hall Wheelock (New York, 1961), 172.

first twenty-four are eight lines each; the last is fourteen. For several pages, the octaves are unrhymed, but by stanza 20, rhymes have begun to take predictable places, and in the twenty-fourth, all the lines are rhymed in a predictable pattern. The final stanza is a sonnet, though its rhyme scheme is not quite a textbook model. Part of this poem's effect is that of a sonnet preceded by twenty-four attempts at its first eight lines. But throughout the octaves, there is a careful balance between discreteness and continuity; what emerges, rather slowly, from the progression is an example of a subgenre, the voyage poem. The metaphor is stale, perhaps; but there is always room for one more, if the vision is distinctive enough. In this poem, as various figures for the body's slow decline are taken up and then passed over, the lightening of burdens becomes almost palpable, and the fact of death almost consoling:

> There, on the ocean floor, ships may ride
> in impossible attitudes, toe-dancer poses,
> stand on their noses, or roll over like kittens
> and dream what they like in the weatherless aimlessness.
> We think of our own manifests and, seasick,
> fear their gloom and silence less than the freedom
> catastrophe offers. Richly encrusted, they sport,
> make pets of monsters, have learned how to settle.
> (RH, 72)

And so, in the end, one prays to be set loose from "clamorous mouths and tyrannical organs," and

> The earth,
> making its late amends for the trauma of birth,
> opens, receives, quiets our grumbling dust.
> (RH, 75)

The many approaches to the sonnet, and the repetitive structure of "Rounding the Horn," come to seem like warm-up exercises for something more ambitious—such is the distorting power of hindsight—when we come to *Dozens* (1981), which is a long, loosely structured poem consisting of 144 numbered stanzas of twelve lines each. It is a brilliant success, partaking of roughly equal parts of journal and fiction, "confession" and elaborate satire. Many of the stanzas appear to be set in the speaker's home city, wherever that may be; it is a modern urban nightmare of the east-coast sort. Other stanzas are set in a tropical dictatorship where something like Spanish is the primary language, and corruption, indolence, and inertia are the primary spiritual qualities. The comedy of the imaginary police state, though, becomes less comic as the boundaries between these two worlds become less well defined, and the strategy of the poem reveals itself. In the fourteenth stanza, one of a few that make direct reference to the poem itself, the imaginative task is set out:

> If stanzas are rooms, then poems must be buildings,
> and volumes, streets, whole towns, impositions
> of minds upon topography. A harbor,
> a defensible hill may prompt, but the human eye,
> full of its own humors, orders the prospect
> and fails—one's best vision being blind.
> These dodecahedrons then are living rooms
> in a random dwelling. I sit in its dark, guessing
> what city would least disresemble mine,
> what square, what series of shops, what gable,
> slick in the streetlit rain, reverberate right
> to the footsteps I want to take, or want to have taken.[6]

The tropical world is a caricature, its denizens gathered at the Hotel Magnifico, sporting names like El Jefe, Il Grande del Prospettivo, and Coronel Corrupcion, pondering the decline of their civilization; and the poet, sometimes there and sometimes nearer home, shows us that most middle-class city dwellers are as remote from the poor as the Hotel Magnifico is remote from, say, Philadelphia. The poem shifts rapidly in tone, from breezy cynicism to regret, as in this first sentence from stanza 40:

> The picador horses around. The matador
> does dumb tricks with his cape, veronicas,
> betties, archies . . . It's the exterminador
> I cheer for from my seat on the sombre side,

---

6. David R. Slavitt, *Dozens* (Baton Rouge, 1981), 7. Hereafter cited in the text as *Dozens*, followed by a page number.

with his can, his pump, and the sweet smell of a death
I hope will be exquisite, lingering, and thorough.
(*Dozens*, 20)

These changes of attitude serve the poem well at those moments when it comes closest to a direct treatment of the ills of our civilization; Slavitt avoids excessive didacticism, but manages to provide chilling moments of realization. Stanza 69 begins with a jaded description of the local electrical system, which goes out from time to time, causing appliances to fail;

                    and there's a buffet
of what would spoil, sumptuous, candle lit,
delighting our reactionary tastes.
It's not the end of the world but, say, the fun
of the end of the world. And then the lights come on,
radios blare, and we reset our clocks.
(*Dozens*, 35)

The use of the first-person plural helps to keep the satire from becoming too Swiftian for its own good; by the end of this wonderfully imaginative excursion, when the poet finds himself and his son and daughter in New Haven "on an ordinary evening," there is still the possibility of the affirmation that the writing itself has consistently implied:

                    Let our havens
always be new and the broken down world heal
as the poets have taught us to think it may. It may
if we say so often enough and loud enough.
(*Dozens*, 72)

The balance between love of the world, and life, and contempt for human behavior, is more precariously maintained in *Big Nose* (1983) than in any of Slavitt's previous books. The title poem recounts an appalling episode in the history of Rawlins, Wyoming, where a forgotten outlaw named Big Nose George Parrott was captured, tried, hanged, and finally flayed so the hide could be turned into a pair of boots for the sheriff's office window. Slavitt imagines the town's turning against this act, until the sheriff could stand it no longer, and disappeared into Saskatchewan, still pursued by the vision of what he did—as the speaker, driving on eastward, is pursued by the memory of the story, having been shown a reminder of what we are. The sheriff miscalculated; all he wanted to do was provide a lesson. And the poem contains other, almost incidental reminders of the cost of carelessness, taking well-known phrases from Robert Frost, or the conventions of the law, and remarking, by the way, on their absurdity:

> Two roads diverge . . . if they didn't there wouldn't be two roads
>   but only the one, as any greenhorn kid
> can plainly see. Correctly, it's the one road that diverges
>   to make the two.[7]

And in the account of Parrott's end, there is this:

>   [they] hanged him by the neck
> —as judges say who dislike creative prison wardens
>   trying to hang men by their ankles or nuts.
> (BN, 41)

Big Nose opens with an excoriating address "To His Reader," railing against the idiot culture of our time, in which the attention typically paid to poems is worse than inattention. The poem ends, "You and I / depend thus on one another, and serve, / but you are not my friend. Nor am I yours" (*BN*, 6). Despite this declaration, one remembers Baudelaire's "Au lecteur," a similarly scornful accusation, and its ending: "—*Hypocrite lecteur,* —*mon semblable,* —*mon frère!*" That Slavitt knows this poem well was wittily demonstrated years ago, when his first Henry Sutton novel, *The Exhibitionist* (1967), was dedicated to a couple of gentlemen who turned out to be a garbageman and a septic-tank cleaner—"*mes semblables, mes frères.*"

That sort of wicked enjoyment characterizes many poems gathered at the end of *Big Nose* under the spendthrift title "Throwaways and Encores." "Titanic" advances the curious yet convincing notion that most of us would book passage on that boat if we had the chance: "We all go: only a few, first-class" (*BN*, 50). And "Ramon Fernandez Recollects" describes Wallace

---

7. David R. Slavitt, *Big Nose* (Baton Rouge, 1983), 39. Hereafter cited in the text as *BN*, followed by a page number.

Stevens from the standpoint of the man addressed in "The Idea of Order at Key West":

> What he remembers is the portly yankee,
> down for a good time, walking the beach
> to clear his head from the drink or to get drunk
> just on the salt air the way they can,
> and a girl singing. He got very excited,
> yammering on and on about the sea,
> her song, Christ knows what. He wasn't rowdy
> but pointed at the fishing boats and the sky
> and talked and then fell silent. It was his tie,
> the way he never unbuttoned his collar button
> or loosened his tie. That's what made him crazy—
> not enough blood gets to the brain. In Hartford,
> are they all like that? It must be very odd.
> Still, he paid in cash and he tipped well.
> (BN, 57)

Poets are sometimes scolded for collecting their slighter poems, as if more serious poetry were too sacred to be thus adulterated. It's a silly notion, of course, carried over from the "high seriousness" of Arnold; the desire to write the best poem in the world possesses all poets to some extent, but the smaller things delight, and keep the poet sane.

Slavitt's next collection, *The Walls of Thebes* (1986), dwells more on the ugly side of things than is the case in his earlier books; but it opens with a poem that reminds us of transient pleasures. "Visions" is about those gifts from the world that catch us up and hold us momentarily, like "those half dozen hot-air balloons in flotilla, / a progress of dowager queens across the sky";[8] they turn out to be hard to remember, sometimes; they fade, and cannot be saved up. "But it isn't such hoarded visions that can redeem us / so much as the hope that their like may happen again" (*WT*, 1). Despite the violence, and the close questioning of justice and belief that occur in the poems that follow, this hope of redeeming visions does not diminish as the book proceeds; and therein lies its triumph: it is easy to give up, and to justify

---

8. David R. Slavitt, *The Walls of Thebes* (Baton Rouge, 1986), 1. Hereafter cited in the text as *WT*, followed by a page number.

doing so; it is much harder to provide reasons for giving up, and then convincingly to show how and why not to do so.

Once in a while, there is a burst of exuberance characteristic of Slavitt's
earlier poems, as in the opening of "Herz-Werk":

The eyes and ears, let us say, bite, and the brain
digests, chewing the cud, but the heart absorbs:

this is the system by which the soul is nourished
and it builds—as fat and muscle accrete—wisdom.

Comes then like some tv-fitness bozo
with a program of strenuous calisthenics, Rilke!
(WT, 2)

But the tone of many of the shorter poems is pessimistic. *The Walls of
Thebes* has two central sources of power. One is "Bloody Murder," about the
murder of the poet's mother, who was bludgeoned to death by a burglar whom
she surprised in her house; the other is "Amphion's Lyre," a 555-line retelling
of the Greek legend about the musician whose lyre caused the walls of Thebes
to rise up of their own accord. On one hand, these poems say, here is the
terrible way things often are; on the other, here is what is sometimes made
of what we do. Many of the other poems in the book take their places somewhere along the spectrum between these points of view.

"Bloody Murder" opens with a stanza composed of didactic statement,
then moves to the particulars; it's a rugged transition:

Beauty and truth may dally together,
but when it comes time to pop the question,
it's ugliness that settles in
to take the vows with truth for the long
haul, the enduring and faithful companion.
The difficult lesson we all must study
is how to be children of such a marriage
and honor what we cannot love.

After the burglar bludgeoned my mother
to death with a bathroom scale and a large

bottle of Listerine, the police
recommended Ronny Reliable's
Cleaning Service—one of a growing
number of firms that make it their business
to clean up after messy murders,
suicides, and other disasters.
(*WT*, 7)

A surprising number of things are being done here with apparent effortlessness; this is not the place to name them all, but notice that in treating a
subject of such intrinsic power, in such conversational language, the poet
would trouble to achieve the metrical parallelism between the first lines of
each stanza. That sort of wit is rare in any age, and the wisdom to control it
is even rarer.

There are several poems in *The Walls of Thebes* that are directly illumi-
nated by "Bloody Murder"; an indirect light from that poem shines on several
more. "Old Photo" even draws some of its power from it. A brief meditation
on a roll of film left undeveloped for years, this poem might merely be a fine
little evocation of one of those stern reminders of time's ravages; all the
information we would need is there. But the presence of "Bloody Murder" in
the collection gives added poignancy to certain passages in "Old Photo":

> The Quinlans' tree
> had not yet been cut down. Neither had Mother.
>
> . . . .
>
> Mother's face in the one shot is far away.
> Dad doesn't even appear. I close my eyes
> to see better, but not better enough.
> (*WT*, 15)

"Jephthah's Prayer," "The Last Dalmatian," and "Parodos" are among
the other poems whose close scrutiny of dark realities seems to arise from the
opening proposition in "Bloody Murder." All three poems are concerned
with loss; "Jephthah's Prayer" is an imaginative reconstruction of the story in
the Book of Judges, in which Jephthah prays for victory in battle, promising
God that on his return, whatever first emerges from his door will be sacrificed
as a burnt offering; this turns out to be his daughter, and this time, there is
no reprieve, as there was in the case of Abraham and Isaac; and so Slavitt

imagines Jephthah abandoning his faith at the moment his daughter dies.

"The Last Dalmatian" takes its point of departure from an imaginative proposition that has come to seem typical of Slavitt's wide-ranging wit: imagine, early in this century, the last aged speaker of a dying language, Dalmatian, gradually losing her vocabulary as occasions to use her language become ever scarcer. In the same way, we all suffer losses of things we once knew, or nearly knew:

> I am a parrot, can say, "Hello, hello,"
> and utter at inappropriate moments a few other
> simple phrases, telling all I know.
> (WT, 10)

In "Parodos," a term denoting the ode sung by the classic chorus upon their first entrance, Slavitt's meditation on the chorus' effect becomes a moving evocation of what community is, and what balm a prayer can be, even to the nonbeliever.

As grim as the subjects of these poems are, Slavitt's artistry is more than equal to the task of lifting the subjects from the realm of individual suffering to the realm of literature. Almost as if to emphasize that he has done this, he has included in The Walls of Thebes a few poems that explore directly some of the relationships between art and the life depicted in art. Some of these are more amusing than solemn, though all of them are, finally, serious. "The Whippets" begins as an account of a minor disaster in a production of Der Rosenkavalier; that opera contains a scene in which, among the "supernumeraries filling the stage" (WT, 28) there is a man offering small animals for sale; in some productions he is given a caged bird or a monkey; on this occasion, he has a pair of whippets on a brace lead, and they disrupt the performance by giving in to their amorous urges. The poem goes on to present the main characters' reactions to the interruption, the gradual restoration of order, and a conclusion describing the lesson learned. An arresting feature of the poem is that the distinction is blurred between the characters and the singers who perform the roles; the interior monologues of Octavian, the Marschallin, and the Baron are presented from the point of view of the characters, but they take note of their stagy surroundings, hovering between being characters and performers. The Baron concludes his observations by noticing the conductor:

> the maestro raises his baton
> for us to resume the pursuit of our quarry of meaning,
> driven, perhaps hounded, but not forgetful
> of who we are or where we are in the score.
> (*WT*, 30–31)

The complicated irony of "not forgetful / of who we are" is introduced so gracefully that the careless reader might miss it; there is no apparent strain in the speakers' ability to inhabit two worlds at once, or in the poem's brilliant realization of a seldom-articulated truth: if we often use art as an escape from "real life," there are also times when, for the sake of our health, we flee in the opposite direction.

This inexhaustible theme is explored further in several other poems, notably "Wilson's Pen," an intelligently playful ramble around the idea of the pen's might, prompted by recollection of a headline on the eve of the treaty of Versailles; it should have read WILSON'S PEN IS READY, but a dropped space between two words had embarrassing results; Slavitt's ability to play with this in a manner both witty and tasteful is one of the high points in this collection. "Guts," "Tambourine," and "Mocking Bird" also work productively in the difficult, blurred area between what is lived and what is made.

The last sixteen pages of *The Walls of Thebes* contain "Amphion's Lyre," a magnificent poem in eleven parts, in which Slavitt's ability to make classical myths speak to our time is at its best. The legend itself has most of the more powerful ingredients: a set of twins, fathered by Zeus, abandoned on a hillside only to be saved by a shepherd and allowed to grow up, learn their true identity, and wreak revenge; a king whose lust for power and for women leads him into self-destructive error; and the magic of the maker, in this instance represented by the musical ability of one of the twins. When the twins return to their actual homeland and take power, the walls of Thebes come into being:

> Zetus built the wall; Amphion played his lyre—
>   as simple as that. Anyone who was there
> can tell you Zetus planned it, supervised the masons,
>   even worked beside them himself, sighting
> the hewn stones along the taut strings and plumb lines.
>   His brother, worse than useless, was only a nuisance
> good manners contrived to overlook. But the story

> is still told—how the walls around the city
> of Thebes somehow sprang up, grew together, built
>   themselves, because of the music Amphion played.
> To call it magic is not to dismiss it as arrant nonsense.
>   Miracles happen. Mysteries aren't mere
> demonstrations of how we need more information.
> (WT, 49)

In meditating on the myth's aptness to our time, the poet puts both hope and pessimism in their places; in the face of impending death, the work of the artist goes on, and there is always the chance that the believer is right,

>   and I, in my unbelief, am wrong,
> too cautious, too timid, lacking in the real imagination
> in which there is said to be tranquillity
>
> and a peace I can almost imagine that I imagine.
> (WT, 49)

The power of narrative to transform the events it recounts is among the most rewarding mysteries by which we can be absorbed. David Slavitt is among the most accomplished living practitioners of that art, in both prose and verse; his poems give us a pleasurable, beautiful way of meditating on a bad time. We can't ask much more of literature, and usually we get far less.

JACKSON MAC LOW Gristlier Translations, Arcane Pronouns

> There are people who say, "If
> music's that easy to write, I could
> do it." Of course they could, but
> they don't.
>
> —John Cage

I

When poetry delivers less than the reader expects, the reason is usually nothing more than the poet's relative incompetence, or the reader's inability to overcome prejudice. Once in a while, however, a poet strips away much that readers have come to expect; whatever the poet's private reasons for doing this, the results may suggest that usual expectations need adjustment, that poetry has some essential qualities that are in danger of being forgotten, or that yet one more writer has succumbed to misconstrued myths of the avant-garde.

Prevailing prejudices make it easy to dismiss experimental writers, whether they are talented and serious, or merely taking refuge in elected scorn. Among the myths of the avant-garde are the notions that experiment always results in superficial departures from the expected; that "making it new" is an activity in total opposition to that of "making it old"; and that what has been done before is not worth doing again. With mischievous usefulness, Jorge Luis Borges teases these propositions in "Pierre Menard, Author of *Don Quixote*."[1]

---

1. Jorge Luis Borges, *Ficciones*, edited and with an introduction by Anthony Kerrigan (New York, 1962), 45–55. "Pierre Menard" is translated in this edition by Anthony Bonner.

Menard's peculiar project begins with the premise that distant memory of a book read in youth may resemble the author's conception of the book before it was written. Starting there, and absorbing with impossible thoroughness the time, culture, and language of the original author (and forgetting three centuries of history), Menard attempts to write *Don Quixote* without looking at it; after immense labor, he produces two chapters. The story proceeds to compare a passage by Cervantes with one by Menard; they are verbally identical, yet differences emerge, based on culture and time. Menard, a contemporary of William James, has made something "infinitely richer." The story is a parable for readers of almost any theoretical persuasion.

The comparison between the two passages depends entirely on knowledge of their respective origins; work "is valued as it is aimed," as Hugh Kenner has noted: "The same paper, the same ink, the same design, will earn one man, working for the Bureau of Engraving and Printing, his salary, and another, working for his art, hanging space in museums, and another, working for the mob, twenty years at Leavenworth."[2]

Moreover, though it is traditional to value the struggle perceived in apparent absence of it, and not to excuse a poem's perceived faults on the grounds that it was written quickly, readers often overlook or praise the mechanical accretion of paradoxes in Chidiock Tichborne's "Elegy," whose subtitle (often printed "Written With His Own Hand In the Tower Before His Execution") has become a part of the poem. Not a bad night's work, as workshop students sometimes say, usually in blissful innocence of nights so bad as Tichborne's last. Since knowledge or suspicion concerning a poem's origins will influence judgment of it, the creative process may include contriving origins for poems that will lend them an interest they might not otherwise have.

Here, for example, are a few lines by Jackson Mac Low:

Recognize I neither sure, All I
O neither
These, he emptiness
Sure, emptiness liver front,
O recognize
"These, he emptiness

2. Hugh Kenner, *The Counterfeiters* (Bloomington, 1968), 56.

O neither emptiness
Who he O
I sure,
All these
Must O must emptiness neither these,
Recognize I quite he these,
These, he I sure,
I neither
Front recognize O neither these,
O front
Understands sure. . . .[3]

Mac Low is a well-known poet and composer of performance pieces for voice and music, the author of *Stanzas for Iris Lezak, The Pronouns: A Collection of Forty Dances for the Dancers* (1979), *Asymmetries 1–260* (1980), *The Virginia Woolf Poems* (1985), and *Representative Works: 1938–1985* (1986), all of which contain large amounts of work produced by the systematic application of chance or nonintentional methods to the business of arranging words on paper. These books constitute a small fraction of Mac Low's total *oeuvre*, which has been surprising, baffling, and delighting readers and audiences for many years.

It is easy to acquire the kind of literary education that leaves one badly prepared for an encounter with Mac Low's work. I first saw his name in William Packard's *The Craft of Poetry* (1974), a collection of interviews from the *New York Quarterly*. At that time I was unwilling to read anything that had been produced by the following means:

> [The poems in *Stanzas for Iris Lezak* are] completely acrostic—stanzaic acrostic. Every one of the *Stanzas* poems is in some way an acrostic of either the title or some other word string. (I call such a series of words an "index string.") Each word of the index string determines a line, and each whole "spelling out" of the index string constitutes one complete stanza. Often I use units (each beginning with an "index letter") longer than single words, such as phrases or large fragments of sentences or whole sentences. In some

---

3. Jackson Mac Low, *Stanzas for Iris Lezak* (Millerton, N.Y., 1971), 162. Hereafter cited in the text as *Stanzas*, followed by a page number.

stanzas the units are repeated every time the letters with which they begin
are repeated in the index string. In other stanzas they aren't repeated.[4]

The lines thus determined are made of words drawn from other texts, or
from the environment; the poems are not "written" at all, in any sense other
than "transcribed." I put Mac Low from my mind.

A few years later, while visiting my sister in Connecticut, I went with
her to a charity flea market and found among the books a copy of *Stanzas for
Iris Lezak*. Tempted not to ignore whatever forces had brought me and the
book together upon a lawn in Darien, I bought it, brought it home, and,
encouraged by the calm good sense in the *Craft* interview, gradually discovered a way of reading it. I open the book at random, having decided by
tossing a coin to flip from there toward the front to the first page on which a
poem begins. This time, it is the passage above.

These are the opening lines of "Rinzai on the Self, or 'The One who is,
at this moment, right in front of us, solitarily, illuminatingly, in full awareness, listening to this talk on the Dharma.'" The lines quoted are acrostics
on the first seventeen words of the title or "index string"; in accordance with
one of his more usual practices, partially described in the passage from the
Craft interview, Mac Low has selected the index string, then read through
the source text (not precisely identified in this case), seeking the next occurrence of a word beginning with the letter he needs to continue the acrostic.
In the first line, an acrostic on "Rinzai," he has settled for an *s* word in the
fourth position; elsewhere, in all probability, he has skipped over words in
the source that lack what he calls "semantic weight,"[5] since there are no
articles, conjunctions, or prepositions in the passage. There is also a typographical error: lines 10–13 are based on the words *at, moment, right,* and
this, in that order. So the passage can be proofread at a level of organization
more complex than that of a random list of words.

Stanzas for Iris Lezak runs to 394 pages, not counting the 25–page essay
at the end, "An Afterword on the Methods Used in Composing & Performing *STANZAS FOR IRIS LEZAK*." This essay announces that the book
"comprises all of the poems I wrote between some time in April or May &

4. William Packard, *The Craft of Poetry* (New York, 1974), 244–45. Hereafter cited in
the text as *Craft,* followed by a page number.
5. Jackson Mac Low, *Asymmetries 1–260* (New York, 1980), 243. Hereafter cited in the
text as *Asymmetries,* followed by a page number.

Halloween Week, 1960" (*Stanzas*, 399). Six months, then, or a little over two pages a day—a high rate of production, as poetry goes.

Many widely held convictions about the nature of poetry make it easy to dismiss such work; nevertheless, some readers have been attracted by the recurrence of words and phrases, and the knowledge that they have, as it were, found their own places; whether or not he is paring his fingernails, the author here is nearly as remote and detached from the work as it is possible to be. Mac Low has often said that among the influences or desires that turned him in this direction was "a result of a certain interpretation of the Buddhist doctrine that the ego is an illusion. Both John Cage and I were very much influenced by Zen, especially by D.T. Suzuki's seminars in Zen and Kegon Buddhism at Columbia in the middle and late '50s. Cage and, through his influence, I began composing by means of chance operations in the '50s in an attempt to escape the dominance of the ego—especially the personal passions—in art" (*Craft*, 250). Mac Low has also composed music; the context of this passage suggests that that may be what he is talking about, but the same principles apply to much of his writing.

Some of Mac Low's experiments have resulted in work that has more (perhaps illusory) coherence than the *Stanzas*; this is "5TH DANCE—NUMBERING—17 February 1964," from *The Pronouns:*

All of you begin naming things.

Then each of you jumps,
comes on as a horn,
numbers anything or anyone,
darkens something,
& then hammers on it.

Then one of you starts fingering a door.

Soon another one of you begins rewarding someone for
   something or going up under something.

At the end all of you are numbering things.[6]

6. Jackson Mac Low, *The Pronouns: A Collection of Forty Dances for the Dancers* (Barrytown, N.Y., 1979), 18. Hereafter cited in the text as *Pronouns*, followed by a page number.

This is a distinctive mixture: unpredictability and a definite tone take turns undercutting each other, and the vaguer words—*things, something, someone*—blur the focus as often as *horn* and *hammer* sharpen it. The poem provides other pleasures: that of visualizing a troupe of dancers trying to perform it; of noting that repeated syntactical elements and words, many of them nouns and verbs, nudge baffling opacity in the direction of attractive mystery; or of knowing something about its origin.

The method of composing "NUMBERING" is explained at the end of *The Pronouns,* in "Some Remarks to the Dancers (How the Dances Are To Be Performed & How They Were Made)":

> Many of the actions of the 40 dances that comprise *THE PRONOUNS* were drawn by a systematic chance method (outlined below) from a "pack" of 56 filing cards, on each of which are typed one to five actions, denoted by gerunds or gerundial phrases, e.g., "jumping," "having a letter over one eye," & "giving the neck a knifing or coming to give a parallel meal, beautiful & shocking." 170 different actions are each named once in this pack of cards, & three more, "jumping," "mapping," & "questioning," are each named twice. . . . [explains that all the words in the action phrases "were drawn, with the help of the Rand table of a million random digits, from the 850-word Basic English Word List."]
>
> I decided to write a dance-instruction-poem for every word listed as a pronoun in the Merriam-Webster Dictionary (most linguists would now call such words as "everybody" nouns rather than pronouns, but I went by the book). After having written 40 of them, I thought I'd written enough of them, so there are no poems for some of the less-used pronouns (or pronoun-like nouns).
>
> In composing each dance, I would first shuffle the pack & then cut it & point blindly to one of the actions on the card cut to. This action became the title of the dance. Before or after determining the title, I would also choose which *pronoun* was to be the subject of all the sentences in that dance-poem. The title was then used as a "diastic index" to determine the successive actions of the dance & also, necessarily, their number. That is, the letters of the title determined the actions drawn for the dance. (*Pronouns,* 69–72)

Diastic is a word Mac Low has derived from *acrostic*; in the dance-poem above, the title, "NUMBERING," provides the first letter of the first action, *naming,* the second letter of the second action, *jumps,* the third letter of the third, "comes," and so on. According to a note at the end of *The Virginia Woolf Poems*, Mac Low began to develop the "diastic" method in January of 1963. In the *Craft* interview, he says that this method brings about a considerable amount of repetition, since the word that fills the bill may be another occurrence of the index-string word; he likes this, because of the repetitive music, and because such repetition can give the piece a "feeling of subject matter" that is often absent from purely acrostic pieces (*Craft,* 246).

Mac Low is careful to let us know that he freely chose the various conjunctions and adverbs that connect the phrases into sentences and the sentences into strophes of *The Pronouns*. Though he has composed texts in which nothing is left to choice, and others in which everything is, he also works rewardingly with methods that are not purely either. Note, in the passage above, the ease with which the texts are called "poems," "dances," or "dance-poems."

II

Though a large number of Mac Low's poems, performance works, and musical compositions have been published widely in magazines and anthologies, many of them have also been performed. The texts in *The Pronouns*, especially, are both poems and instructions for dancers. Treated purely as instructions, they leave a great deal up to the dancers. Performances of earlier works by Mac Low follow careful directions involving randomly drawn text cards, playing cards, cards with numbers on them, numbers in text regulating silences, and regulations governing tempo, dynamics and manners of delivery; in a play, a dice player selects the times when randomized playing cards bearing action directions are given to actors. However, most of Mac Low's instructions also contain a strong recommendation that the performers always remain alert to their surroundings, to the other performers, and to their own impulses. The wit and imagination of the dancer will have much to do with what happens when "Soon another one of you begins rewarding someone for something or going up under something."

Among the choices Mac Low leaves to others is whether a performance of *The Pronouns* will include audible renditions of the instructions themselves. When it does not, the question whether they are poems does not arise; but when it does, or when Mac Low publishes them or includes some of them in a poetry reading, their similarities, their dependence on pronouns, and the recurrence of phrases and images, are mysteriously evocative, whether or not they are also hilarious. The tenth and eleventh dances have as their subjects "thou" and "ye," respectively; Mac Low's touch with archaic usage, and the unpredictable sequence of images and actions, make a rich blend:

Thou comest by.

& then thou goest about between & through unserious-seeming goings-on,
& thou hammerest.
.   .   .   .
Thou dost something in the manner of a sister whose mind is happy &
    willing,
thou writest with a bad pen,
& either thou hast curves or thou hast to put weight on a bird
while thou puttest something slow under an insect,
& thou hast or seem'st to have serious holes,
albeit thine ending be one wherein thou reactest to orange hair.
(*Pronouns*, 24)

I have often read this and other *Pronouns* poems aloud to classes and to audiences in various parts of the world, and have developed a fairly dependable set of expectations concerning the reactions they will evoke. Some people, of course, conclude that if I will read that to them, they are probably in for a troublesome evening; but invariably there are also listeners who visibly "follow" the poems, carried along on the authority of the rhythm, the humor or spookiness of the unpredictable imagery, and the security of closure, which is sometimes achieved simply by including the word "end," "ending," or "finally" in the last line.

In its relative coherence, and what may be felt as an ironic tension between the archaic language and the actions, this is far from Mac Low's earliest chance-generated work, "5 biblical poems," begun late in 1954. The poems are strictly formal, but not traditionally so; throws of a die determined the "meter," which is based on an "event" consisting of a word or a silence; a silence lasts as long as it would take the performer to say a word—of the performer's choice. The die determined the number of lines in the poem (which is also the number of stanzas in the poem), the number of events in corresponding lines of the stanzas, whether an event is a word or a silence, whether to count from the top or the bottom of a column to get to a word, how many lines to count, and how many words to count. However, the successive words in the whole series were each taken from successive columns in a copy of the Hebrew Scriptures. The silences must be indicated one at a time, so a typographical bristliness may slightly interfere with imagining how the words might sound in performance. These are the first three stanzas of "5.2.3.6.5.,the 3rd biblical poem" (the numbers in the title indicate the number of events in each line of a stanza):

sustenance L_____/ and L_____/ L_____/
L_____/ L_____/
L_____/ L_____/ bullock,
of twenty L_____/ L_____/ L_____/ children
hands, L_____/ came and L_____/

L_____/ weight threescore L_____/ the
upon L_____/
Shechem L_____/ L_____/
L_____/ L_____/ he L_____/ his against
L_____/ L_____/ Jephthah, cities L_____/

L_____/ L_____/ L_____/ not children
L_____/ thee?
ten the L_____/
L_____/ said for eater But L_____/
L_____/ L_____/ done to and[7]

A complication is introduced in "21.21.29.,the 5th biblical poem(for 3 simultaneous voices)the 1st biblical play"; each part consists of three stanzas of long lines, but each part was separately composed. Chance provides for coincidence, in parallel locations over the three parts, of word with word, or word with silence; performers' options may prevent these typographical co-incidences from occurring, and bring about others.

About six years later, Mac Low began composition of a series of "Gathas"

---

7. Jackson Mac Low, *Representative Works: 1938–1985* (New York, 1986), 24. Hereafter cited in the text as *RW*, followed by a page number.

in which words in performance may be reduced to phonemes. As he says in an introduction to some of them in *Representative Works*, "The Sanskrit word *gatha*, 'verse' or 'hymn,' was adopted for them, on analogy with its use to designate versified sections of Buddhist sutras and short poems by Zen masters and students, because I considered Gathas to be Buddhist performance texts" (*RW*, 234). These items consist of a mantra, a name, or a series of "non-mantric English words," written on graph paper, one letter to a square. In a few instances, chance determines which of the top ten squares to start with in each vertical transcription; in others, the vertical phrases "hang" on a horizontal axis consisting of the phrase itself, or two or three of the letters in the phrase; in some examples of this mode, the axis is a prolonged "OM": AAAAAAAUUUUUUUUMMMMMMMMMM. Performance of a gatha can include both voice and instruments; if the latter are used, each letter in the mantra has a prescribed tonal equivalent. Each performer "moves" from square to square in any direction, including diagonally, speaking or singing the sounds or names of letters, or syllables, or words. Occasionally a performer may wish to "jump" to another part of the page. "When performing mantric Gathas, one *must* repeat the mantra once or several times before 'jumping.' In Vocabulary Gatha performances the name on which the Gatha is based *may* be spoken before a 'jump'" (*RW*, 234).

As with Concrete Poetry, it is a particular violence to such an item to quote it partially; but here is a section of "1st Milarepa Gatha," which is written on quadrille paper 34 squares wide and 44 deep. The mantra is Tibetan, and goes "JE MILA ZHÄDPA DORJE LA SÖLWA DEBSO"; it is written vertically 34 times, each column beginning in one of the top ten squares. The upper left square of this excerpt is 16 down and 14 across:

```
HAZ P DA
Ä  HAO
DDÄ RZ
P ODD J H
AR P OE Ä
  J AR  D
DE  J LP
O  DE AA
```
(*RW*, 242)

In 1976, Mac Low and Sharon Mattlin recorded a seven-minute performance of this Gatha for distribution on a 45-rpm disc (Edizione Pari & Dis-

pari, Cavriago, Italy); their realizations of letters range from unvoiced plo-
sives through prolonged diphthongs to sung vowels, over a wide range of
tempi and moods. There are moments, especially toward the end, when traf-
fic noise is audible; by fortunate chance, since the performers could not have
predicted when a distant motorist might blow his horn, these sounds cue an
improvised coda in which the performers echo and take off from the horns.

The fact remains that the performance consists almost entirely of sounds
without denotations, although it includes some English and French words
fortuitously produced by letter contiguities and puns. Readers and listeners
unfamiliar with Tibetan can seldom find meaning, other than their own,
even in the mantra when it is spoken; Mac Low does not provide a translation. Plenty of sensible people will deny that this kind of thing is poetry,
even after considering what Jerome Rothenberg has said about it in his preface to *Representative Works:*

> I got the "idea" early along, but I really *got* the idea sometime mid-60s in a
> performance of one of the "gathas." . . . The old Japanese words, resonant
> from earlier readings, & the recognizable *aum* as mantric axis line that held
> the piece together, appeared & disappeared as phonemes & syllables began
> to move around the space in which we had dispersed ourselves. I had never
> so clearly heard or felt my own voice or Voice Herself as carried by the
> others—the separation and recombination of sounds that related back to a
> fixed string of sounds & to a meaning that I didn't reach but that I knew
> was there. It was something very old & very new: Jackson's arrangement &
> invention but vibrant with the source itself. (*RW*, x)

Rothenberg describes something that can happen, and names things,
like "Voice Herself," over whose actual or metaphorical existence poets do
better not to quarrel. This is demonstrable in several ways other than par-
ticipation in a performance of Mac Low's work. If the linguistic realms in
which some of these demonstrations occur seem far removed from poetry, it
may be because generations of poets have emphasized poetry's distance from
vulgar speech, even when claiming to draw heavily on it; hierarchical clas-
sifications of speech and writing are often conceived selfishly. It is unlikely
that even a habitual reader of poetry, asked to identify the sources of a dozen
lines including "Walk with light," will remember that the sentence is affixed
to a lamppost at a nearby pedestrian crossing.

In "How to Talk Double Talk," Elmer Roessner does not create a context that brings poetry immediately to mind, though he does say that the
accomplished double-talker "may go into the movies, *he may write a book*, he
may become a military expert" (emphasis added). He is concerned to explain
how double-talk can be used to confuse people, put them off or down, to
exercise power. The method is simple, but takes practice. One selects a number of "word parts," preferably not babbling and onomatopoeic noises like
"uggle," but groups of syllables that sound as if they might be parts of words:
urment, eton, ogion, izans, onate and twenty others are listed in his article,
along with injunctions that the expert is master of a hundred such fragments,
and knows how to adjust the proportion of double-talk to actual talk, as in
Roessner's concluding sentences:

> His art is a hacqueton to soften the world's blows; hyratory though his pho-
> nate onslaught be, it is no whigmaleerie. It may become a logion that the
> violescense of his wit is no outgrowth of hypoplasia. It seldom vesicates.
> Nor is his a canzicrans humor. It is mature, straightforward, and risorial.[8]

As Rothenberg might say, this approaches a meaning it does not quite
reach; the feeling that it may be there, or ought to be there, is tentative, but
not to be ignored. Mac Low has produced some kinds of texts that resemble
Roessner's, though the differences between the kinds is considerable.

The earlier kind is exemplified in "Asymmetry 81," from *Asymmetries
1–260* (1980); this group of poems was composed beginning in 1960, as a
departure from the symmetrical poems in *Stanzas for Iris Lezak*. Mac Low
adjusted the rules by which he used chance and source texts, so that lines
would be more various in length, and word-fragments and portmanteau words
might also be admitted. In an afterword to *Asymmetries 1–260*, he remarks
that he was led in this direction partly by "admiration for the irregular verse
of Ezra Pound and of such contemporaries of mine as Paul Blackburn and
Larry Eigner" (*Asymmetries*, 245). It is instructive that Mac Low's work is
not immune to such influences.

"Asymmetry 81" contains incomplete words, because the method of
counting toward usable items in the source text overlooks, or includes, spaces
between words:

8. Elmer Roessner, "How to Talk Double Talk," *Esquire*, January, 1940, pp. 30, 168.

"It"
    troed
ingplanspot,
       be
         "Ourth."
           upfirsttono
              perprothis
       notby outlay.

          thows ben getnec
hisscion pokesev ingcoundid soven
sadjust ell dressconder jorto
leke os notbutdin subluteones
painlongcame "ir trebe."
thes:
    heve Irth standnow.
(*Asymmetries*, 89)

The pleasures available here include the tantalizing way in which sounds move into and out of recognizable words, a few of which drift between possibilities, like *s / adjust* and *sad / just*; the sonic parallelism between the opening and the closing, suggestive of an equivalency between *Ourth*, *Irth*, and Earth; the notion that the manner in which "painlongcame" is best conveyed in a phrase from something like German, the quotation marks making nearly audible a cozy "as it were"; and gleeful acknowledgment that if there are no *subluteones*, they should be invented, whether pronounced *sub-lute-ones* or *sub-luty-owns*.

Conservative readers object that more traditional poems can provide quite similar pleasures, along with the richness of denotative meaning; but this poem's relative incomprehensibility, and the knowledge that it was generated by chance, isolate and magnify its features. The difference between this, produced by a serious poet, and the concluding sentences of "How to Talk Double Talk," produced by a professional smart aleck, does not lie entirely in understanding their respective aims and origins, but as Kenner suggests above, it is largely there: listening to something offered as a poem, we hear it differently than we hear most jokes, though as Howard Nemerov has shown, poems and jokes have similar ways of taking us by surprise.[9]

9. Howard Nemerov, "Bottom's Dream: The Likeness of Poems and Jokes," in his *Reflexions on Poetry & Poetics* (New Brunswick, 1972), 3–18.

III

Mac Low has not always depended on chance methods to produce poems and other texts. His early work ranges from "cubist" fragmentary items to quite competent traditional sonnets; in 1970 and 1971 he wrote over a hundred "Odes" for Iris Lezak, in four-line syllabic stanzas, all written directly; and his recent *Pieces o' Six* (forthcoming from Sun & Moon Press, Los Angeles), which comprises poems in prose that are often discontinuous and fragmentary in denotation, but sinuous and controlled in rhythm and syntax. In May, 1961, he developed a procedure in which he writes directly between "nuclei"—words, phrases, and so on, given by one or another nonintentional method—that limit and govern his choices; works of this sort include the poems "From Nuclei" (1961), "The Presidents of the United States of America" (1963), and the "Light Poems" (1962 to the present), all in *Representative Works.* [10]

Some of Mac Low's directly written work is less effective than one might wish; the "Odes," especially, flatly declare love and the gradual dawning of disappointment, as if, in shifting to a mode in which he could say something, he was overcome by the desire to get it denotatively said. In "The Presidents," however, the method of choosing images yields striking results. Each poem's sequence of images is based on the Phoenician meanings of the successive letters of the president's name; the meanings are taken from Sandra Lawrence's *The Roman Inscriptional Letter,* which gives these meanings for the letters in James Madison's name: *J,* "hand"; *A,* "ox"; *M,* "water"; *E,* "window" or "look!"; *S,* "tooth"; *D,* "door"; *I,* "hand"; *O,* "eye"; *N,* "fish." This is "1809" (titles are first inaugural years of their subjects):

> James Madison's hand cd lead an ox to water
> and he'd look at him while he drank
> > > letting it
> > spill down from grassy teeth.
>
> After he'd water'd his ox
> > > James Madison'd
> > push open his door with his hand

---

10. "From Nuclei," 128–31, "The Presidents of the United States," 152–69, "Light Poems," 136–51, all in *RW.*

> & then his teeth'd
> grind and mash up all but the bones & eyes of a large fish.
> (*RW*, 156)

The chronological appropriateness of "ox" and the amusing contractions lift this above the level of pure word-games. The sequence goes through Fillmore, and the repetition of images in different contexts adds a note of cheerful irreverence.

In the Light Poems, too, the poet allows himself the freedom of connecting as he may the "nuclei," in this instance various kinds of light. Usually these light names begin with the letters of the dedicatee's name and appear in their order in the name. Most have been taken from a chart of light names by random selection, but in "32nd Light Poem: *In Memoriam* Paul Blackburn—9–10 October 1971" (*RW*, 221–23), Mac Low announces that he will "choose the kinds of light," though they begin with successive letters of Blackburn's name; the first four kinds of light to appear are "pale light," "Amber light," "umber light," and "Lightning." The frequency with which these references occur is freely chosen; the four above are spread over the first two-thirds of the poem, which is a powerfully moving recollection of Blackburn's courageous fight against cancer, and of his success, at a poetry festival in Michigan, in concealing from some of his friends the imminence of his death:

> I see Paul standing in the umber light
> cast on his existence
> by his knowing that his death was fast approaching
>
> Lightning blasts the guilty dream
> & I see him
> reading in the little auditorium
>
> & hear him
> confidently reading
> careful of his timing
>
> anxious not to take
> more than his share of reading time
> filling our hearts with rejoicing

seeing him alive
doing the work he was here for
seemingly among us now
(RW, 222)

The final third of the poem recalls an earlier time with the poet, and the news of his death. It moves from "black light" through "*no* light" as Blackburn's name supplies the letters Mac Low must use, and ends with the "poems' light" as consolation, "The unending light of your presence / in the living light of your voice" (RW, 223). I have quoted enough of the poem to illustrate its directness and simplicity, but the poem's overall rhythm, and the moving details of lives devoted to poetry, give the simplicity its emotional power.

IV

In *Pieces o' Six*, a method close to Elmer Roessner's produces something richer than Roessner's practical joking. Mac Low uses few invented words; instead, he chooses words that do not make usual sense in the contexts he is constantly on the verge of seeming to create. Meanwhile, the sentences move convincingly, like those that Frost said could be understood if one heard them as through a closed door, the words not quite audible.[11] This is the beginning of XXI in the series:

Once the kenurdlers had settled on a schema, the new pipes were brightened. The quiet pitches were liberated. When the fleets flamed, the deals were offensive, though the foolers increased their pretense. Nodules were soaked. Labile oaks listed as they listed, and boats tinkled as whistlers particularized threats, but tony coal heavers heavily bested durational scissors when nets were portioned among panic thieves. Live pachyderms were picked for street engulfments. The daily cascades were defaced by facile derangements, though any cousin might have known the difference. Rigid diligence seemed to be in order that day, for discipline Castilian as hills was praised, and whoever alerted the picnickers was nowhere to be seen when

11. *Robert Frost: Poetry and Prose*, ed. Edward Connery Lathem and Lawrance Thompson (New York, 1972), 261.

the lines were down. Ices were consummated soon. The Druse monotones filtered through a cuckold's initial cacklings. Pheasants were dropped and drastic features annealed. Nobody's sleeves were tinted. Sluices gave way to crevices wherever an annular violence was detected, and orphaned wigglers lifted wizened visages just as the clocks of the tin situation were primed to be filled. That was the time of the zoological. (*RW*, 334)

The piece goes on in this manner to the length of about 1,000 words. The past tense, and the use of conjunctions and such modifiers as *when, once,* and *soon,* give the sentences the sound of cause-and-effect narrative, yet expectations are jarred almost word by word; no narrative emerges, except as a stylistic ghost. The passage has the feel of texts that must be read before an examination, when the reader mistakenly believes that just looking something over will be sufficient: yes, yes, yes, live pachyderms, discipline, sleeves and sluices, the tin situation.

Pieces o' Six is among Mac Low's most mysterious successes, perhaps because it has not yet appeared with a preface or an afterword explaining the methods of its composition. In a brief telephone interview in 1987, Mac Low told me that the piece quoted above was written directly, without recourse to systematic chance operations; he "made it up."[12] I know of no other writing, including that of the people called Language Poets, which rejects ordinary "meaning," personality, and narrative with this much thoroughness, at

---

12. In a letter dated February 22, 1991, Jackson Mac Low provided me with the following account of *Pieces o' Six:*

The 33 poems in *Pieces o' Six* are of many kinds, some like the one in *Rep Wks,* but some like essays or nearly normal, but possibly "short-circuited" stories, and a few were made systematically, two drawing from journalistic sources (*Scientific American* and *The Village Voice*), others working systematically, but not aleatorically, with materials first appearing in the earlier sentences of the poems. They started out being written longhand in a particular notebook, similar to the ones in which *Stanzas, Asymmetries,* "The Presidents . . . ," *The Pronouns,* and most of my other work written before I had a computer was written. The first one occupies exactly the first six pages in the notebook, so I decided to fill the notebook with six-page poems in prose. . . . However, in typing them up, they sometimes were revised so that if written again in the notebook they would've occupied *more* than six pages, so the rule became that the first *draft* would occupy six pages. Then, beginning with #31, I began writing them on computers, so that the rule then became "six computer pages in the first draft." The only other "rules" are that they are all prose of some kind and that they are all, by intention, poems.

the same time that it displays this much verbal prodigality and understanding of sentence movement and its effects. It is extremely difficult to think of the unexpected word without relying on perceptible association; it is hard to imagine how Mac Low could produce, on so smooth and compelling a syntactical framework, such frequent departures not only from expected sense, but also from what might be called expected nonsense.

Readers accustomed to more usual sorts of coherence may wonder why anyone would reject meaning, personality, and narrative, which have been among the foundation stones of literature. One answer is that words and the conventions according to which they follow one another may be even closer to the foundation than the matters they have traditionally carried, and that profound pleasure can be taken in watching them move gracefully under a different burden. The pleasure is more complicated than that which some people take in listening to a language they do not know. In that case, sound is almost everything; but in this case, most of the individual words have recognizable denotations, and their refusal to add up produces a continuous, if highly localized, suspense.

Mac Low had earlier made some experiments that probably contributed heavily to his success with *Pieces o' Six*. There were "word events," in which a performer realizes a word in all the permutations that come to mind—a letter at a time, anagrams, fragments, etc. More systematic are the "vocabularies," which employ words that can be formed using the letters in one person's name. The most ambitious of these is "A Vocabulary for Annie Brigitte Gilles Tardos," derived from the baptismal name of Mac Low's wife, the painter and performance artist Anne Tardos (*RW*, 293). The description of the procedures for composing, visually presenting, and performing this work are detailed on pages 293–98 of *Representative Works*. They are extremely careful, even for Mac Low, whose prose discussions of procedure and composition history are extraordinarily detailed. According to Mac Low, these instructions are "the most complete and precise description of the methods for realizing one of the author's performance works. Performers of his other works would do well to read it" (*RW*, 298).

This "vocabulary" is founded on a "lexicon" that "comprises 5,000 entries, including general words and geographical, biographical, and personal names. Many entries include both a base word and several word forms derived from it by adding suffixes. . . . Any particular letter appears in any single word form only as many times as it appears in the whole name, e.g., no form can include more than two A's" (*RW*, 293).

A computer was used to generate 3,000 lines, each consisting of one to ten randomly selected entries in the lexicon. Mac Low then composed sentences from lines in the printout, selecting a word form from each entry, and sometimes supplying connectives spelled only with the letters in the name. Many of these sentences sound very much like sentences in *Pieces o' Six*: "Steele's greatness is to Bennie's lobar andirons as rondels are to tablas" (*RW*, 302). This sentence occurs in a reproduction of a graphic realization of the vocabulary, in which the sentences were typed on strips, and mounted in various orientations to the horizontal, some sentences changing direction. A more traditional-looking spinoff from the project is "Antic Quatrains," which begins thus:

Along a tarn a delator entangled a dragline,
Boasting o' tonnages, dogies, ants, and stones
As long as Lind balled Gandas near a gas log
As it late lit rigatoni and a tag line.
(*RW*, 304)

There are twelve stanzas in the poem, which is also the number of letters in Tardos' name; in alphabetical order, they are A, B, D, E, G, I, L, N, O, R, S, and T. This limitation results in frequent recurrence of sounds, in words, names, and phrases as conceptually remote as *senile Tiresias, gerardias, gristlier translations, Liebig, Alger, Ingersoll, Ginsberg, Seeger, Aretino,* and *Lister*. The effect is analogous to those produced in exercises once suggested by Fred Bornhauser: write poems using the letters typing manuals assign to either hand. The results might be adroit or gauche, dextrous or sinister.[13]

In recent years, Mac Low has taken the logical step of using a personal computer to perform many of the operations he used to carry out "by hand," with the aid of such cumbersome tools as the Rand table of a million random digits. It is relatively easy to automate the process of searching a text for a word with the next required initial letter, or even with the next required letter in the required position. Between March and August of 1989, Professor Charles O. Hartman of Connecticut College perfected DIASTEX4, a program that performs Mac Low's "diastic" search of a text and prints the result to another file. A few years earlier, beginning in 1984, Hugh Kenner and

---

13. Fred Bornhauser, in conversation with the author, Charlottesville, Va., early 1960s.

Joseph O'Rourke produced TRAVESTY, a program that reads a text file and generates pseudo-text based on letter-combination frequencies in the original. As the authors of the program put it in an introductory article in *Byte*, "The connection of the output to the source can be stated exactly: *for an order-n scan, every n-character sequence in the output occurs somewhere in the input, and at about the same frequency.* That is all, yet it is enough to account for an eerie similarity." [14] In running the program, the operator can set *n* between 3 and 9; the lower "orders" produce something close to gibberish, and the higher ones contain more phrases from the input file. The following three utterances are 100-character "travesties" of the quotation above:

> Order-3: The can be some in the con to the sequency. The out to the in the in be con ther an be connected about to the in out at abours sequency. The output the in the same for and at at the in of th
>
> Order-6: The connection of the source can be stated exactly: for an order-n scan, every n-character sequency. The connection of the same frequence in the output occurs somewhere in the same frequency
>
> Order-9: The connection of the output occurs somewhere in the input, and at about the same frequency. The connection of the output occurs somewhere in the output to the source can be stated exactly:

When run on longer texts, the results can be more entertaining; an order-6 travesty of "Lycidas" has yielded such lines as "What could not float upon the selfsame hills" and "great vision forehead of the guarded mouths!"

Mac Low has in the past three years produced a number of texts using both TRAVESTY and versions of Hartman's diastic-text program. Production of the ten-page "Reveal Realistic Levulin Live," for example, began with an order-7 travesty of Mac Low's intuitively written *Twenties*, one hundred five-quatrain poems. He then ran an early version of DIASTEXT on the travesty; this version of the program used the entire input file as the index string, instead of a shorter phrase or name. The result was over one hundred pages of single-spaced text. Mac Low has been "mining" this vast storehouse for many months, for shorter and longer poems, deciding at various times whether to keep or modify portmanteau words, and how much to edit toward the illusion of normal syntax. [15]

14. Hugh Kenner and Joseph O'Rourke, "A Travesty Generator for Micros," *Byte*, IX (November 1984), 449.

15. Letter, Jackson Mac Low to HT, February 22, 1991.

The results are quite similar to the earlier work Mac Low produced by nonintentional means, except that the travesties introduce more words that had not previously existed: *absentertained, coelentertainment, torrefaction, mescalation, apprentinental, embittersweeten,* and *absentences* all appear on the second page of the poem, but so does *runcible,* one of Edward Lear's favorite adjectives. The poem ranges from word-strings that feel quite random, to illusions of syntax reminiscent of "XXI" of *Pieces o' Six,* as in these lines:

Iridescence's lax nexus glances stippled perm prank snow leafmold.
Apprentinentality dashes professions' palliative foundation.
Embracement baccalaureated professional ornament. [16]

It is fun to notice *coalheavers* on page 8, since it constitutes a motif; it appears (as two words) in the above excerpt from *Pieces o' Six,* and obviously occurred to Mac Low again during the composition of *Twenties.* Among the strengths of Mac Low's work is that it will not reveal why this happened.

It is obvious from such poems as "32nd Light Poem" that Mac Low is not always concerned to exclude the ego and the personal passions from the process of composition. In fact, he has admitted that even when working with systematic chance, he may take pride in the methods he has devised. [17] And so he should: many writers and readers are more consistently dependent on the idea that a single consciousness is responsible for a given literary work, but much of Mac Low's poetry constitutes a dazzling reminder of what the language—"Voice Herself"—can do with a minimum of authorial interference.

In one respect, however, pre-computer projects like *Stanzas for Iris Lezak* are likely to have been emotional in ways that the poems can hardly convey. Having selected a source text and a method of extracting words from it, the process itself might be a rapid series of small disappointments and jolts of elation, as attractive words must be passed over, and as intelligible patterns

16. Jackson Mac Low, "Reveal Realistic Levulin Live," *Hot Bird Mfg,* I (February, 1991), 1–10.

17. Jackson Mac Low, "The Poetics of Chance and the Politics of Simultaneous Spontaneity, or the Sacred Heart of Jesus (Revised & Abridged) July 12, 1975," in *Talking Poetics from Naropa Institute,* ed. Waldman and Webb (Boulder, 1978), 175.

briefly emerge and vanish. The same reactions may occur on a larger scale as the poet moves from method to method, in a spirit of honest exploration, and in generous recognition "that we've extended the possibilities of music and poetry through use of systematic chance, but not that we've invalidated intuitive methods of making art works" (*Craft,* 251).

WILLIAM JAY SMITH Enter the Dark House

I

The poetry of William Jay Smith is widely praised for its deftness of form and tone. A few of his best-known poems are light verse, if the genre is defined with sufficient breadth. He can be very funny, in memorable meters employing startling rhymes; but poems with these qualities make up only part of his work, now handsomely gathered in *Collected Poems 1939–1989* (1990), and of those, a very small number are untouched by a strange gloom, an awareness that we are never far from nightmare or atrocity.

This dark side has always been evident in Smith's work, but *Collected Poems* emphasizes it, partly by the generous addition of previously uncollected poems, especially from the 1940s, and partly by the qualities that have distinguished much of Smith's poetry since 1966, when *The Tin Can* introduced his poems in sinuous long lines. The new poems at the end of the book, however, are among the strongest representatives of Smith's power to hover among various tones in descriptions of strange and threatening occurrences or states of mind.

"The Players," the final poem in the book, is one of two that take up the shameful history of America's treatment of its natives. This is a new subject for Smith, though he has often referred to his Choctaw ancestry. "The Players" opens with a background note on an odd historical fact that, if it were not true, few writers besides Smith could have imagined: "In May 1840, during the Second Seminole War, the players of a traveling Shakespearean troupe left their baggage unattended near St. Augustine, Florida, and a band of Seminoles made off with it into the swamp." At Fort Cummings the following spring, a general of the U.S. Army met to discuss a treaty with the Seminole chief Coacoochee ("The Wild Cat"), who with his followers appeared in Shakespearean dress. The poem is cast in the present tense, and the moment is allowed to develop slowly toward the realization that the situation is odd, but not very funny:

> A curtain of green divides—and there they are:
> the Wildcat Hamlet, black-caped, plumed, and nodding,
> Horatio at one side, and on the other,
> in silken turban, an opal at one ear, Othello—
> or is he the slave who fled the Georgian whip?—
> then Richard, grim and brooding in his royal purple,
> together with the Fool, whose cap and bells
> capture the faintest breeze like wind-chimes . . .
> and slowly they advance toward you, General,
> seated before your table in the clearing.[1]

At first, this combination of present tense and second-person address of the General serve to bring the past close to us; it soon becomes clear that this is not merely a literary effect, but a disheartening reminder of a long history of military folly. The tapping of rain on the barracks roof is "as unending as the oratory on the Congress floor / to justify an unjustifiable war" (253).

The General has a vision of his battlefield; its details are precisely Floridian, but the swampy fecundity recalls Viet Nam:

> green, unfolding fans, striped scarves, and spotted feathers,
> the stately live oak trailing gray Spanish moss
> (the shredded rags of Lear upon the heath),
> the cypress knees protruding from the water
> (the knuckles of your fallen dead

---

1. William Jay Smith, *Collected Poems, 1939–1989* (New York, 1990), 252. Hereafter cited by page number in the text.

whose ghosts have grappled with the mist),
the purple cape of sunset dragging its ermine edge
across the mangrove thicket,—
all are mirrored here before you, General: your enemy
has come in the nightmare clothing of the swamp.
(253)

Lines become a little shorter, and stanza breaks more frequent, as the Chief approaches the General's table; the effect is that of a series of still shots blending into slow motion, as individual images of Hamlet, a skull that may be only a piece of coral, and the paper on the table bring this charged and static moment to its close:

—A wild wind rakes your fort, a hurricane
across the tense peninsula . . .
                    and in the silent eye
a voice that cleaves the quiet water:

"There will be no surrender, General. There will be no peace;
only the murderer who waits, only the poetry that kills."
(254)

It is historically true that the Seminoles "withdrew into the Everglades and never surrendered," as Smith's headnote puts it; it is still noteworthily risky that the final clause in *Collected Poems* refers to "the poetry that kills." Literally, this evokes the power some cultures have found in shaped and ordered language, but it also brings back to the foreground the Shakespearean costumes that the Seminoles have transformed. Nevertheless, the phrase keeps pulling free of its immediate referents to take on a larger and vaguer identity, a force that is waiting to be released.

One possible way of looking at this force is given in another of the new poems, "Journey to the Interior." The quatrains here are deceptively formal, since they portray someone in unproductive, angry introspection:

He has gone into the forest,
to the wooded mind in wrath;
he will follow out the nettles
and the bindweed path.
(246)

The ease of the stanza's movement almost conceals the oxymoron in "bindweed path," a way of considerable resistance. The poem goes deeper among "tangled roots" and "fungi," and then enters a more sterile landscape:

he will pursue each dry creek-bed,
each hot white gully's rough raw stone. . . .
(246)

According to the poem's geography, this arid country is deeper in the mind than the uncontrolled vegetation at the outer edges. What lies beyond the desert seems to be nothingness:

and trees around grow toothpick thin
and a deepening dustcloud swirls about
and every road leads on within
and none leads out.
(246)

It is a hallmark of Smith's work that the bleakness of such a vision is somehow mitigated by the sound of the words; there is pleasure in the form, in the phrasing, that keeps the poem from blatant pessimism, though there are no denotative suggestions of hope or optimism.

These two poems exemplify a surprising number of the virtues Smith's poetry has displayed from the beginning. Lush landscapes, odd animals barely within view, startling but wholly plausible shifts in consciousness, imagery that borders on the surreal without becoming precious or arbitrary, and a profoundly sensitive ear for sound and suggestion—all these recur in Smith's poems, whether or not the effect is finally gloomy or cheerful.

II

Smith has arranged his early poems in four sections of *Collected Poems;* the first consists of only three, one of which, "Quail in Autumn," was not first published until the 1960s; it begins, as several of his later poems do, with a walk in the woods, this time in late autumn; at the snap of a twig, a covey of quail flies up:

> Like brightness buried by one's sullen mood
> The quail rise startled from the threadbare wood;
> A voice, a step, a swift sun-thrust of feather
> And earth and air come properly together.
> (3)

In the next section, earth and air are often apart, or improperly together; "Dark Valentine" gathers fifteen poems of World War II. Six appeared in Smith's first book, *Poems* (1947), and some, like "Pidgin Pinch" and "Barber, Wartime," were composed during that period and withheld from publication until the appearance of *The Tin Can*. "Villanelle," which appeared in *Poems* and is now carried forward for the first time, derives some of its oracular quality from the villanelles of William Empson, but its context, and its final stanza, make it somewhat less mannered than Empson's "Missing Dates," for example. If the first stanza is seen as a comment on military life, it gives no hint of arbitrariness:

> You rise to walk yet when you fly you sit;
> The young are not so young as the old are old:
> People with hair are always combing it.
> (25)

The poem proceeds through a sequence of instances of disorder, each reined in by one of the refrain lines. The "wings" in the penultimate stanza are those of a plane, and also of something like apocalypse:

> We comb the country for the shoes that fit;
> The mushroom grows where now the wings unfold:
> People with hair are always combing it.
>
> The laurel has been cut, the flares are lit;
> The people wait, the pilot's hands are cold:
> You rise to walk yet when you fly you sit;
> People with hair are always combing it.
> (25)

The progression of the images of disorder, and the return of the refrain lines, keep progress and stasis in a tense equilibrium. Most of the other poems

from wartime are arranged at various points along the spectrum between the
soldier's alternatives: some, brittle and sophisticated, are about killing time;
others, more nearly dirgelike, are about killing people.

"Barber, Wartime" and "The Barber" wittily exemplify the transition
between the "Dark Valentine" poems and "Celebration at Dark," the third
section of *Collected Poems* (the title is that of Smith's second book). The
barber in the first poem, "Seaman First Class, name of Cartocelli / . . . Trims
the dormant intellects"; meanwhile,

> . Off there, the long white razor of the reef
> Slashes lather through the slender trees . . .
>
> .   .   .   .
>
> What are life and death to Cartocelli,
> Who shears the domes his dimming glass reflects?
> Night falls; men die—to him details are silly,
> And trim, the dormant intellects.
> (21)

The discomfort of a sophisticated young man, caught up in the business
of war, is the pivot on which the poem balances slang and formality.

"The Barber," on the other hand, consists of eight lines that seem to
begin in a real enough world of haircuts; but even here, apparently in peacetime, the narrative unfolds with a strange disorientation:

> The barber who arrives to cut my hair
> Looks at his implements, and then at me.
> The world is a looking glass in which I see
> A toadstool in the shape of a barber chair.
> (29)

The word "arrives" in the first line raises questions that cannot be answered
with complete confidence; but it undercuts some usual expectations. There
is something hesitant in the whole scene, as if both the speaker and the
barber were mildly surprised at the situation. The end of the poem makes
sense of these apprehensions:

> The years are asleep. A fly crawls on the edge
> Of a broken cup, and a fan in the corner whines.

The barber's hands move over me like vines
In a dream as long as hair can ever grow.
(29)

As the speaker's world slows down and the dream takes over, the poem itself abandons its pattern, letting go of the rhyme between the first and fourth lines of each quatrain. The result, accomplished with unobtrusive deftness, is that the poem opens outward, propelling the reader into reverie.

In "Celebration at Dark" and the fourth section, "The World Below the Window," most of the poems bring close to perfection the delicate combination of light-verse rhythms and dark, surreal, or frightening images, as in these stanzas, the third and seventh, from "Galileo Galilei":

Apple trees are bent and breaking,
And the heat is not the sun's;
And the Minotaur is waking,
And the streets are cattle runs.

. . . .

Galileo Galilei
Comes to knock and knock again
At a small secluded doorway
In the ordinary brain.
(61–62)

By combining images of devastation with rhythms reminiscent of Edward Lear, Smith found a haunting and memorable voice in which to speak to his own time. Some of his most famous poems—"Mr. Smith," "The Ten," "American Primitive"—operate according to this principle. To call it a "principle" is by no means to suggest that it can be mastered by any and every poet; although it is composed partly of recognizable techniques, one of the essential ingredients is the vision that can make, as in "The Ten," a nightmare out of a casual newspaper statement that Madame Henri Bonnet is one of the ten best-dressed women of a given year:

Mme Bonnet is one of the best-dressed ten;
But what of the slovenly six, the hungry five,

The solemn three who plague all men alive,
The twittering two who appear every now and again?
(104)

The effect created by looking idiosyncratically at the ordinary is not always so creepy; "The Closing of the Rodeo," Smith has often said, originated
with a straightforward announcement in the New York *Times* that the rodeo
that had been at Madison Square Garden was about to close. From this unlikely beginning Smith made a brilliant miniature; a version of it appeared in
Poems, and the perfected version has appeared in each of Smith's subsequent
retrospective collections:

The lariat snaps, the cowboy rolls
        His pack, and mounts and rides away.
Back to the land the cowboy goes.

Plumes of smoke from the factory sway
        In the setting sun. The curtain falls,
A train in the darkness pulls away.

Good-bye, says the rain on the iron roofs.
        Good-bye, say the barber poles.
Dark drum the vanishing horses' hooves.
(49)

The quiet, declarative tone of these lines, and the precision of words like
"snaps," enable the poem to remain completely "factual" in tone, even
through lines that might have appeared in one of Smith's poems for children.
Aside from articles, conjunctions, and prepositions, only three words—*cowboy, away,* and *Good-bye*—occur more than once, in a pattern that underscores the permanence of this closing, and suggests extinction.

"Independence Day" relies for some of its power on the repetition of
quiet, declarative phrases; it begins, "Life is inadequate, but there are many
real/Things of beauty here" (80). Dedicated "For S.H. in his melancholia,"
the poem addresses someone who has

> turned away
> To a mirror of completion and of certainty,
> To clocks that tick, and have no time to tell.
> (80)

The last stanza contains some of these "real things of beauty," suffused with sadness at the friend's condition:

> Upon a cliff of sadness the trees bend
>   Strangely toward the sea. . . .
>   The day
> Is bright, the cloud bank white with gulls.
>   And while we lie, and watch the ocean roll,
> The wind, an Indian paintbrush, sweeps the sky.
> (81)

Though "Independence Day" is composed of three stanzas of eleven lines each, the meter is frequently varied, and rhymes are unpredictably placed. The effect is different from that of "The Barber," where a pattern establishes itself sufficiently that breaking it is noticeable; here, the nearly equal lines move through occasional rhymes that make a rhythmic or conceptual point, while internal rhymes almost conceal the fact that unrhymed lines outnumber rhymed ones by about two to one.

Up through 1957, Smith worked rarely but successfully with this delicate balance between tight form and free verse. "Chrysanthemums," "The Girl in Glass," "Nukuhiva," and "The Descent of Orpheus" are all, finally, formalist in spirit, however subtly they elude stricter classification; but they give ample evidence of the occasional rewards of an expanded field of operations, which Smith came to explore in several poems first collected in *The Tin Can*. In these, he found a way of working with extremely long lines, typographically suggestive of Whitman or Ginsberg, but rhythmically and stylistically his own. The expansive unrhymed lines allow for a more leisurely pace, without sacrifice of intensity. The most nearly flawless of these poems is "Morels," an account of finding, preparing, and eating

> These mushrooms of the gods, resembling human organs uprooted, rooted
>   only on the air,

Looking like lungs wrenched from the human body, lungs reversed, not
    breathing internally

But being the externalization of breath itself, these spicy, twisted cones,

These perforated brown-white asparagus tips—these morels, smelling of
    wet graham crackers mixed with maple leaves. . . .
(153–54)

In the mid-1960s, when these poems first appeared, readers were conditioned to expect certain qualities of looseness, even windiness, in poems that
look this way on the page. "Morels," which is a single sentence always under
control, is a powerful reminder that dispensing with rhyme, meter, and brevity can be managed without loss of economy. The other poems in this section
that are cast in long lines tend toward a more ambitious scope and vision,
culminating in "The Angry Man" and the final poem, "The Tin Can."

"The Angry Man" is arranged as a series of four visions; they are connected by the epigraph from Goya ("El sueño de la razón produce mon-
struos"), and by the narrative, in which the speaker struggles toward resolu-
tion by way of giving himself over to his rage. The first turns inward to "the
terrible isolation" of anger, where the images tumble from spooky porten-
tousness to bitter triviality:

I am a passenger on a ship in the shape of a carving block bearing a cargo
    of bones;

I know the language spoken by cats and dogs, all peripheral tongues; I
    invent new words, every syllable detailing disaster;

I am the King of Buttons, enriched by bottle-caps, profligate with
    paper. . . .
(176)

The second section of the poem turns outward, still in a waking nightmare,
as the world turns under its burden of waste and horror; in the third, "the
monsters of the mind's making" have overcome the speaker, bound him in
iron rope and hung him from a brink that seems at first a precipice and then
a ceiling, though the room is blackly overgrown, and walls are meaningless:

> Rivers are nailed above me, their bird-fish flying, teeth dragging the
>   marbled water, and their debris lining a painted dome of tin cans,
>   bottles, rusted and twisting knives. . . .
> (178)

The fourth section releases the speaker from the iron hoops, only to set him down in a courtyard in a desert, where he lashes at "soft flying creatures" with a whip that has materialized from the coils that bound him; after he has littered the courtyard with their bleeding bodies, he climbs to a narrow bed and lies down; the whip, which has bound him and partially released him, still seems an extension of himself as it "rests limp at [his] side—a tassel, a tail, a reed" (179).

Among the sources of this poem's power is the steadiness with which it balances the speaker's surrender to rage against controlled diction and syntax; the speaker is no less polished in his diction than Smith himself is, and he refuses to succumb to easy breathlessness, or to exclamation points, even at his most nearly insane moments. "The Angry Man" is disturbing in many ways, especially in its grim recognition that even during the most disoriented of his visions, the speaker retains his identity: "I wasn't myself" is not among the explanations available to him.

"The Tin Can" takes its title from a Japanese expression, explained in the epigraph: "When someone gets off by himself to concentrate, they say, 'He has gone into the tin can'" (187). It is among the few successful recent poems overtly to be concerned with the search for the right words under the always difficult circumstances of trying to write. It avoids the self-indulgence of most such poems in the same way that Smith has always avoided it: the speaker calls himself "I," but there are no embarrassing self-revelations; the poet withdraws behind the teeming images suggestive of loneliness, fear, lust, ambition, and, finally, of the hope that comes with a recollection of playing in a dump near a cannery, festooned with bright ribbons of tin. This image might provide the impetus needed to leave behind "the raging women, and the sickening mould of money, rust, and rubble" (193).

III

Smith's exquisite touch with difficult forms has sometimes led him into genuine light verse, as well as "nonsense" verse for children; in a few instances, he has applied the techniques of such work to poems that children doubtless enjoy, but whose audience knows no age limit. Twenty-one examples of his "satires, epigrams, and nonsense," representing the period from 1950 to 1980, are included in *Collected Poems*, in a section that falls between the poems through 1957 and the poems from *The Tin Can*. "Mr. Smith" is here, with its eerie shift of tone; from jolly indebtedness to Edward Lear it slides almost without transition into poignant acknowledgment of fear and mortality. Here, too, are a couple of Smith's famous ornithological discoveries, "The Bay-Breasted Barge Bird" and "The Typewriter Bird," and two domestic tragicomedies, "The Floor and the Ceiling" and "The Antimacassar and the Ottoman."

This section, however, overlaps its neighbors not only chronologically but tonally and thematically as well; a few of the "satires" could as easily appear elsewhere in this book, along with those that do. "Light," for example, moves briskly along in octosyllabic couplets, but it portrays an epidemic mode of withdrawal from the world:

> By television day and night
> The people lean to see the light.
> (130)

The children grow up: the daughter marries, the son goes off to war and does not return; behind their bolted door, the people go on as before:

> And something deep within them throbs;
> They set the dial, they work the knobs,
>
> While elephantine shadows fall
> And faces leap from the parlor wall.
> (130)

Finding this poem, or the deft and touching epitaph for a lawyer, in a section called "Light Verse," provides a brief and unobtrusive lesson in reading Smith's poetry, none of which is shaped by heavy hands, or pitched at a single tone.

"The Tall Poets," for example, has the look of a satirical bagatelle, a snatch at the opportunity provided by the sailing of the tall ships up the Hudson on July 4, 1976. In part, it seems a complaint against whatever fates have conspired to keep the speaker, a poet named William, out of the front rank of contemporary poets. It is more than either, though it includes those ingredients. Smith's place in contemporary poetry is secure enough; the poem satirizes the tendency to verify this by looking at the list of his prizes, rather than at his poems. It has fun lampooning what often passes for the best poetry of our time; but it is also hilarious on the subject of William, his appearance, his Louisiana background and his elegant wife, "the Swan of Strasbourg," and his difficult struggles with the writing of poetry. The whole thing balances precariously on an unstated point, which is that many poets are torn between desire to be of the Establishment, whatever that is, and the urge to stay outside it, chucking well-aimed rocks at the elegant leaded windows.

IV

Since *The Tin Can* appeared in 1966, Smith has not published a full-length collection devoted entirely to new poems. But aside from those included in *New & Selected Poems* (1970), there have been three small limited editions, a collection of critical essays, and four collections of verse translation from six languages. During this burst of activity, Smith managed, when he wrote his own poems, to keep his attention focused on matters of considerable ambition, in both technique and theme.

Of the poems first collected in 1970, the most interesting and enduring are "Fishing for Albacore" and "What Train Will Come?" The first balances the excitement and comradeship of a father and son on an offshore fishing expedition against the blood and chaos of a successful catch. The second takes its epigraph from a line "found scrawled in a subway station": "What train will come to bear me back across so wide a town?" It is an echo of a line from Tolkien: "What ship will come to bear me back across so wide a sea?" As the speaker descends toward the turnstile of the subway station, the gritty scene inspires meditation on urban waste and contemporary violence. He recalls walking through a town after a tornado, thinks of Darwin's account of Talcahuano Bay after an earthquake, and moves on to the televised

war in Viet Nam, in which "men kill men, and all three inches tall" (216).
The next section of the poem turns inward:

> Three inches tall (in memory) I wander up and down . . . Ah,
>   once I loved a stone, the shape of water winding through
>
> Wild rose, sweet-william, Indian paintbrush, and in the woods a
>   woman (was it my mother?) walking in yellow lace
>
> Through violet shadows, nodding and talking . . . And I left
>   her there by the stream . . . and then that night found her
>   again
>
> Locked in a little room at the top of the stairs, moaning and
>   calling as if from underground,
>
> And the club that had beaten her rested like some heraldic
>   emblem beside the door where the drunken man had placed it;
>
> And I knelt down, staring into my own vomit, helpless, dazed,
>   and dumb . . .
>
> *What train will come?*

(216–17)

This recollection, or imaginary recollection, is convincing in its weird
elusiveness; the whole poem captures the way in which a shifting consciousness will fasten on details one at a time without logically connecting them.
It is extremely difficult to combine long lines and rhyme, but each of the
poem's eight sections is constructed like this one, the long lines moving perilously close to prose until they come upon the rhyme and the refrain. The
poem ends with a realization that "the way out is never back, but down," and
the epigraph at last appears entire, a desolate question made of what had
been a graffito, a joke.

Smith has published several more long-line poems in the past few years;
if many odd catalogues of half-seen sights had not given the genre a bad
name, three of them might be called travel poems: "At Delphi," "Venice in
the Fog," and "Journey to the Dead Sea." They are grouped together with

"The Traveler's Tree," the title poem of the new and selected volume Smith published in 1980, and the four poems reveal themselves as parts of a sequence, however strong any of them is alone. Like "Morels," these poems explore life's joys more deeply than its pain, and make deep sense of a career in which the dark side of things is often turned toward the light.

"At Delphi" is addressed to Allen Tate on his seventy-fifth birthday; the spring at Delphi, surrounded by dry heat, "guarded by the python coiling from its seismic chasm," brings to mind Tate's "The Swimmers," "Where the drowsing copperhead kept watch beside the water 'that bells and bickers / All night long.'" The poem affirms the power of language to survive, and night "draws fully in, thread over fine, thin fingers at the center of the earth" (222–24). The water of the spring, and of Tate's creek, is part of the stream that connects the four poems. In "Venice in the Fog," mist rising from the canals makes the city's buildings seem to float free of the earth, as the speaker himself does when he recognizes the love of his life, who comes in from a walk in the fog, takes a warm bath, and lies down with him, transforming all he sees.

"Journey to the Dead Sea" is the longest of these poems, and the most various in tone; the speaker reacts to the wiseacre guide and his ancient jokes, to the landscape and the cast-off cars, oil drums, and whatnot that defile it; when the tourists get off the bus to enter the Dead Sea, they all remind him of animals, mostly birds. But below all this runs the ground bass of ancient history and its modern aftermath, so that the oasis of En-Gedi breaks on his parched consciousness like the waterfall itself, that

Falls on a clear pool, tilting with stars, encircled with smooth rocks and cress,

On that healing place this side of death that can be reached only through knowledge and pain.
(235)

These three poems are based directly on actual journeys; "The Traveler's Tree" doubtless partakes of Smith's many wanderings over the world, but the traveler here is addressed in the second person; the speaker does not refer to himself as "I" until the last line. The poem takes its point of departure from a paragraph by Thomas H. Everett, author of *Living Trees of the World*, in which is described a palm-like tree in the shape of a fan, in the hollow bases of whose leaf stalks travelers could find water. The poem itself is an imaginary journey through remembered scenes to various exotic landscapes, culminating at a small dark house beside which one of these trees is growing:

> And breaking off that branch, you will break off your dream
> and be again a boy in a small boat
> drinking from a paddle
> the transparent water of a mountain stream.
>
> Then cross the threshold and enter the dark house.
> You will be welcome. I will be waiting. I will be there.
> (238)

A demonstration, almost a parable, of the power of the imagination, this poem is clear evidence that Smith continues to range fruitfully over the variety of verse forms at his disposal. The sequence of four poems is like a lifetime compressed, the changing waters bearing the speaker through rediscovery of language, love, reverence, and imagination, on toward the most recent poems in this splendid collection, where restless curiosity and formal inventiveness, as in those of "A Sculptor, Welding," bring "out of life's formlessness, now form" (243).

JAMES WRIGHT In the Mode of Robinson and Frost

When a poet's career is substantial enough for us to start talking about his early work, we face some problems of critical perception. We may not be able to solve them, but we should at least keep an eye out for the traps they set for us. This is especially true in the case of James Wright, who set his earlier work apart from the rest with unusual ostentation.

Almost anyone can avoid the absurdity of referring to *The Green Wall* and *Saint Judas* as apprentice work, as if the poems in them were written with an eye toward *To a Blossoming Pear Tree.* But it seems harder to avoid the equally fallacious tendency to think of *The Branch Will Not Break* as the moment when Wright "found his real voice," as if the first two books constituted some sort of ventriloquism.

Certainly *The Green Wall* contains some poems that got in because this was a first book, and certainly Wright's poetry developed along lines most obtrusively introduced in *The Branch Will Not Break.* But in this discussion of the first two books, I hope to keep in mind the following points.

First, *The Green Wall* and *Saint Judas* are anything but false starts. In the poetic climate during which they appeared, they displayed, in their way, the self-reliance that characterizes most of Wright's work. The problem of perception here is that it is hard to re-create, imaginatively, the climate of the late fifties; but I will set down a few reminders.

Second, Wright's well-known shift in style was a necessity, a survival tactic. *Saint Judas* is a splendid book, but it contains considerable evidence of Wright's growing impatience with the style in which most of it is written. Moreover, the shift seems to have been more stylistic than thematic. I do not deny the new subtlety of perception, the new sensitivity, in Wright's later work, but I am suspicious of claims that the shift was a cataclysmic transformation of the whole man. The problem of perception here is insurmountable; time has condemned us to hindsight.

Third, many of Wright's early poems may still be ranked among his best. As Richard Howard has suggested, Wright's having declared a moratorium on his earlier manner ("whatever I write from now on will be completely different") is not the same thing as declaring that he should never have written those poems in the first place.[1] In assembling his *Collected Poems* (1971), Wright discarded only five, all of them underachieved pieces from *The Green Wall*. The rest were brought forward, and they can still stand the light.

Finally, it will be noticed that Wright's abandonment of rhyme and meter was not absolute. Each of his books contains at least a few poems in traditional forms. But it must be noticed, too, that these are inheritors, not only of the early style, but of the new style as well.

We cannot go back to the days when Wright was putting together his first two books, but we can spend a little time among relics of the period. There is the first edition of *New Poets of England and America*, which appeared in 1957. One reads vast stretches of it with half-amused bafflement, wondering what has happened to some of these people, noticing that all five of the selections by Robert Bly are metrical, and agreeing, mostly, with James Dickey, who said of these poems, "It is easy to like them, but difficult to care about them."[2]

There are also such reference works as *The World Almanac*, which reminds us that from 1956 through 1960, the Pulitzer Prizes for Poetry went to Elizabeth Bishop, Richard Wilbur, Robert Penn Warren, Stanley Kunitz, and W. D. Snodgrass. The National Book Awards for the same period went to W. H. Auden, Wilbur, Warren, Theodore Roethke, and Robert Lowell.

1. Richard Howard, *Alone With America* (New York, 1969), 576–77.
2. James Dickey, *The Suspect in Poetry* (Madison, Minn., 1964), 42.

That is how things seem to have been. Other important forces were at work, but they were not widely felt until the early sixties.

In his introduction to another anthology, the Penguin *Contemporary American Poetry*, Donald Hall, writing in 1961, took some notice of these other forces:

One thing is happening in American poetry, as I see it, which is genuinely new, and so new that I lack words for it. In lines like Robert Bly's:

In small towns the houses are built right on the ground;
The lamplight falls on all fours in the grass.

or Louis Simpson's:

These houses built of wood sustain
Colossal snows,
And the light above the street is sick to death.

a new kind of imagination seems to be working.[3]

It is tempting to say, with Flannery O'Connor's Mrs. Crater, that "they wasn't as advanced as we are." This is nonsense, of course; things change, for better or worse, whether we like it or not. In 1960, Gregory Orr was thirteen, and Carolyn Forché was ten.

In the 1950s, despite the commandments that came down from the Black Mountain, it was quite usual for young poets to try to accommodate their own voices to forms inherited from England. Wright, though he began with a strong talent and notable independence, was not exceptional in this respect. In *The Green Wall*, the process of accommodation is tentative and slow; several of these poems, successful in many ways, sound like no one in particular; this is from "Witches Waken the Natural World In Spring":

And though she made a leaflet fall
I have forgotten what she said:

Except that spring was coming on
Or might have come already while

3. Donald Hall, *Contemporary American Poetry* (New York, 1962), 24.

We lay beside a smooth-veined stone;
Except an owl sang half a mile
Away; except a starling's feather
Softened my face beside a root:
But how should I remember whether
She was the one who spoke, or not?[4]

Wright early acknowledged an indebtedness to E. A. Robinson, and this passage reveals some of the things that master could teach, though the awkwardly enjambed *Away* is not one of them. Here are the careful setting, the question that deepens the mystery by being somewhat baffling in itself, and the significant details that are sometimes hard to visualize, despite the specificity of the words ("except a starling's feather / Softened my face beside a root").

Something more fully achieved appears in a short poem called "To a Hostess Saying Good Night." It combines formal craftsmanship with occasional clichés and colloquialisms, to produce a low-keyed extravagance:

Shake out the ruffle, turn and go,
Over the trellis blow the kiss.
Some of the guests will never know
Another night to shadow this.
Some of the birds awake in vines
Will never see another face
So frail, so lovely anyplace
Between the birdbath and the bines.

O dark come never down to you.
I look away and look away:
Over the moon the shadows go,
Over your shoulder, nebulae.
Some of the vast, the vacant stars
Will never see your face at all,

4. James Wright, *Above the River: The Complete Poems* (New York, 1990), 30. This new collection is now more accessible than the *Collected Poems* to which the essay refers, so page numbers following quotations will refer to it.

Your frail, your lovely eyelids fall
Between Andromeda and Mars.
(24–25)

This is the courtly tradition in somewhat modern dress, allowing itself nods toward its forerunners: the careful parallelism of the two stanzas, the shift from earthly to astronomical praise, the O. Yet under all this runs a diction flexible enough to include a word like *anyplace*.

This flexible diction, expanding at times to an enormous inclusiveness, soon found a subject or a set of subjects to which it was appropriate. Throughout his career, Wright was concerned with "social outsiders," as Auden called them in his introduction to *The Green Wall*—bums, drunks, whores, murderers, homosexuals, and so on. He also returns often to the vast, gritty landscape of his youth in Ohio, and the nature of love and death in such a place.

The union of style and subject approaches perfection in many of Wright's poems; some of them, though not as ambitious as others, transcend the manner of their time. Such a poem is "An Offering for Mr. Bluehart," the third poem in *Saint Judas*. It is a model of formal organization, its three-part narrative falling without excessive tidiness into three tightly rhymed stanzas of iambic tetrameter. The first two stanzas evoke a boyhood time and place, when the speaker and his friends raided an orchard while "the lean satanic owner" cursed them, even shot at them. But now that the old man is dead, there is touching honesty in a small gesture:

Sorry for him, or any man
Who lost his labored wealth to thieves,
Today I mourn him, as I can,
By leaving in their golden leaves
Some luscious apples overhead.
Now may my abstinence restore
Peace to the orchard and the dead.
We shall not nag them any more.
(51)

The surprisingly appropriate last line is brilliantly prepared for, even metrically: in the first two stanzas, the rhyme scheme is $a\,b\,a\,b\,b\,c\,b\,c$; but in this stanza the poet goes to a fourth rhyme in the fifth and seventh lines, thus avoiding *grieves* at the same time that he leads us to expect it.

If Wright brought his early style to a high degree of excellence in several poems, he was also finding in other poems, both good and bad, that the style could betray him, or he the style. His oft-quoted statement on completing *Saint Judas* reveals his impatience: "Whatever I write from now on will be completely different. I don't know what it will be, but I am finished with what I was doing in that book."

This statement seems to have been made some time before its use in promoting *The Branch Will Not Break;* when it appeared on the jacket of that book, Wright had learned something about what his new direction would be. But when he made the statement, he was evidently more interested in quitting a style than in defining a new one.

Mastery of traditional forms can sometimes be accompanied by the illusion that within those forms there is a finite way of doing things. Clearly articulated, the idea is not convincing; but as a sneaking suspicion in the mind of the poet, it can have unhappy results. Certain habits of phrase, rhythm, and rhyme come along more often than the poet cares to notice, and some poems seem less themselves than versions of earlier poems. The poet is able to apply too much prior experience to each new poem, and not enough invention. (It should go without saying that all these traps await the worker in open forms as well; but in this century the opponents of traditional form have produced the stronger propaganda.)

That Wright's poetry had reached some such impasse can be deduced merely from the ends of the lines in his first two books. The following words appear anywhere from nine to thirty-four times each: *snow, bird(s), dead, down, gone, ground, stone(s), tree(s), face(s),* and *air.* Every one of the sixty-six poems carried forward from the first two books into *Collected Poems* uses at least one of these end-words; a few use almost all of them. *Stone* and *air* are durable, but not indestructible.

"All the Beautiful Are Blameless" is a fine example of various uses of these habitual moves. An account of a girl's drowning in a lake, and of the recovery of her body, it is one of my favorite poems in *Saint Judas.* I came upon it when I was an undergraduate, and I still read it with an echo of that first surge of certainty that this was the kind of poem I liked. Much of the tension in the poem arises from the intrinsic power of the subject matter, but even more is produced by the two views of what happened. One point of view is unswervingly romantic, and the other is realistic, sometimes to the point of brutality. "Out of a dark into the dark she leaped / Lightly this day" (63), the poem begins, but the tone quickly moves into its rapid alternation of tones and viewpoints:

> Two stupid harly-charlies got her drunk
> And took her swimming naked on the lake.
> The waters rippled lute-like round the boat,
> And far beyond them, dipping up and down,
> Unmythological sylphs, their names unknown,
> Beckoned to sand bars where the evenings fall.
> (63)

These shifts in diction are deftly modulated, and establish a wide range of sensitivity. The voice launches a few lines later into something close to preciosity, as the imaginative attraction of the subject is clarified:

> Slight but orplidean shoulders weave in dusk
> Before my eyes when I walk lonely forward
> To kick beer-cans from tracked declivities.
> If I, being lightly sane, may carve a mouth
> Out of the air to kiss, the drowned girl surely
> Listened to lute-song where the sylphs are gone.
> The living and the dead glide hand in hand
> Under cool waters where the days are gone.
> Out of the dark into a dark I stand.
> (63)

Orplidean is interesting, not least because I have seen no dictionary that contains it. But it has the sound of a real word, all right, and it turns up again in *To a Blossoming Pear Tree*, where Wright gazes lovingly across a part of Italy he calls "my orplidean country." The word seems to be a coinage based on Orplid, an imaginary country of fantastic loveliness invented by the German poet Eduard Mörike. This word, then, strikes an extraordinarily literary note, which reverberates through *declivities*, *lute-song*, and *sylphs*, to the last line of the stanza, where the distinction between *a dark* and *the dark* is echoed from the first line of the poem. The sensibility thus depicted is brought up short in the next two stanzas:

The ugly curse the world and pin my arms
Down by their grinning teeth, sneering a blame.
Closing my eyes, I look for hungry swans
To plunder the lake and bear the girl away,
Back to the larger waters where the sea
Sifts, judges, gathers the body, and subsides.

But here the starved, touristic crowd divides
And offers the dead
Hell for the living body's evil:
The girl flopped in the water like a pig
And drowned dead drunk.
(63–64)

As in the passage quoted from "Witches Waken the Natural World in Spring," there is a small syntactical mystery in the first sentence above. "Down by their grinning teeth" is hard to visualize: does *by* mean *beside,* or *by means of*? To the speaker, it does not matter; the violence of the image, blurred as it may be, is enough, and its very confusion is a symptom of the speaker's state of mind; he can see what he wishes to see only if he closes his eyes. In the final stanza, a reconciliation between the two ways of seeing is almost achieved:

So do the pure defend themselves. But she,
Risen to kiss the sky, her limbs still whole,
Rides on the dark tarpaulin toward the shore;
And the hired saviors turn their painted shell
Along the wharf, to list her human name.
But the dead have no names, they lie so still,
And all the beautiful are blameless now.
(64)

The long second sentence of this stanza is a fine fusion of the romantic's way of talking and the realist's way of seeing. But the first and third sentences tilt the balance in favor of a romantic fuzziness. "So do the pure defend themselves" is an interesting summation of the girl's leap; it seems also to reach out farther into the poem, to speak for the romantic visionary's defense as well. And the last two lines demand more assent than they quite deserve.

They are prepared for in several ways: the unknown names of the "unmyth-ological sylphs," and the "ugly" who "[sneer] a blame," give the lines a ground to grow from. At the same time, however, the lines fail to make quite enough literal sense; we are free to take or leave their assertions. All this leads to a suspicion that the lines may have been written earlier than other parts of the poem, and were worked toward. This cannot be proven in the absence of worksheets, but that is not the point; that they sound like a pre-arranged conclusion is a considerable deficiency in the poem, even though the lines themselves have a memorable loveliness.

Another illustration of Wright's increasing frustration with his early style is the trio of poems about men condemned to death: "A Poem about George Doty in the Death House," from *The Green Wall,* and from *Saint Judas,* "American Twilights, 1957," and "At the Executed Murderer's Grave." All three poems are somewhat oratorical, and contain passages of inflated rhetoric. The last of them is explicitly concerned, not only with the executed murderer, but with the problem of poetic style and posturing.

"A Poem about George Doty in the Death House" reveals Wright's early style at something close to its best. Formally, it consists of almost inappropriately delicate eight-line stanzas of rhymed iambic trimeter, but within that framework Wright masters his flexible diction. The speaker begins by describing the prison, and then imagines in more detail one prisoner, George Doty, an Ohio rapist and murderer. Beside his cell, "hardy perennial bums" are said to complain of hunger and cold, while Doty's desperate need for love, and his pathetic failure, are the occasions for the speaker's sympathy:

Now, as he grips the chain
And holds the wall, to bear
What no man ever bore,
He hears the bums complain;
But I mourn no soul but his,
Not even the bums who die,
Nor the homely girl whose cry
Crumbled his pleading kiss.
(26)

The unusually exclusive sentiment in this stanza is implicitly rejected in "American Twilights, 1957," which is dedicated to Caryl Chessman, famous for staving off execution at San Quentin until he finally went to the gas chamber in 1960. The poem is in two parts, the first a description of the hopeless routine of prison life; the second takes the oratorical stance, pointing to public obliviousness, and calling for God's mercy on the public as well as on the outcasts. The tone is somewhat artificially elevated by means of repetition ("God, God have pity") and occasional poeticism ("Lo now, the desolation"). However, it mourns, not one soul to the exclusion of others, but everyone caught in the human predicament.

"At the Executed Murderer's Grave" returns to the subject of George Doty, and by occasion takes up the situation of the poet, identified in the first line as James A. Wright. Most of the poem is in irregularly rhymed iambic pentameter, but the lines are often violently colloquial, stronger even than the "realistic" sections of "All the Beautiful Are Blameless":

> I walked here once. I made my loud display,
> Leaning for language on a dead man's voice.
> Now sick of lies, I turn to face the past.
> (82)

One could hazard a guess that "the dead man" is E. A. Robinson, in whose mode Wright had "tried very hard" to work; but the tone is enough to tell us, not what Wright thinks of the dead man or his voice, but what he thinks of his earlier "loud display":

> Doty, if I confess I do not love you,
> Will you let me alone? I burn for my own lies.
> The nights electrocute my fugitive,
> My mind. I run like the bewildered mad
> At St. Clair Sanitarium, who lurk,
> Arch and cunning, under the maple trees,
> Pleased to be playing guilty after dark.
> Staring to bed, they croon self-lullabies.
> Doty, you make me sick. I am not dead.
> I croon my tears at fifty cents per line.
> (82–83)

This passage repudiates not only the earlier Doty poem, but also "She Hid in the Trees from the Nurses," an excessively wistful characterization of a girl in a sanitarium evading the curfew. Wright works himself up to brutal energy in the next section, describing Doty as an idiot, a thief, a piece of filth; then he makes a double-edged declaration:

> I waste no pity on the dead that stink,
> And no love's lost between me and the crying
> Drunks of Belaire, Ohio, where police
> Kick at their kidneys till they die of drink.
> Christ may restore them whole, for all of me.
> Alive and dead, those giggling muckers who
> Saddled my nightmares thirty years ago
> Can do without my widely printed sighing
> Over their pains with paid sincerity.
> I do not pity the dead, I pity the dying.
> (83)

The anger in this passage seems to radiate in all directions, until the last line focuses the poet's rage. Wright himself is among "the dying," as he makes clear in the fourth and fifth sections of the poem. In the fifth section, the meter expands surprisingly, as does the vision, and we are given a glimpse of things to come:

> This grave's gash festers. Maybe it will heal,
> When all are caught with what they had to do
> In fear of love, when every man stands still
> By the last sea,
> And the princes of the sea come down
> To lay away their robes, to judge the earth
> And its dead, and we dead stand undefended everywhere,
> And my bodies—father and child and unskilled criminal—
> Ridiculously kneel to bare my scars,
> My sneaking crimes, to God's unpitying stars.
> (83)

"The last sea" is like those "larger waters" in "All the Beautiful Are Blameless," "where the sea / Sifts, judges, gathers the body, and subsides." That all will be judged leads the poet to the poem's conclusion where, as he reverts to meter, he faces the realization that he cannot fully separate himself from

> the rotted face
> Of Doty, killer, imbecile, and thief:
> Dirt of my flesh, defeated, underground.
> (84)

Though it sometimes skirts the edges of self-indulgence, the flexibility and unpredictability of this poem mark it not only as a recognizable precursor of Wright's later style, but also as one of his best poems in either style.

But if Wright came to distrust his early manner, and could even articulate that distrust in good poems, there are other poems in which the form is simply there, not visibly separable from the poems, which are as good as anything in Wright's work. These very successful poems tend to be concerned with the same themes that Wright always returned to with some regularity.

"The Assignation," for example, still ranks as one of Wright's most impressive poems. It may be that few poets now under forty will admire it; certainly few enough of them have the skill to have carried it off, even on a dare. Like "My Grandmother's Ghost," "Come Forth," "The Ghost," "The Alarm," and "But Only Mine," the narrative concerns revenance or resurrection, presented in this instance not as a dream, but as the thing that really happens. The poem is surprisingly controlled, given its length—eighty-eight lines—and the melodramatic nature of the story. By an intricate spell, a ghost rises and is enabled to return to a picnic ground, a place significant to her and her lover when she was alive. She fails to find him, and takes a demon as a surrogate; but still the pain of her loss keeps the ghost yearning for her lover, and accusing him of failure to keep an old promise:

> You sat beside the bed, you took my hands;
> And when I lay beyond all speech, you said,
> You swore to love me after I was dead,
> To meet me in a grove and love me still,
> Love the white air, the shadow where it lay.
> Dear love, I called your name in air today,
> I saw the picnic vanish down the hill,
> And waved the moon awake, with empty hands.
> (41)

In one view, this poem may be taken as a *tour de force*, a contemporary attempt at Coleridgean evocation of the supernatural; as such, it is successful, which is remarkable enough. But in the particularity of its details, the poem becomes a convincing character study as well, taking hold of the reader and not letting go until it has made a point; the reader senses the unimaginable permanence of the separation between the living and the dead.

The poems about revenance, or the "graveside" poems like the second one about George Doty, are almost all quite moving in their presentation of the impossibility of communication between living and dead. In one case, "Devotions," there is a hard and honest edge to the speaker's frustration, as he stands before the grave of a childhood enemy, regretting that it is too late even to gloat:

> I cannot even call to mind so clearly,
> As once I could, your confident thin voice
>   Banishing me to nothing.
> Your hand crumbles, your sniffing nostrils barely
>   Evoke the muscles of my loathing;
> And I too die, who came here to rejoice.
> (81)

In the presence of his enemy's bodily deterioration, which of course he can only imagine, the speaker is "shaken" by the same realization of futility that overtakes the final address to George Doty. In language quite similar to that of his later work, Wright addresses to the dead enemy a final stanza of unusual power, evocative of losses that cannot be regained; at this cemetery, there is

> Nothing to mark you off in earth but stone.
> Walking here lonely and strange now, I must find
>   A grave to prod my wrath
> Back to its just devotions. Miserable bone,
>   Devouring jaw-hinge, glare gone blind,
> Come back, be damned of me, your aftermath.
> (82)

At its most extreme, Wright's early mastered ability to combine traditional form and colloquial diction sounds increasingly like his later poems. "A Note Left in Jimmy Leonard's Shack," for example, arises from the same grimy background that produced such later poems as "Autumn Begins in Mar-

tins Ferry, Ohio"; the speaker is a boy, apparently a re-creation of the young
Wright, who had had to deliver a message to a drunken bum. Jimmy Leonard's brother Minnegan has been found unconscious beside the river. The
boy is afraid to try rousing Jimmy out of his stupor, and is already apprehen-
sive about having broken family rules in "coming up this far, / Leaving a
note, and running as I came" (53). Here is how the voice sounds at the end
of the poem:

> Beany went home, and I got sick and ran,
>   You old son of a bitch.
> You better hurry down to Minnegan;
> He's drunk or dying now, I don't know which,
> Rolled in the roots and garbage like a fish,
>   The poor old man.
> (54)

And here, from the end of a poem published almost fifteen years later, is
the voice of a man recalling another unsavory episode; the poem is "Ohio
Valley Swains," from *Two Citizens* (1973):

> You thought that was funny, didn't you, to mock a girl?
> I loved her only in my dreams,
> But my dreams meant something
> And so did she,
> You son of a bitch,
> And if I ever see you again, so help me in the sight of God,
> I'll kill you.
> (234)

What is notable here is not merely the shared epithet, but the continued
inclusiveness of diction; Wright's later manner is sometimes said to be free of
old-fashioned rhetoric, but it can still find room for a line like "I loved her
only in my dreams."

The publication of *The Branch Will Not Break* elicited various reactions,
most of them extravagantly favorable. Moreover, after Wright mastered his
open forms, retaining in them the voice and character that always gave his
poems their extraordinary strength, it is not hard to conclude that he moved
in productive directions. But two things need to be remembered. First, as I

have said, Wright never completely abandoned traditional forms; and, second, many of the earliest poems in the new manner are boring, derivative failures. At the same time that Michael Hamburger was claiming that "it is only in the new collection that Wright has found this wholly distinctive voice," George Garrett, in a virtuoso essay called "Against the Grain: Poets Writing Today," expressed less certainty about the distinctiveness of this voice: "The triumph of Bly is all too obvious in the 'new' James Wright. Wright began as a disciple of Frost, developed as one of the finest poets we have. But *The Branch Will Not Break* is quite close in style and mannerism and even subject-matter to Bly's *Silence in the Snowy Fields*; and, in fact, one of the poems is called 'Mary Bly,' after Bly's daughter."[5]

Sure enough, there are some poems in Wright's third book that are virtually indistinguishable from most of the poems in Bly's first book. There is the insistent absence of meter, the flatness of statement, the heavy dependence upon image alone; this is a kind of poem that absolutely anyone could write, after having seen a few examples, such as "In the Cold House":

> I slept a few minutes ago,
> Even though the stove has been out for hours.
> I am growing old.
> A bird cries in bare elder trees.
> (138)

It can be argued that this little poem is held together by the contemplation of time; it moves from minutes to hours to growing old. Unfortunately, it goes on from there to *elder*, which suddenly becomes a pun that must be explained away somehow, like the end of this sentence from Frost's "Mending Wall":

> Before I built a wall I'd ask to know
> What I was walling in or walling out,
> And to whom I was like to give offense.

But of course Wright was more often successful with the new style, especially when he made it his own; poems like "A Blessing" still stand up very

---

5. George Garrett, "Against the Grain: Poets Writing Today," in *American Poetry*, ed. Irvin Ehrenpreis (London, 1965), 234.

well, and the fierce gentleness of vision in Wright's subsequent books kept him in the first rank of poets writing since World War II.

The rhymed and metered poems that continued to appear are interesting, not merely because they are there, though that is something; but even in that mode Wright developed and extended his art. "Two Horses Playing in the Orchard," included in *The Branch Will Not Break*, may possibly be left over from years when *Saint Judas* was being written; but its delicately truncated grammar, especially in the final stanza, is unlike anything in the first two books. The first two stanzas describe the horses, raiding the apples in an orchard where they do not belong; the poem begins, "Too soon, too soon, a man will come / To lock the gate, and drive them home" (133). The last stanza echoes this beginning, expresses a view somewhat different from that taken in "An Offering for Mr. Bluehart," and achieves a magical ambiguity in the last line:

> Too soon, a man will scatter them,
> Although I do not know his name,
> His age, or how he came to own
> A horse, an apple tree, a stone.
> I let those horses in to steal
> On principle, because I feel
> Like half a horse myself, although
> Too soon, too soon, already. Now.
> (134)

From this point onward, it is almost safe to say that the vagueness goes out of Wright's poetry. In later poems in traditional forms, there is a new kind of bluntness in the tone acquired during the mastery of open forms. There is also a new willingness to speak somewhat cozily about the problems of the formalist poet, as in "Speak" (*Shall We Gather at the River*) or "To a Dead Drunk" ("New Poems," *Collected Poems*). In the first of these, the tight form is abandoned momentarily ("rhyme be damned"), and in the second, a line that ought to rhyme with miracle is a parenthetical aside: "(Listen, what rhymes with miracle?)" There are other examples of this calculated lapse into self-consciousness, even the use of metrical terminology such as *hendecasyllabic* and *amphibrach*. At the same time, Wright continued to turn faultless stanzas to good uses, as in "With the Shell of a Hermit Crab" (*To a Blossoming Pear Tree*).

It appears, then, that certain features of Wright's career are less important than has sometimes been claimed. Many poets of Wright's generation—Rich, Merwin, Kinnell, and Simpson, among others—shifted from closed to open form at about the same time. Some poets simply find it necessary to keep moving. What is extremely unusual in Wright's career is that through great industry, independence, and vision, he developed an increasingly large and flexible command of technique. His flexibility saved him from the rigid allegiances to open or closed form that are sometimes declared by other poets, and which often make current American poetry seem less artistic than political. Through all of Wright's poetry, though there have been some underwrought failures and some ill-suited postures, there runs a strong thread spun of compassion and technical brilliance. It is a tough combination.

INDEX OF POEM TITLES

GENERAL INDEX